Peeking at Peking

China, India and the World

Peeking at Peking

China, India and the World

Gp Capt (Dr) R Srinivasan VSM (Retd)

HOW
ACADEMICS
an imprint of Highlyy Publishing LLP

ISBN: 978-93-95522-03-8 (Hardback)
First Published : 2023

Cataloging in Publication Data--DK
Courtesy: D.K. Agencies (P) Ltd. <docinfo@dkagencies.com>
Srinivasan, R., 1961- author.
Peeking at Peking : China, India and the world / Dr R Srinivasan.
pages cm
Includes bibliographical references.
ISBN 9789395522038

1. Geopolitics--China. 2. China--Politics and government. 3. China--Foreign relations. 4. China--History. 5. China--Foreign relations--India. 6. India--Foreign relations--China. 7. World politics. I. Title.

LCC DS736.S65 2023 | DDC 951 23

Published by : HOW ACADEMICS
an imprint of Highlyy Publishing LLP

Correspondence Address:
4/30 A II Floor, Double Storey Buildings
Vijay Nagar, Delhi-110009
Editorial: +91 9811026449
Sales : +91 9999953412
Email: info@howacademics.com
Website: www.howacademics.com

Printed in India

Contents

Section IV – Concepts, Strategies and Think Tanks

Dedicated to the memories of

The gallant men of 2nd Rajput, 6th & 13th Kumaon, 8th & 9th Gorkha, 1st Jat, 4th Dogra, 9th Punjab, 4th Grenadiers, the valiant of Ladakh Scouts and the erstwhile J&K Militia, together with herein unnamed battalions of the Indian Army;

Brigadier Hoshiar Singh, Major BK Pant, Major Shaitain Singh, Captain BN Singh, Lieutenant Bikram Singh Rathore, Lieutenant AS Khatri, and herein unnamed officers whose leadership and sacrifice is immortal;

Wing Commander Jag Mohan Nath, Sqn Ldr CS Raje, Squadron Leader Chandan Singh, Squadron Leader Arnold S. Williams and the herein unnamed Mi4 helicopter and transport pilots of the Indian Air Force.

Preface

Joseph Needham (1900-1995) commenced his career as a chemical embryologist. His books entitled Chemical Embryology (1931) and Biology and Morphogenesis (1942) had already secured him recognition in those fields. His chance interaction with three Chinese researchers in mid-1930s however changed the course of his life forever. Today, he is celebrated as the Erasmus of the Twentieth Century for his scholarship on China. During his work in Chonquing and elsewhere, his discoveries led him to assert that it was China that first developed printing, magnetic compass and gunpowder weapons in the world. Needham's discoveries about the advanced scientific knowledge in ancient China have till now been published in 24 volumes with more work awaiting to be published.

As of now, USA alone lists 77 well-known sinologists topping the list of over 250 sinologists the world over. To apportion this interest on China to the present world scenario alone would be like developing botany as a science since we just now discovered a weed in our lawn. China has held the attention of the world from millennia before Christ. There is little emphasis to saying that it will continue to hold our interest in future.

Home to a sixth of humanity, its sheer size and geographical location makes China indispensable to the world. It commands nearly a fifth of global GDP at 18.56 percent and accounts for 30 percent of global manufacturing output. At $710 billion USD, as of 2021 China is the world's largest exporter commanding 14.7 percent of the world, with the USA trailing behind at 8.1 percent. With over 2 million active duty personnel, China's military is the world's No. 1 and its technological advancement both on ground and in the space continue to stoke the curiosity of the world, giving rise also to apprehensions. Apart from the economic and military muscle that it displays, China's outreach in the past decade through its Belt and Road Initiative (BRI) to 147 countries across the world is perhaps the most compelling reason that holds the attention of scholars and analysts, and again, not without some trepidation.

The rise of China in this manner is of immense concern to the comity of nations since not all its actions are seen as synchronized with international principles contributing to world order and peace. Especially, the creation and militarization of artificial islands in the South China Sea, the results of cheque book diplomacy in Sri Lanka, Pakistan and elsewhere, its unwavering posturing on the Taiwan issue, and its bonhomie with Russia have evoked anxieties as to its intent to dominate the world order.

Even amidst developments leading to these angsts, China's actions on its western front have stood out as the biggest concern to nations in South Asia, specifically to India. Seen as the most potent rising power in Asia, India's concerns are rightfully centered on the border issues with China affecting its domestic and international politics. Apart from the border contests, China's reach to Pakistan through China Pakistan Economic Corridor and its immense presence in other neighborhood like Afghanistan, Nepal, Bangladesh, Myanmar, Sri Lanka and Maldives lend credit to the 'string of pearls theory', prompting even more concerns to India. The port project at Gwadar (Pakistan), the permanent military base at Djibouti, ports of call by Chinese naval and survey ships in Indian Ocean Region and their permanent presence off the Somali coastline (albeit for counter-piracy mission) add to these concerns.

Indian and international scholarship generally tends to view these developments as India specific or as BRI specific, unilaterally tailoring them into the world's concerns over South China Sea. Freedom of navigation on high seas, the question of Taiwan or in general the question of democracy since China avowedly practices the Maoist version of communism, are also part of the discourses. These views are in no less measure stimulated by Chinese refusal to abide by the arbitral award in favor of Philippines, its domineering role in WTO, the "don't-blink-it's-not-me" response to the genesis of Covid19 virus and the apparent ability to posture against USA. China's high seat in UNSC and its relationship with Russia in any case, are ever green subjects for international criticism.

The front side of the portrayal of China in the contemporary world leads one to believe that it is a hegemon which needs to be countered by collective international will. Such an impression had prevailed against some powers earlier too in world history, to cite Napoleon Bonaparte and Hitler as examples. However, to presume that whatever they did or failed to do was driven only by an ambition to dominate the world, may be only partially correct. History tells us that even the most powerful nations suffer from internal and external compulsions, perhaps guided by their vanity and such like factors, prompting them to do or omit to do what they did. The three Afghan Wars that the British Indian Empire undertook were guided by the eagerness to checkmate Czarist Russia, engendering the Great Game that continues to affect the world today. It is quite ironical that the same British Empire gladly gave up its claims when the Czar merely pressed his railway line 100 miles closer to Afghan border and offered a compromise in exchange of Constantinople, though subsequently. The Czar's plan for invasion of India was never seriously intended. It is from historical instances such as these, this book has taken form.

In its first three chapters, the book attempts to understand China's border disputes with India, its quest for maritime power, and its engagement with Pakistan, Afghanistan, Australia and the larger world through BRI (CPEC), RCEP and international lending. The final chapter examines how China appears to be learning new strategies from Taiwan, Turkey and global think tanks. The book ends with evaluating two important agenda that India has embarked upon in recent years, the Theatre Command Concept and defence production for Atma Nirbhartha (self-reliance). India has not stated both the last two aspects as a response to Chinese posturing against it. However, the connection is hardly a matter of mere presumption.

The most compelling arguments through all the chapters in this book may be synthesized to just two: China needs to be understood through a holistic appreciation of its history and, if the Chinese actually deserve countering, it must be done by an intelligent assessment of its very mind. Western and non-Chinese view of the conduct of China otherwise is unlikely to be comprehensive. Acting upon such analysis will likely result in opportunities that perhaps are more in Chinese interest than the world may only acknowledge in retrospective.

For example, the prevalent analysis of Sino-Indian conflict of 1962 apportions Nehru's forward policy and Dalai Lama's asylum as the most compelling reasons for its genesis. It also apportions the Indian military debacle to poor preparation, hasty deployment and failure of leadership. While all these reasons have merit, a closer examination of China reveals that it chose to squander the numerical superiority and battlefield victories voluntarily and unilaterally for an internal benefit. In the aftermath of the failure of the Great Leap Forward, Mao needed to establish the supremacy of his ideals over those of rebel forces in CCP by showcasing his leadership. He used the PLA to divert national attention, built a halo around the faithful army through 'quick victory' which in turn, brought the internal rebellion under control. His able emissary Chou Enlai played up the Hindi-Chini-Bhai-Bhai merely to keep India guessing. Asylum to Dalai Lama inadvertently provided the excuse.

Again, the willing and abrupt withdrawal from Eastern Ladakh post-Galwan in 2020 was eagerly and patriotically apportioned to the gallant actions of Indian soldiers. It is evident that Indian Army is far more prepared. Resolute political and military leadership is apparently visible. However, a small step across Northeast India reveals that at the same time, Myanmar had plunged into anarchy with the arrest of democratically elected President Aung San Suu Kyi. The way Military Junta takeover of Myanmar would go depended on unpredictable factors. With over $20 billion USD investment in Myanmar, it made better sense for China to move 10000 troops there to protect its investments. Apparently, dealing with India can wait for some other time. As things turned out, the 15th and 16th Joint Working Group Meetings and Military-to-Military Meetings post Galwan have yielded nothing credible thus far.

In order to find answers as to how do Chinese think, the articles in this book step aside from contextualized frameworks. Using historical analysis as a backdrop, each article attempts to view and understand China through a Sino-centric lens. The objective is to facilitate a greater understanding on China and how its mind works.

It is important to acknowledge that the authorship of the contents does not originate from substantial expertise in dealing with China. The sinologists and strategic analysts of the world are far more comprehensive in their appreciation of anything Chinese. It rather originates from an intense yearning to understand a China that single handedly has kept the world engaged and appears poised to do so for some more time to come.

Coimbatore, India — Gp Capt R Srinivasan VSM (Retd), PhD

Acknowledgement

This book contains some articles by me that were published by Chennai China Centre for China Studies (C3S), Defence Research and Studies (DRaS) and Kalinga International Foundation (KIF) over the past two years. I am indebted to them for permitting me to collate and republish them in this form. I am grateful to them for the encouragement to pen those articles and publish in their web portals,in the first place.

I also acknowledge with gratitude Professor S. Utham Kumar Jamdhagni and Vij Publishing Group for their permission to include my paper on 'Post colonial Approach to Understanding China's Quest for Maritime Power'in this book. This paper was first published titled Dragon in the Sea: A Post-colonial Approach to China's Quest for Power by them as part of an edited volume under the title India's Blue Pulse: Preparing for a Maritime Future, in Jan 2023.

My interest on China was fostered by my parents Shri V. Rajamanickam and Mrs. Kalavathy Rajamanickam. Their patriotic fervor aside, the illuminating discussions on history at home guided my thought processes towards learning more about China.

My wife Chitra Srinivasan walked every step during my career in the Indian Air Force, always reminding me to seek understandings beyond what the tenures merely demanded. She also patiently listened to the narrations in this book, debating my insights and the text of my writings. I owe her a gratitude beyond mere words.

My two sons, Deepak and Sashank, have always been enthusiastic listeners who extracted an explanation for every perception that I hold. They dare me with their wit and never failing curiosity to probe the merits of my thoughts. I have no words to acknowledge their encouragement in this endeavor.

Mr. Kanav Kansra of HOW Academics is a demanding publisher, even though his discussions are couched in utmost civility. This book has taken shape through his complete attention to details and substance. To him, I owe a special gratitude apart from the entire team of HOW Academics.

Coimbatore
14 Feb 2023

R Srinivasan

Introduction

Peter Frankopan in his preface to The Silk Roads: A New History of the World makes a pertinent observation: there were alternative ways of looking at history, ones that did not involve looking at the past from the perspective of the winners of recent history. The profound meaning of this statement is the underlying motive for this book.

I was about thirteen months old when the Sino-Indian conflict of 1962 occurred. My father used to hold me in his lap while avidly listening to All India Radio broadcasts almost on the hour, covering the progress of war. A patriotic history teacher, the ignominious events that unfolded during October-November 1962 affected not just him, but the whole country. When the Indian Army was retreating on ground but Jawaharlal Nehru addressed the nation on November 20th saying:

> Huge Chinese armies have been marching in the northern part of NEFA. We have had reverses at Walong, Se La and today Bomdila, a small town in NEFA, has also fallen. We shall not rest till the invader goes out of India or is pushed out. I want to make that clear to all of you, and, especially our countrymen in Assam, to whom, our heart goes out at this moment.

Some 3000 km away, my father broke down and cried. Nehru's heroic radio broadcast was dramatically nullified by his Chinese counterpart, Chou Enlai who announced a unilateral ceasefire on the same day! Thus, Nehru's first option to deal with the invaders was ironically fulfilled by the invaders themselves.

I was too young to understand the events or even to appreciate my father's emotions. But then, time had a way of teaching me something about both. I was four years old when, Pakistan attacked India in 1965 and all of 10 plus, when 1971 War happened. In between, my father presented me with a book that carried the exploits of the gallant men in 1962, who had battled the Chinese at Bomdila, Se La and Ladakh, earning for themselves Param Vir Chakra, Maha Vir Chakra and Vir Chakra posthumously. It seemed that time had determined the course of my life in the years to come.

I served in uniform for over three decades in all the frontier provinces where some of the most grueling battles during these wars took place – Ladakh and NEFA (now Arunachal Pradesh).

In Ladakh, I was privileged to meet the man who repulsed Chinese with such ferocity that the local populace went on to deify him – Colonel Chewang Rinchen, Maha Vir Chakra & Bar, Sena Medal (Gallantry); in NEFA, I visited the very battle ground in the Namti Plains where the gentle Lohit River ran red with the blood of the Kumaon, Dogra, Sikh and Gorkha troops. I was present thirty years after 1962 at a location when one more skeleton of a Kumaoni soldier was found still holding the butt of his rifle at an invisible Chinese column advancing towards him. In the most fitting epitaph to these glorious men, Lieutenant General RP Kalita, GOC Spear Corps, dedicated a statue of 'Kumaoni Soldier' on December 5th, 2020 at the very spot where the battle had taken place.

My thirst for understanding China was tempered and shaped through these and some other events in my professional career. Most importantly, a venerable military dictum - know your enemy - caused me to search and research into China. As a freelance researcher now, opportunities to remain a curious student have encouraged me to look at different facets of China with the intent to further my understanding. The succeeding paragraphs present the synopsis of my attempts at understanding China.

From time immemorial, China has held the curiosity of the world. The travelogues of Marco Polo, Fa-Hian & Hiuen Tsang and such like travelers portray China as a mythical, incredibly rich culture that held sway over the imaginations of the west and east alike. From Xia Dynasty of 2100 BC to the Qing of 1912, the emperors of China (in all its avatars and names) have held their court over a vast proportion of humanity. Even today, China is home to a sixth of all of humanity. Whether its empires were confined to the Han heartland or eventually expanded to include Inner Mongolia, Xinjiang and Tibet as we see today, it attracted tribute, trade and invasion alike throughout its time. The influence of Confucian thought, distinctive culture and the Chinese way of life have been the connecting threads through its trials and tribulations in the annals of history, as much as its accomplishments. Extensive trade through ancient Silk Road connected China with the rest of the then known world. Its influence on the way of life elsewhere is quite unique even today. We still call the tableware at our homes as Chinaware or porcelain (derived from porcellana that Marco Polo used to describe the pottery that he saw in China during his stay of 17 years between 1271 to 1295 in China), even if it is made in our own country.

The perception that China is the hegemon that the world must counter now is, in my opinion, a matter of debate. History of the world is testimony to such perceptions by the powers who mattered at different phases of its course of events. Attila the Hun, Genghis Khan the Tartar both are classical examples portrayed as villains the world could have done without, but were quite different when the mirror of perceptions is just turned around. Genghis Khan is the one who introduced currency notes, printed books for spreading knowledge, established the courier system and improvised agriculture in the plains of Persia centuries before Europe adopted such practices. Historical evidence suggests that he forgave more easily than the barbaric annihilation of innocents that we are made to believe that he did. Incidentally, he was Mongol, not Tartar.

His son, Kublai Khan the Mongol, united the provinces across East Asia and sculpted the country that we call as China today! Kublai Khan merits a little indulgence for he realized the importance of both 'a strong army and good propaganda, but the third element of his strategy came from good administration and policy'. While he drew inspiration from the Confucian ideals that appealed to the upper class in the society whose imaginations expressed unified China 'as an ideal or romantic image in the poetry, calligraphy and essays of the intelligentsia', he set about creating the administrative fabric across his vast empire with the objective of garnering popular support of the peasantry and rural masses. Even though China was home to a great civilization, for most parts of its history it remained fragmented with the cultured upper class deeming itself far superior to the peasantry and speaking a different language. In contrast, the rural populace spoke a different language and toiled under the yoke of regional satraps. Kublai Khan, himself an illiterate Mongol herdsman, succeeded in creating a unified China that appealed to the sensibilities of both the classes of the society. In more than one way, this historical facet is reflected in the Chinese society even today. Centuries later when Mao Zedong undertook the Great March, his appeal to the peasantry played a critical role in forging the communist China that we see today. It is also quite distinctive from Soviet communism that apportioned the revolution to the wisdom of the proletariat (the working class). The Chinese communism is the imagination of Mao drawn from the wisdom of its peasantry and rural folk.

In the years that led to the Opium Wars of the 19th century, the combined armies of Britain, France, Germany, Dutch, and the United States, vandalized and laid to waste China, bringing the emperor on his knees and even burning down his Summer Palace at Yuan Ming Yuan (Beijing). Alongside the motive for profiteering, the evangelization by western missionaries played a crucial role in wrecking the society and pushing it to the brink of chaos through Boxer Rebellion of 1899-1901. China was subjected to what President Xi Jinping is fond of recalling often as the Century of Humiliation. History is again witness, for the motives that drove the western armies to wreck China are the same evils at the core of the fight against drugs and trafficking by the western powers in the modern world.

The Qing Dynasty that eventually abdicated in 1911 witnessed nine rebellions during its reign from 1644 till it collapsed under their weight. The Revolt of the Feudatories (1671-74), the White Lotus Rebellion (1796-1804), Eight Trigrams Uprising (1813), Taiping Rebellion (1850-64), Nian Rebellion (1851-68), Du Wenxiu Rebellion (1856-72), two Dungan Revolts (1862-77 & 1895-96), Boxer Rebellion (1899-1901) and Xinhai Revolution (1911-12). These combined with the successes of the expeditions by Seymour, Gaselee and by Eight Nation Alliance of Austria-Hungary, France, Germany, Italy, Japan, Russia, the United Kingdom and the United States in 1900 ended the history of imperial China. They paved the way for the Great March and the birth of Peoples Republic China.

Perhaps the most grueling experience that China went through were the Japanese invasion in 1937 and the civil war that ensued in the aftermath of Japanese surrender in 1945. The Nanking Massacre is conceivably the most macabre example of what occupation could bestow a society. On December 13, 1937, Japanese armies reached Nanjing (Nanking or Beijing as it is known now). In the six weeks that followed, it was estimated the 200000 civilians were massacred and over 20000 women raped systematically. Nearly three decades later, on September 29, 1972, Prime Minister Kakuei Tanaka said to the people of the People's Republic of China:

> The Japanese side is keenly conscious of the responsibility for the serious damage that Japan caused in the past to the Chinese people through war, and deeply reproaches itself. Further, the Japanese side reaffirms its position that it intends to realize the normalization of relations between the two countries from the stand of fully understanding 'the three principles for the restoration of relations' put forward by the Government of the People's Republic of China. The Chinese side expresses its welcome for this.

From the making of China under Kublai Khan till the eventual fall of its imperial dynasties in 1912, its relations with the rest of the world could broadly be classified into two: with its immediate neighbors and with others. A careful survey into its history reveals that China tended to treat them in a threefold manner, quite akin to three concentric circles within each other (See Fig 1). In the core was China itself, its immediate neighborhood in the second and the outer circle consisting of the rest of the world. Imperial China adopted again a threefold foreign relations policy to deal with these three circles. The core China was directly under imperial rule. The middle circle consisted of vassal states, tribute paying states and barbarians. To this extent, we may imagine the middle circle consisting of three layers. The outmost circle were nations and societies whom the 'benevolent emperor looked upon with condescending eyes'- not equals but then not vassals too. This Chinese conception of the world is at the core of the popularly discoursed Middle Kingdom syndrome of China. This is a pertinent facet of the Chinese mind that begs understanding from the oriental perspective, if that expression could be employed. It also facilitates an appreciation of how China perchance still views the world.

Fig 1: Imperial China's View of the World

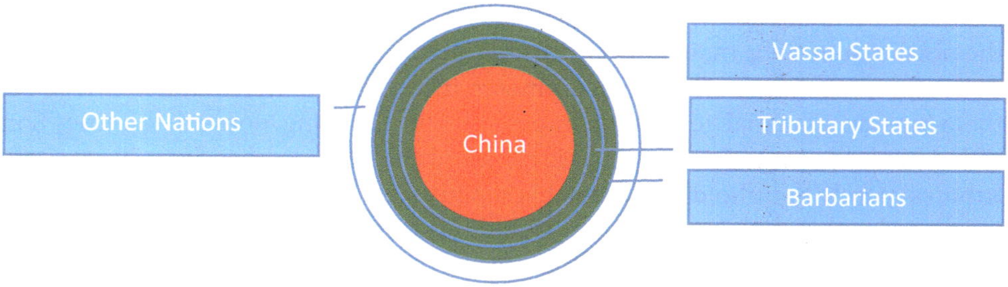

To the western mind, this Chinese perception is a bit complex. In the west, empires viewed the world as friendly or inimical, black or white, as is seen from European history. European kings viewed what lay in their neighborhood as territories to be conquered or brought into alliance through marriage or other such filial relationships. Everything that lay beyond the neighborhood were classified as barbarians to be subjugated. India was perhaps an exception though it was not in Europe's neighborhood. To exemplify through a fact of history, the Portuguese King who commissioned Vasco da Gama to find the sea route to Indies, India was already given to Christ. It had to be brought back to the fold. In so far as Africa was concerned, the pagan population had no soul and therefore did not qualify to be brought into the fold. It had to be subjugated[1].

The benevolent view of India was neither motivated by Christian faith nor the belief that people outside Europe could also qualify as human. It was motivated by economics. History tells us that Saladin the Great who built the first ever Islamic empire of Egypt and Syria and critically countered the Third Crusade, left behind an empire that was viewed as economically unsustainable to European interests. The Arab traders made more money bringing goods from China and India than what European markets could ever make. The silver and gold from European households traveled all the way to India and China in return for the spices, silks and porcelain that European gentry could not live without. The problem lay with the Arabs since the galleys from Sparta, Athens, Venice, and Lisbon had to procure these goods at the cost determined by Arabs. The overland Silk Road that was the economic spine of the world in pre-Christian and the 1st post-Christian millennia,

1 Panikkar, KM (1959). Asia and Western Dominance: A Survey of the Vasco Da Gama Epoch of Asian History 1498-1945, George Allen & Unwin Ltd, p 26 & 27.

ended at Constantinople and Venice through the Persian Empire of Isfahan, the Caliphates at Baghdad and Cairo. Either way, the Arabs were seen as milking the European empires handsomely. The direct sea route to India and further to China was therefore a more compelling economic necessity, than an exemplifier for the adventurous spirit of Europe[2] or its Christian faith.

Chinese mind did not view the world in the stricter compartments that the west did. To China, even the barbarians like Tartar who controlled territories to the northeast of their mainland were essential to the survival of the empire. While militarily deterring the Tartars, commerce in furs and other requirements with them was an essential feature of imperial policy. Having donned the title 'Son of Heaven', the imperial court had it recorded that the supplies from Tartars are tributes merely to uphold the inviolable sanctity that the halo around the emperor warranted. A closer examination would also reveal that Annam (Vietnam) gathered its name from what it means – the Viet (non-Chinese) of the South. Even though Annam came under the rule of the Chinese emperor in around 111 BC, it gained complete political freedom by 938 AD. The 1000 year of Chinese suzerainty was marked by comparative political freedom with only the annual tributes mandated by the emperor. The relationship was that of tribute and trade through which China attempted to maintain regional order[3]. However, this continues to feed the imagination of Annam being a tributary in the Chinese mind even today. The rise of communism in Vietnam and the American intervention to checkmate communist expansion in Southeast Asia in the 1960s and the inglorious withdrawal of America from Vietnam served only to bolster this imagination. When the history of Yunnan, Xinjiang and even Tibet are visited, a similar strain of connectivity can be distinctively inferred. Mao's famous Five Finger Policy stands testimony to this inference and apparently continues to influence modern Chinese political thinking.

Curiously, the Sun of Heaven's benevolent view of diplomatic exchanges as a tribute (implying suzerainty over that state) included even India in a way. The empires of South India, the Chola in particular, extended their empires overseas though they never directly exercised sovereign control except in the case of Sri Vijaya (modern Sumatra, Indonesia). Chola navies and merchant vessels freely coursed through the Malacca Straights and South China Sea up to modern Borneo. Rajendira I, son of the famous Rajaraja I, sent emissaries and gifts for the Chinese emperor[4]. While there is no evidence as to battles between the two empires, Chinese

2 Ibid, p 22.

3 Muhlhahn, Klaus (2019). Making China Modern: From the Great Qing to Xi Jinping, The Belknap Press of Harvard University Press, p 80.

4 Sastri, Nilakanta K A (1958). A History of South India: From Prehistoric Times to the fall of Vijayanagara, Oxford University Press, p 176.

courtiers gladly and apparently recorded these emissaries and gifts as tributes to the Son of Heaven.

It is an interesting insight into Chinese mind that throughout its early history, being blessed with 14500 km of coastline by geography, it remained curiously a land-focused society. It is not till Kublai Khan that China actually took a keen interest on the sea. The Indian, Malay and Sri Vijaya mercantile fleet took care of the commercial interests of China. The ancient Maritime Silk Route originated in Nara (Osaka, Japan), touched Guangzhou (Canton), Poduka (Madras/Puducherry), Muziris (Cochin), Zanzibar, Muscat, Jedda and traveled partly overland ending at Alexandria. It then traveled through the Mediterranean, reaching Venice. China apparently was more content with bulk of its trade moving through the over-land Silk Route that traveled from Xian to Ephesus (close to Izmir in modern Turkey today), for it provided larger markets through established civilizations living along the route and subject to minimal risks unlike piracy on the high seas.

The inference that China remained landward looking in terms of maritime prowess requires a little more understanding. The Han dynasty, also known as the House of Liu or the Eastern Han of 202-220 BC took interest in developing a navy that remained largely confined to the rivers and coastal areas. History records naval engagements from the Han period till the Mighty Qing. Most notable among the battles in which naval might was used in that era is the Battle of Chibi (208 AD) in which the Northern Alliance was resoundingly defeated by the Southern Alliance on the South Banks of the mighty Yangtze River. Sinologists such as Rafe De Crespigny note that even though ships and about 50000 marines were used, the battle was clinched by a mammoth land army consisting of over 200000 soldiers[5]. It took almost a millennium for China to look seawards and develop a navy under the Song Dynasty (960-1279 AD). A century later when the Ming Dynasty ascended to the throne in 1363 AD after the Battle of Lake Poyang, squadrons of ships and fire fleet were still used for what was predominantly a land dominated victory. However, the Ming commenced the entry of China into the blue waters of East and South China Sea. Their Treasure Fleets dominated the Asian waters, enabling the Ming to send governors to Luzon, Palembang, and reach commercial missions to Sri Lanka and India. The Treasure Fleet of Admiral Zheng He is of particular interest owing to its sheer size and the seven voyages that Zheng He undertook successively.

> In autumn of 1405, the fleet of 317 brightly painted junks with a total crew of more than 27,000 men was ready to depart from Nanjing.... The destination of the treasure

5 Crespigny, Rafe De (2007). A Biographical Dictionary of Later Han to the Three Kingdoms, (23-220 AD0 (Handbook of Oriental Studies, Section 4), Brill. ISBN 9789047411840

ships was Calicut-the powerful city state in Kerala on the west coast of India that had a market for spices and rare woods that attracted traders throughout the Indian Ocean. Here, in this isolated coastal region west of the Ghat range, grew cardamom, cinnamon, ginger, turmeric, and precious pepper, worth its weight in gold[6].

Zheng He made seven voyages to India and beyond and developed personal friendship with the Zamorin of Calicut[7]. Chinese held the Zamorin in high respect for the courtesies extended, efficient administrative system and the strong military and naval power that Zamorin possessed, as can be inferred from the travelogues of Ma Huan[8].

It is also pertinent to note that the Ming navy was able to rout Portuguese in several naval engagements, as seen from the Battle of Tunmen (1521) and the Battle of Xicaowan (1522). They defeated the Dutch and a Chinese Pirate force in the Battle of Liaoluo Bay (1633) and the Taiwanese Kingdom of Tungning in the Battle of Penghu (1683). These naval exploits were not without subsequent reverses. However, they promoted a whole school of scholarship on warfare including the naval dimension like the Wujing Zongyao (by Zeng Gongliang in 1044, dealing with riverine ships, catapults, etc), Huo Long Jing (by Jiao Yu and Liu Bowen in the 14th century), Wubei Zhi (compiled by Mao Yuanyi in 1621) and the Jixiao Xinshu (written by Chinese General Qi Jiguang of the Ming Period). There are at least 13 well known treatises on war and strategy in the China of pre-modern era[9].

It is evident that the fleets of riverine and coastal navy that China started with in the 2nd century before Christ had developed into ocean going fleets of formidable quality by the onset of 15th century BC. This development took place not without resistance from Confucian scholars of the imperial court, for they contended that the power of the land armies and the divine nature of the Son of Heaven were

---

6 Levathes, L.E. (1994). When China Ruled the Seas: The Treasure Fleet of the Dragon Throne 1405-33, Oxford University Press, p 88.

7 Zheng He reportedly died at the end of his 7th voyage at Kozhikode (Calicut) in India in 1433, though there is another version of his death at Nanjing in 1435. See: Dreyer, Edward L. (2007). Zheng He: China and the Oceans in the Early Ming, 1405–1433. Library of World Biography. Pearson Longman. ISBN 978-0-321-08443-9.

8 Mills, JVG (1970). Ma Huan: YING-YAI SHENG-LAN, The Overall Survey of the Ocean's Shores (Translated from the Chinese text edited by Feng Ch'eng-Chün with introduction, notes and appendices), The University Press, p 137-146.

9 The Art of War (Sun Tzu), The Methods of the Sima (Sima Rangju), Six Secret Strategic Teachings (Jiang Ziya), Wei Liaozi (Wei Liao), Wuzi (Wu Qi), Three Strategies of Huang Shigong (various authors including Wu Qi), Questions and Replies between Tang Taizong and Li Weigong (Emperor Taizong and Li Jing), Sun Bin's Art of War (Sun Bin), Thirty-Six Stratagems (various authors), Wujing Zongyao (Zeng Gongliang), Huolongjing (Jiao Yu and Liu Bowen), Jixiao Xinshu (Qi Jiguang), and the General's Garden (Zhuge Liang). See: https://en.wikipedia.org/wiki/List_of_Chinese_military_texts

sufficient to defeat enemies. The proceedings of the Opium Wars when diviners and God-men were used to engage with western armada provides testimony to this lingering belief of the imperial court. This aspect will be dealt with in the opening chapter of this book.

Notwithstanding such beliefs, the Chinese were not entirely lost to the importance of naval might. The Qing Dynasty that came to power in 1636 embarked upon building four navies - Beiyang Fleet (North Sea Fleet based at Weihaiwei), Nanyang Fleet (South Sea Fleet based at Shanghai), Guangdong Fleet (based at Canton, present day Guangzhou), and the Fujian Fleet (based at Fuzhou, founded in 1678), respectively.

Even though the Chinese had developed their navies to undertake military missions through the 14th and 15th centuries rather successfully, the reckoning moment as to their inadequacies came through two important instances in their history. The first was the 1st and 2nd Opium Wars (in particular the 2nd of 1856-1858) when 300 Chinese naval ships were blown out of the contest by a mere 56 Anglo-French and other foreign ships. The second was the Battle of Yalu River 1894, when on a single day (September 17, 1894) the mighty Beiyang Fleet was routed by a smaller Japanese Fleet and thoroughly rendered ineffective at the Battle of Weihaiwei shortly thereafter.

In the aftermath of Japanese invasion later in 1937, Chinese navy literally ceased to exist. Post Pearl Harbour, the resounding victory of America and eventual surrender of Japan was through the role played by US Navy and its aircraft carrier fleet. China under Mao did not fail to register this lesson and as is customary, China unobtrusively worked through the Cold War and its aftermath to beget for itself a navy that is hugely impressive now. That the Chinese navy has modern muscles to display was noted in many of the press briefings of the US Navy brass commanding the US fleet in South China Sea.

> "We certainly have a lot of respect for them given their ability to learn and evolve," Admiral Michael Gilday, chief of US naval operations, said at the Centre for Strategic and International Studies in a discussion of the US Navy's future[10].

China's growth as a global power is not on account of its increasing maritime prowess. The civil, political and economic transitions from 1949 have played mammoth roles in shaping its course through contemporary times, intrinsically weaving the lessons from its history into its foreign policy. Mao for example

10 Magnier, M (Apr 29, 2022). US Navy chief says 'phenomenal growth' in China's military requires a strong response, South China Morning Post (online). See: https://www.scmp.com/news/china/military/article/3175909/us-navy-chief-says-phenomenal-growth-chinas-military-requires

ascended to power in a country that was hugely depraved. The war with Japanese having practically destroyed Han China, the civil war between Mao and Chiang Kai Sheikh (the Kuomintang) further rendered the country asunder. The retreat of Kuomintang to Formosa laid the seeds for the present-day Taiwan crisis. The United States also became embroiled into the PRC versus RoC issues forever since it had assisted Chiang Kai Sheikh during Japanese occupation and the filial connections remained. It is necessary to appreciate the Sino-US Relations through history in order to understand the complexities surrounding the Taiwan question.

United States formally dispatched diplomatic consuls to Imperial China as way back as 1784. The Chinese Court did not recognize the American Consul as a representative of the state though. Both countries recognized each other, without formally entering diplomatic or trade relations. It is in only on June 16, 1844, that US Consul was formally received by Qing officials and negotiation on trade, etc, truly commenced. Full US Consuls were present in China at various locations from 1844 to 1947, though these relations were interrupted in 1912 when the Qing abdicated and in 1924 when Provisional Government of Republic of China (RoC) was formed at Nanjing by Chiang Kai Sheikh. With the full recognition of RoC, the diplomatic relations were resumed in 1928. During the Japanese occupation of China from 1937 to 1945, the US Consulate continued to function from Nanjing, Chonqing and Guangzhou till 1946. When the communist uprising threatened RoC and the capital moved to Taipei, the US embassy also moved to Taipei. When the People's Republic of China was proclaimed on October 01, 1949 by Mao at Nanjing, USA refused to recognize PRC and continued its diplomatic relations with RoC till 1972. President Nixon during his visit to Beijing in February 1972 agreed to endorse the 'Shanghai Communique 1972' under which US established a Legation at Beijing in May 1973. On January 01, 1979, USA formally recognized PRC as the sole legitimate government of China and withdrew its recognition of RoC at Taipei. On March 01, 1979, it appointed its formal Ambassador to China at Beijing[11].

Quite curiously, USA also passed the Taiwan Relations Act on Jan 01, 1979, the opening paragraphs of which read:

> Taiwan Relations Act - Declares it to be the policy of the United States to preserve and promote extensive, close, and friendly commercial, cultural, and other relations between the people of the United States and the people on Taiwan, as well as the people on the China mainland and all other people of the Western Pacific area. Declares that peace and stability in the area are in the political, security, and

11 Office of the Historian (n.d.). A Guide to the United States' History of Recognition, Diplomatic, and Consular Relations, by Country, since 1776: China, https://history.state.gov/countries/china Retrieved 01 Nov 2022.

> economic interests of the United States, and are matters of international concern. States that the United States decision to establish diplomatic relations with the People's Republic of China rests upon the expectation that the future of Taiwan will be determined by peaceful means and that any effort to determine the future of Taiwan by other than peaceful means, including by boycotts or embargoes is considered a threat to the peace and security of the Western Pacific area and of grave concern to the United States. States that the United States shall provide Taiwan with arms of a defensive character and shall maintain the capacity of the United States to resist any resort to force or other forms of coercion that would jeopardize the security, or social or economic system, of the people of Taiwan[12].

An important provision that the Taiwan Relations Act 1949 makes pertains to supply of nuclear material to Taiwan in the following words:

> Prohibits any United States agency, commission, or department from denying an export license application or revoking an existing export license for nuclear exports to the people on Taiwan based on the lack of diplomatic recognition by the United States of the Government of Taiwan[13].

The Taiwan Relations Act of 1979 effectively ended the earlier Sino-American Mutual Defence Treaty 1955 (SAMDT) under which USA had provided some guarantees to RoC to secure it against an invasion by PRC. The SAMDT also extended to Japan and Philippines. Its lapse in 1979/1980 was replaced by assurance of supplies in Taiwan Relations Act, further enhanced by similar acts in later years. USA has neither formally relinquished its recognition of PRC till now, nor has it recognized the RoC as a sovereign country, not withstanding its overtures towards Taiwan.

It would appear as though the US government keeps its options open, either guided by the bitter lessons of Korean and Vietnam wars and its policy to contain expansion of communist influence or a strategic ambiguity that prevails owing to the clash between its economic and political objectives.

Reverting to China, Mao paid more attention to building the PRC through lateral relations with USA as well as USSR. His honeymoon with Leninist form of communism ended a decade later around 1959, when he was cold shouldered by Khrushchev. USSR withdrew thousands of Russian engineers and technical experts from China. Before they departed, China had however extracted from USSR more than what the world realized-it had become a nascent nuclear power. In the years

12 US Congress (Jan 01, 1979). H.R.2479 - Taiwan Relations Act, Conference report filed in House (03/24/1979). Retrieved from https://www.congress.gov/bill/96th-congress/house-bill/2479#:~:text=Taiwan%20Relations%20Act%20%2D%20Declares%20it,other%20people%20of%20the%20Western

13 Ibid.

that led up to the 1967 border clashes with Soviet Union, China had managed to get its industrial infrastructure take off to decent levels. While there are contradictory versions as to how the border issue with USSR was resolved, it is apparent that China settled it without much loss of face finally in 1989. In the interim, China had fought in Korea, in and with Vietnam and with India. It also had its border issues settled with most of its neighbors excepting India.

Even before his death in 1976, Mao had secured a seat for China at the UNSC and established ties with USA though his relations cannot be labeled as warm. It is pertinent to note that the maturing of economic relations had to await the rise of Deng Xiaoping, though Mao's distinctive policy regarding opening of Chinese economy to foreign investments appears to guide China's economic policy even today. The Asian Financial Crisis of 1997 led to China reforming its till then state controlled socialist economic policy, paving the way for its membership of WTO in 2001.

Mao's period in Chinese history is marked with certain events that have profound impact on India, its other neighborhood, and the larger world. The most prominent amongst them merit brief visitations.

Distinctive brand of communism. The Leninist brand of communism based on the teachings of Karl Marx and Engels was a product of the industrialization that occurred in Europe. The exploitation of labour and oppressive practices of the age of industrialization placed the proletariat at the heart of Soviet communism. The socialist model relied upon state control of all productive endeavours. The China that Mao grew up was predominantly agrarian and its peasantry had characteristically differed from its Confucian elite in language, customs, and monumental sufferings because of internal upheavals and foreign interventions. Mao preached a different form of communism that goes by his name, Maoism, today. It places the peasantry at its heart, especially the landless masses.

> Indeed, in so far as Mao recognized and encouraged the view that the Chinese revolution was largely a peasant revolution in which the peasants could assume a leadership role, he distanced Marxism from its European and Soviet counterparts which had insisted on a working-class leadership of any revolution with socialist goals.[14]

South Asia and Southeast Asia (as is South America and the colonial world elsewhere) are characteristically agrarian and the appeal of Maoism sways their rural masses. The industrial growth seen as the panacea for developmental deficits

14 Knight, N. (1997). Mao Zedong and Working Class Leadership of the Chinesne Revolution, 1927-1930. China Information, 12(3), 28–45. https://doi.org/10.1177/0920203X9701200302

by governments in these countries engenders the clash between development and sustainable livelihood, underwriting the class struggle that is ascribed to Maoism.

Even though China itself embarked upon industrial development, the eventual opening of its economy to investment, control over production and trade by the government, much to the discomfiture of European and Western world, is indicative of the influence of Mao's beliefs in policy making in contemporary China.

The Five Finger Policy. Mao's speech on November 15, 1939, has been attributed as the source of his Five Finger Policy that placed Tibet at its palm and designated Ladakh, Nepal, Bhutan, Sikkim, and Arunachal Pradesh as its five fingers. Mao apparently included these territories in his grand vision for China. Analysis of his concept of 'New Democracy' that he passionately advocated reveals a lack of distinction in his mind between minority nationalities and sovereignty in his overarching vision for China[15]. Whether there was ambiguity or clarity, that he emphatically included the Tibetans, Uyghur, Miao (Arunachal Pradesh), Yi (Vietnam and Thailand), Chuang (partly in Yunnan and Myanmar) in his construction of the Chinese society provides ample evidence to support the inference of his 1939 speech.

> China has a population of 450 million, or almost a quarter of the world total. Over nine-tenths of her inhabitants belong to the Han nationality. There are also scores of minority nationalities, including the Mongol, Hui, Tibetan, Uighur, Miao, Yi, Chuang, Chungchia and Korean nationalities, all with long histories though at different levels of cultural development. Thus, China is a country with a very large population composed of many nationalities[16].

In the years following its occupation of Tibet in 1957 compelling the Dalai Lama to seek political asylum in India till most recent Galwan clashes in Eastern Ladakh, the pattern of conflicts with its neighbours gives some insight into the prevalence of Five Finger Policy in China's foreign policy. This aspect is dealt in a chapter in the book.

Settling Border Issues. Commencing from the north, China settled its border issues with USSR rather in a compromising tone by 1989. In the process, it gained control over Inner Manchuria where Mongols continue to face suppression under

15 Howland, D. (2011). The Dialectics of Chauvinism: Minority Nationalities and Territorial Sovereignty in Mao Zedong's New Democracy. Modern China, 37(2), 170–201. http://www.jstor.org/stable/23053322

16 Marxist.org (Selected Works of Mao Tse-tung: The Chinese Revolution And The Chinese Communist Party, December 1939, Chapter I-Part 1-The Chinese Nation. Retrieved from https://www.marxists.org/reference/archive/mao/selected-works/volume-2/mswv2_23.htm on 01 Nov 2022.

its rule. In the east, Japan continues to be engaged with the claim over Senkaku where Diaoyu Island is under Chinese control surrounding which China has constructed several artificial islands and militarized them.

To the Southeast, Philippines, Brunei and Vietnam are locked horns with China over Spratly and Paracel Islands that are at the core of South China Sea disputes.

To the south, having supported North Vietnam during the war with South Vietnam that attracted American intervention, China abruptly withdrew from North Vietnam in 1968. Its border issue with Soviets at that time was the primary reason. However, unified Vietnam faced incursion by Chinese PLA in February 1979. The conflict lasted 26 days resulting in impacts beyond the two countries. Soviet Russia, a staunch ally of Vietnam, found it is helpless to intervene; China found that its supposedly victorious battles could not dislodge Vietnam from Cambodia; and the rest of the world merely stood and watched. China gained some territory through border negotiations and quite surprisingly used the same corridor for building Hanoi-Kunming Highway in 2007 that has become a mark of vibrant Sino-Vietnamese relations.

Even though Mao expressly said 'As for Thailand, she should be treated like the fascist satellite states in Europe'[17], by 1970s and 80s China's relations with Thailand had metamorphosed into a vibrant bilateral cooperation. Notwithstanding the small border issue between Thailand and Cambodia, both of them are staunch allies of China in and outside ASEAN[18].

To the south west, China settled its border issues with Burma (Myanmar) voluntarily applying the Thalweg Principle[19]. China's eagerness to concede without much confrontation was guided by two aspects. First, in the years following

---

17 Mao, Tse-tung (1945). On Coalition Government April 24, 1945. Chapter 10. The Problem of Foreign Policy, Selected Works Volume III (political report made by Comrade Mao Tse-tung to the Seventh National Congress of the Communist Party of China). Retrieved from https://www.marxists.org/reference/archive/mao/selected-works/volume-3/mswv3_25.htm#p21

18 Chambers, M.R. (2005) 'The Chinese and the Thais are Brothers': the evolution of the Sino–Thai friendship, Journal of Contemporary China, 14:45, 599-629, DOI: 10.1080/10670560500205100

19 *Article VIII.* The Contracting Parties agree that wherever the boundary follows a river, the midstream line shall be the boundary in the case of an unnavigable river, and the middle line of the main navigational channel (the deepest watercourse) shall be the boundary in the case of a navigable river. In case the boundary river changes its course, the boundary line between the two countries shall remain unchanged in the absence of other agreements between the two sides. See: UN Treaty Series, Volume 1010: Nos. 14840-14847, p 142. https://treaties.un.org/doc/Publication/UNTS/Volume%201010/v1010.pdf

formation of PRC by Mao, Kuomintang under Chiang Kai Sheikh had retreated to Yunnan and Burma (apart from Taiwan). Mao's China needed Burma to flush out the Kuomintang to prevent a two-frontier threat to its mainland. Secondly, Burma voluntarily allowed PLA to enter and fight Kuomintang on its territory, enabling China to eliminate the threat to its soft underbelly. The generous settlement of borders with Burma was more in the form of appreciation and gratitude.

With Pakistan, China did not have a border issue when it came into being in 1947. With the accession of Kashmir into India, Indo-Pak hostilities commenced in 1948. When ceasefire was declared by India, a 559 km long Kashmir-Tibet border remained under the control of Pakistan. In 1963, Pakistan and China entered into an agreement[20] by which Pakistan ceded 5180 square kilometers of the 78000 sq km area under its occupation. This remains a bone of contention between India and China till now[21].

With Afghanistan, China settled its 47-mile border peaceably without any dispute through a bilateral agreement on November 22, 1963. The CIA in its intelligence report noted:

> For the past several years, the Chinese Communist Regime has been "tidying up its international boundaries.... The political nature of the settlements is witnessed by the generous terms offered by the Chinese to their smaller neighbors and the acceptance of the "Watershed Principle" where applicable. These positions contrast sharply with the Chinese belligerency towards India and USSR including the flat rejection of the Indian-proposed watershed boundary[22].

A little to the west and north, the erstwhile USSR had settled its border issues with China by 1989[23], and the disintegration of USSR did not create any ripples in its aftermath for China.

That China willingly and accommodatingly resolved its border issue with smaller neighbours stands in stark contrast with its unwillingness to apply

20 Lamb, A (1964) The Sino-Pakistani boundary agreement of 2 March 1963, Australian Outlook, 18:3, 299-312, DOI: 10.1080/10357716408444182

21 See Ministry of External Affairs Note on border disputes with neighbouring countries at Sl. No. 6 at https://mea.gov.in/Images/attach/ans22.pdf

22 Department of State, Bureau of Intelligence and Research (January 14, 1964). The Afghanistan-China Boundary Settlement. Retrieved from: https://www.cia.gov/readingroom/docs/CIA-RDP08C01297R000100120005-5.pdf

23 Dmochowski, T (2015). "The Settlement Of The Russian-Chinese Border Dispute." Polish Political Science Yearbook, vol. 44, annual 2015, pp. 56+. Gale Academic OneFile, link.gale.com/apps/doc/A528328339/AONE?u=tel_oweb&sid=googleScholar&xid=6f51c645. Accessed 3 Nov. 2022. & Maxwell, N. (1987). Sino-Soviet Boundary Agreement: Prelude to Sino-Indian Settlement? Economic and Political Weekly, 22(39), 1643–1647. http://www.jstor.org/stable/4377544

the same principles to its larger neighbours. Even amongst two of its largest neighbours, it accommodated Russian demands in a compromising manner while remaining bellicose towards India. This calls for gauging the complexities involved by prudently assessing the interests of the Chinese state. One chapter in this book deals with this aspect.

Distinctive Socialism. China's brand of socialism has remained complex, at least to the scholars outside China. Mao and his successors including Xi Jinping repeatedly talk of democracy and economic progress in the same words that the rest of the world understands them. However, the practices that China adopts have kept the world guessing as to their content and meaning. Inside China, the perceptions appear to be guided by historical and cultural factors that are being fostered, strengthened and continued in manners that are characteristically Chinese. For example, after two decades of vigorous economic growth through state controlled (socialist) mechanisms, China now appears to be focused on reviving its agriculture and peasantry.

> China's central government's "No. 1 document" for 2021 will boost the development of rural industries, including the development of a more self-reliant domestic seed industry, and integration with manufacturing and services sector aimed at diversifying the income of farmers, according to experts[24].

China has remained focused on its agriculture and peasantry ever since and especially in the past thirty years. However, as US Department of Agriculture noted[25] over a decade ago, the time has perhaps arrived when it is rightfully shifting its focus to integrating manufacturing services and develop market-supporting institutions for its sustained growth. It is important to recall that Mao had classified the poor peasants as the backbone of his revolution and that philosophy yet again is in play after four decades of Mao. But what attracts the attention is China's ability to blend the vision of post-Mao leaders like Deng Xiaoping, Zhang Chunqiao, Yao Wenyuan and Liu Shaoqi, into its policies even though some of those who opposed the Chairman for their belief in capitalist economic models were persecuted. This feature is still visible in China today. It portrays a culture that places value on learning, even though the source of the lesson is unacceptable.

Quite interestingly, China seems to have evolved a unique blend that may be labeled as Maoist-Capitalism which has propelled its spectacular growth till now.

---

24 Global Times (Feb 23, 2021). China to accelerate reform to agriculture, ensuring food security, Global Times (online), https://www.globaltimes.cn/page/202102/1216300.shtml Retrieved 03 Nov 2022.

25 Lohmar, B; Gale, F; Tuan, F & Hansen, J (April 2009). United States Department of Agriculture: Economic Information Bulletin No. 51, p 3. Retrieved from https://www.ers.usda.gov/webdocs/publications/44377/eib-51.pdf?v=0

The middle and lower rung leadership of China has always paid a characteristic obeisance to the elder, who in modern China dons the General Secretary of CCP's cap. To the west, this appears to be sycophantic as a result of oppressive practices by the higher leadership. To the Chinese mind, this is a cultural norm that has been upheld from imperial times. It apparently suits contemporary leadership too, even if their exposure to other cultures may indicate otherwise.

In more than one way, China remains an enigma.

Is China the hegemon that contemporary scholarship makes it out to be, or is it guided merely by its national interests, rooting its ambitions on the lessons from its history? Is it redeeming the Hundred Years of Humiliation that President Xi Jinping is voicing aloud, or has it sets heart to do so in order to reclaim its past glories? Are its claims over South China Sea based on its rights dawn from history, or are they part of a carefully constructed ambition clothed in the garb of history? Does it view the United States and India as its only impediments towards its objectives, or does it view other countries as merely steps in the ladder of its own progress irrespective of their size and potential?

These and several such questions underscore the tons of scholarship on China in our times. The answers may as well be found in the pages of history that are yet to open.

This book makes no claim to provide answers to any of these questions or even pretend to do so. Instead, it examines specific instances of China's engagements with India and the world through a Sino-centric perspective. In doing so, it hopes the findings will facilitate a greater appreciation of China's motives, methods and ambitions.

On April 14, 1933, Jawaharlal Nehru wrote to Indira Priyadarshini on Japan Bullies China. In that letter he said:

> China has the philosopher's temperament, and philosophers do not act hastily...... When an elephant falls, he takes time to get up; he cannot jump up like a cat or dog[26].

Nehru's words have a ring of prescience that may as well caution us to make an attempt to understand China for what China is. With millennia of history behind, it is to be understood from its own perspective, whether we wish to challenge or cooperate with it.

Srinivasan

Note: The chapters in the book are in the same format that they were written originally, some published and others included in this volume ab initio.

26 Nehru, J (1989). Jawaharlal Nehru: Glimpses of World History, Chapter 153: Japan Bullies China, New Delhi: Jawaharlal Nehru Memorial Fund, p 663.

Section I

China and India: Border Disputes and Beyond

1. China's Internal Political Dynamics and its Impact on India

Introduction

John Antonakis (Antonakis, et.al., 2010)[1] attempted to take 'stock of the methodological rigor with which causal claims are being made in a social sciences discipline by reviewing a representative sample of 110 articles on leadership published in the previous 10 years in top-tier journals'. Their conclusion pointed out that:

> Researchers cannot miss this call; understanding the causal foundations of social phenomena is too important a function for society. Important social phenomena deserve to be studied using the best possible methods and in sample situations that can generalize to real-world settings; ideally our goals should be to improve policies and practices.....(with improper measurement of theory, analysis and measurements), researchers "may wind up erecting theoretical skyscrapers on foundations of empirical jello."

One may wonder at the relevance of research conclusions in Applied Psychology to strategic studies in a paper that attempts to explore Sino-Indian relations. Strategic Studies belong to the discipline of international relations, for the strategic intent of any nation and the political, diplomatic, economic, military or even the social capital a nation possess are the instruments through which it expresses its strategic intent in its relations with other nations. David Lake (Lake, 2010)[2] emphasizes this aspect:

> given the crucial role of states in international politics and the pragmatic need to build parsimonious yet powerful explanations, state centric theory will continue to be a valuable—indeed, an indispensable—tool for scholars seeking to understand the world in which we live. Scholars who ignore the state do so at their peril, since no analysis of international relations can do without it.

The state-centric theory that Lake inferred as essential to the study of international relations has been explored by Putnam, Keohane and Milner, and Kahler in path breaking studies. Peter Gourevitch in his seminal work on *Domestic Politics and International Relations* went on to of course sound a caution that 'seeing the domestic and international dimensions as part of a whole does not ease the challenge of understanding. Indeed, it may make it harder, for it raises problems of endogeneity'. He further observes that among the three methods available to address this issue,

> the third body of work, the interaction of domestic and international, is the least well developed and the place that particularly requires further analysis. (Gourevoitch, 2002, P.310)[3]

While these scholarly works imply the inadequacies in relying implicitly on Realist School of thought to understand international relations (especially in the strategic dimension, by inference), they do highlight the dangers of omitting the domestic dimensions in a state's interaction with other nations.

A later paper on China[4] in this book propounds a hypothesis that its internal turmoil instigates a need to aggress on India whenever the political disposition in China faces acute crisis of survival. In arriving at that inference, the domestic politics of China prior to 1962 and the presence of compulsions that a victory in a war with India perceivably helps to address, are covered in that paper.

Apart from 1962, China has engaged in military confrontation with India on the border question a number of times. Taking the cue from John Antonakis, it would be proper that the hypothesis of the later paper is extended to study 'using the best possible methods and in sample situations that can generalize to real-world settings' in order to 'improve policies and practices'.

Locating Sino-Indian similarities and differences

In order to undertake the study of domestic politics vis-à-vis bilateral relations between Asia's biggest neighbors, certain common settings are derived from their histories. When viewed in perspective through the discourses in this paper, they will help in evolving greater understanding.

India and China emerged into the world stage as modern nation states in about the same time, 1947 and 1949, respectively. Curiously both had similarities and differences alike that may be listed as under:

- **British connection**: India was a former British colony. Britain, though it did not colonize China formally, interfered into that country's polity so much through the Opium Wars that the traditional monarchies in China fell, paving the way for communism to take roots. It is also important to recognize that Britain exited India in 1947 as a political power, but it held on to Chinese territory of Hong Kong for another fifty years, exiting only in 1997.

- **Governance Structure**: Though the British connection is common, India was left with a strong administrative structure, sound judiciary and the framework of legislative democracy introduced in the wake of Government of India Act 1935. At independence, India adopted for itself the longest written constitution in the world, expressly creating three independent pillars for its democracy, Legislative, Executive and Judiciary. In a remarkable step, India created a multi-party democratic system for governance, assisted by the Executive in governance, but kept the Judiciary independent of political or executive interference. Again through the seven decades after the Constitution, it adopted constitutionally guaranteed autonomous institutions like an Election Commission, Comptroller & Auditor General (CAG), and a third pillar of governance through Panchayati Raj System that places common citizens in public decision making capacity, etc. In so far as the military was concerned, India kept the military out of political and executive interference by definition. On the contrary, China was sunk into chaos in all these dimensions in the aftermath of British intervention, especially after the Treaty of Nanking in 1841-42. When it formed into PRC in 1949, it evolved a constitution that placed immense powers on a single party and its leadership. Taking Mao's 'Party controls all' policy further, every facet of its governance structure is placed under the direct control of the CCP.
- **Ancient Cultures**: Both India and China are the oldest surviving ancient cultures. Both had reached the pinnacles of their intellectual, spiritual and economic in their times. India's stars went into a decline initially under Mughal dynasties from 13th century and later under the British Rule. China also saw up and downswings in the course of its history. However, the uniqueness of Chinese culture was preserved more or less intact till the advent of Mao in 1949.
- **Societal Ethos**: Introduction of British education, though for colonial purposes, eventually turned India into a knowledge power. It helped in reforming the social ethos without affecting the family structure and cultural values. Independent India adopted for itself a 'secular' constitution that neither expressly supports any indigenous culture or ideology nor deems any culturally relevant institutions like family, practice of faith, etc, as a threat to its fundamental ethos. To be precise, it positively prides itself on the principle of 'unity through diversity'. China's cultural ethos and

family values were seriously impacted with the advent of Mao's Cultural Revolution, an unfortunate byproduct of his Party-is-Supreme Agenda. In addition, China's communist agenda has driven minorities and majorities alike (Buddhist, Muslim, Christian, etc) into rebellion against the regime's policies.

- **Socialist Model of Economy**: India's first PM, Nehru believed that the socialist model of economy viz., state controlled industries and state directed development was the way to uplift millions of Indians from poverty. Even the Indian Constitution adopted in 1950 proclaimed India as a Sovereign, Socialist, Secular and Democratic Republic. Nehru went in for Soviet assistance in building dams (Bakra-Nangal) and the Public Sector Industries to drive the economy. Ports, aerodromes, banks and other such institutions were state owned. Government control over business and industry in the later years (during Indira Gandhi era) earned an epithet 'Licence Raj'. While this phenomenon bred corruption, the Congress or any other political party, per se, did not control or conduct the business of running the economy. China on the other hand, centralized everything under the Communist Party. The CCP owned business, conducted business and even when Deng Xiaoping-style liberalization was introduced, CCP reigned supreme.
- **Internal Security Challenges**: Both India and China have serious internal security challenges. The difference is in their origins and the way they have been addressed. India inherited Kashmir issue based on religious divides and the unfounded imagination of Pakistan. The issue of Northeast was partly due to political handling. However, in the democratic ethos that India believes in, it has brought the insurgents to the dialogue mode more than divisive mode, however faulty that approach could be. In so for Naxalism is concerned, an impartial analysis would reveal that it is an economic issue than an anti-national one. Even there, the government's approach is one of softening the uprising in order to integrate the divisive forces into mainstream life. In none of these instances, India has attempted or even intended a fundamental change in the social ethos of the populations of the concerned region through indoctrination. In the case of China, it created the Tibetan and Uyghur uprising by its politically motivated territorial expansion agenda. The repressions that are driven by communist (Maoist, if we may say) agenda appear to be rooted on vague notions of historical ownership, for expanding its sphere of influence in Asia. At the heart of China's framework for dealing with the populations in Tibet, Xinjiang or elsewhere is Sinification – an attempt to substantially alter the social ethos to those of Han Chinese culture based on communist agenda.

The comparisons stated above are not inclusive. However, the objective of this paper will be best served if these comparisons are kept in mind to understand China's internal dynamics and its effect on relations with India.

Objective

This paper aims to look inside China's internal politics and the compulsions of its ruling elite in engaging with India on courses of collision through the later part of 20th and early 21st centuries. In doing so, it attempts to identify possible connections between its internal stability and aggressive postures with India.

Hypothesis

The hypothesis that its internal turmoil instigates the need to aggress on India whenever the political disposition in China faces a crisis of survival includes its economic ambitions in the world order of our times.

Methodology

This discourse relies on Descriptive Methods, drawing its inferences from published monographs, scholarly papers, books and articles in an effort to examine the perceptions and conclusions.

Considering the hypothesis, a historical narrative and analysis of political dynamics in China as well as India are necessary. Therefore, Part I (Indo-Chinese Border Clashes) follows the below given structure:

a) Brief description of event

b) China's internal situation

c) India's internal situation

After doing so, the hypotheses is tested in Part II, theorizing China's internal dynamics in its relations with India in Part III and then concluding with some recommendations.

Part I: Indo-Chinese Border Clashes

1967 Nathu La and Cho La Clashes

Event: On September 11th 1967, Chinese PLA attacked Indian positions in both these mountain passes in Sikkim.

> The Sikkim clashes came even as American troops were fighting in Vietnam, in the midst of Chairman Mao's unfolding Cultural Revolution, and a few months after China had conducted its first hydrogen bomb test.[5]

Deputy PM of India Morarji Desai who was touring the US at that time, stated to the American Press that China's territorial ambitions are pushing it to undertake such adventures but expressed his confidence that the attacks will be localized. The PM's remarks proved correct in the sense that the decisive victory by Indian Army in both the places sent the PLA packing its bags back home. The strategically important victory was scored by one of India's brilliant military commanders, Brigadier Sagat Singh, who happened to have arrived at Gangtok just a few months before. Sagat Singh's foresight and preparatory moves ensured a quick victory in a sharp five day clash, resulting in PLA's withdrawal with a bloody face.[6]

China's Internal Situation: Switching into China's internal dynamics in the same period, following are observed:

> From 1966 till 1976 China experienced a decade of brutal political turmoil. The Cultural Revolution began when Mao Zedong attacked the Chinese Communist Party itself along with the rest of the institutional structure of Chinese society. Tens of millions of people were affected by criticism, physical assault, suicide, and murder. Vast numbers of urban youth were "sent-down" to the remote countryside, where they spent much of a decade becoming disillusioned and embittered-the so-called "lost generation." Others were imprisoned in China's Gulag; literally hundreds of millions were caught up in the whirlwind of accusation, counteraccusation, self-criticism, and criticism of others.
>
> The ancient spine of Chinese society, the bureaucratic order, dislocated; factions fought each other in large and small work-units; families were broken; systems of communication, transportation, justice, public safety, health, and welfare fragmented. Parents were attacked by children; teachers were assaulted by students; Red Guards-adolescent and young adult revolutionaries-broke into homes, looted their contents, beat their occupants, and destroyed precious objects such as ancestral tablets, heirlooms, and books...Intellectuals were labeled enemies of the people. They were forced to negate the work of a lifetime. Cadres replaced cadres in dizzying swings of power that led to bitterness, recrimination, and revenge. By the late 1970s, though order was restored by the Army and the Party, cynicism, demoralization, and alienation were widespread. Delegitimation spread from a crisis of confidence in the political system to a wholesale questioning of the major indigenous cultural institutions.[7]

By 1966, four years after salvaging his pride and the superiority of his revolutionary ideals as against the revisionist forces within his party spearheaded by Liu Shaoqi and Deng Xiaoping, by first uplifting the image of PLA and then using it to quell dissent in the country side, Mao had found the factionalist forces produced by his Cultural Revolution had gone out of his control.[8]

By deploying the PLA as a militia in the country side, Mao had caused the professional image of a victorious peoples' army that he managed to obtain through

1962 Sino-Indian war to suffer. The surprise with which PLA had operated and the unfortunate but conducive environment on the Indian side in 1962 had played a great role in salvaging his leadership of Chinese nation amidst the precarious circumstances produced by the Great Leap Forward (GLP). The reforms instituted by Liu Shaoqi and Deng Xiaoping had also gone against the grain of Mao's philosophy, for he was convinced that these two lieutenants of him had tilted more towards Soviet Style reforms than the Maoist ideals that he prophesied.

Considering these circumstances, it may be inferred that re-establishing the image of PLA (as a potent tool in his hands) to divert national attention, Mao appeared to have ventured towards India's borders, especially towards the Northeast (NEFA), where he anticipated a quick victory will come forth.

It is also pertinent to recall Mao's famous Five Finger Policy that he had proclaimed almost immediately on coming to power in 1949 in these words:

> Xizang (Tibet) is China's right hand's palm, which is detached from its five fingers — of Ladakh, Nepal, Sikkim, Bhutan and Arunachal (formerly NEFA). As all of these five are either occupied by, or under the influence of India, it is China's responsibility to 'liberate' the five to be rejoined with Xizang (Tibet)[9 10].

By a swift action, if PLA could gain foothold in Sikkim, Mao's dream as expressed in Five Fingers Policy will redeem his prestige and the chaotic tussle for power that he was faced with inside China.

Both Nathu La and Cho La stood. Chinese ambition and Mao's anticipated dividends were quashed by a stronger Indian Army led by its brilliant commander, Brigadier Sagat Singh, on ground.

India's Internal Situation: It is again pertinent to note that Sagat Singh's superiors had issued orders to withdraw (similar to Se La in 1962, where Brigadier Hoshiar Singh was well prepared to meet the Chinese than they had anticipated), by his immediate superior. The order was rescinded by the Eastern Army Commander. Therefore, unlike Hoshiar Singh who died in executing his orders, Sagat Singh stood his ground and history proved him right[11].

What China did not perhaps take into consideration was the changes in Indian internal political and military climates in the years intervening 1962 and 1967. These can be listed briefly as below:

1. Nehru's death in 1964 saw Lal Bahadur Sastri as PM. Contrary to his diminutive physic, Sastri was of iron will and he had cemented together his policy of national progress and military strength by the famous 'Jai Jawan, Jai Kisan' motto which even now reverberates through Indian minds. Sastri's mettle was proven in Indo-Pak conflict of 1965 when the ill-conceived adventures of Pakistan were beaten to dust. It is also to be

noted that much to the discomfiture of US (and probably China), Pakistan succumbed to Russian intervention and agreed to ceasefire to save face. Though outwardly condescending, Sastri was equally tough in the negotiations in Tashkent. The Political climate had changed.

2. On 2nd December 1962, Sam Bahadur Manekshaw was appointed as GOC IV Corps, Tezpur. General Manekshaw undertook to reform the logistic and troop positions in NEFA (Arunachal Pradesh), having learnt the lessons of failure in the war just preceding his appointment. Fortunately, he was supported by an initially hesitant Nehru and his daughter, Indira Gandhi[12].
3. Sam Bahadur later assumed command of Eastern Army Command Kolkata on 16 November 1964[13] where he remained till early 1969.
4. The 1965 War which Pakistan launched believing that a demoralized Indian Army (courtesy 1962) could be beaten to submission, actually redeemed Indian Army's morale. The professional soldier therefore was ready, led by commanders who were loved by their troops. When the Chinese ventured into Nathu La and Cho La, they did not realize that they would be facing an army commanded by Brigadier Sagat Singh at Gangtok and General Sam Bahadur Manekshaw as his boss! And, unlike 1962, the political leadership did not dither, either.

1975: Tulung La, Tawang

Event: On 20 October 1975, Chinese patrols sneak into Tulung La in Tawang District of Arunachal Pradesh and fire at Indian patrol of the Assam Rifles. Four Indian soldiers died but the Indian response got the Chinese retreating in haste.

China's Internal Situation: The political scenario in China and India back then is given below. To start with China:

By 1975, the tussle for power within the CCP had reached a new dimension. Deng Xiaoping, banished and hounded by Mao and Zhou Enlai, had returned to the political spectrum. Mao's failing health and Zhou's ascendency with Mao's support had again factionalized the Communist party owing to the revisionist tendencies that Deng had always displayed. Deng was also seen as 'soft' on America which, despite the setbacks suffered in its Vietnam War, was attempting a comeback in East Asian affairs. To recall:

> The United States used the organization [SEATO] as its justification for refusing to go forward with the 1956 elections intended to reunify Vietnam, instead maintaining the divide between communist North Vietnam and South Vietnam at the 17th parallel. As the conflict in Vietnam unfolded, the inclusion of Vietnam

as a territory under SEATO protection gave the United States the legal framework for its continued involvement there.[14]

However, in 1977 SEATO was formally dissolved after many members realized that their own national ambitions were not served by SEATO. In particular, failure to prevent unification of Vietnam was viewed in China as a strategic failure by US. Vietnam eventually ended up being a communist, one party state, much to the delight of Chinese. It may be recalled that way back in 1954, Mao in his conversations with Nehru had specifically stated that China helped Ho Chi Minh.[15]

With Mao's failing health, he had chosen Hua Guofeng as his successor, contrary to the aspirations of many others who were seen as closer to him. The choice of succession created a tug of war of sorts between the Gang of Four, Deng and those loyal to Mao.

Thus, in the internal political climate of China, it was once again necessary to beef up the image of the ideals that Mao's policies stood for by entering Tawang, historically claimed as Chinese territory. A victory of sorts would have perhaps tilted the scales in favor of Mao and his supporters.

India's Internal Situation: In India on the other hand, Indira Gandhi had become politically ambitious. Her policies and programs were increasingly criticized by opposition parties, media and the actions of her government were seen as detrimental to democratic ethos enshrined in Indian Constitution. In June 1975, she had usurped absolute power by declaring the infamous Emergency. As a consequence, Indian public were under agitated moods, democratic media was throttled and the atmosphere appeared just right in China's favor. Added to the scene were the Bangladeshi refugee situation, which was turning Assam slowly into a cauldron of chaos. The uncompromising mood of the Nagas, especially after the formation of Naga Federal Government with the support of China, also appeared propitious.

China struck again on 20 October 1975 in an attempt to use the PLA for restoring Mao's political power. China once more misjudged the capabilities of an Indian Army that had emerged supremely victorious in the aftermath of 1971. Led by Sam Bahadur Manekshaw, it had created a new country in South Asia fighting on two fronts and demolishing the myth of Pakistani superiority, notwithstanding overt America military aid to Pakistan. And on the political dimension, Indira Gandhi was no weak hearted leader either.

2013, 2014, and 2015

Event: In April 2013, India reported that Chinese troops established a camp in the Daulat Beg Oldi sector, 10 km (6.2 mi) on their side of the Line of Actual Control

(LAC), the de facto border between the two countries. This was later revised to a 19-km (11.8-mi) claim. In an eye ball to eye ball standoff, both countries exercised control and limited their maneuvers to merely testing each other's will. After nearly a month, in May, Chinese withdrew unilaterally without any further provocation.

China's Internal Situation: By 2013, the political climate inside China had changed. Mao's heir apparent, Zhou Enlai died in January 1976. By now an ailing Mao, faced with the predicament of naming a successor, ended up naming Hua Guofeng instead of the anticipated Zhou protégé Zhang Chunqiao. In April 1976, during the Chinese traditional day of mourning (Qingming), the Militia's actions to remove floral tributes to Zhou Enlai in Tiananmen Square led to mass rioting. Deng Xiaoping was blamed for mass incitement and he was literally banished from Peking. Deng and his sympathizers shifted base to Guangzhou[16].

Hua Guofeng, succeeding Zhou in this climate, also took steps to curb the 'Gang of Four' in Shanghai who were viewed as detrimental to China's progress through Maoist ideals. Internal dynamics allowed Deng a comeback into mainstream politics after the 3rd Plenary Session of the 11th Central Committee of the Chinese Communist Party in December, 1978[17].

When he came to power in January 1979, Deng chose to visit the United States first, signaling his willingness to open up Chinese economy to the outside world. He undertook to reform and rescind many of Mao's programs instituted during the Cultural Revolution. He paid particular attention to Guagzhou in developing it as a Special Economic Zone to invite foreign investment. Though his clamping down on the Tiananmen Uprising in 1989 invited worldwide criticism, internally he was praised for reverting Hong Kong to Chinese control in 1997 and Macau later in 1999. He was also noted for his principle of not promoting perpetuity in power by introducing tenures for political office. His successors Hu Jintao and Jiang Jemin were to follow in his footsteps after Deng's demise in 1997. Deng's policy became known as Socialism with Chinese Characteristics (combining free market principles).

However, the rise of Xi Jinping in office and eventually as President of PRC in 2012 saw many of Deng's policies being reversed. Xi reportedly resented the lack of appreciation to his own father, Xi Zhongxun, who apparently played vital role in opening up Chinese economy in Guagzhou when Deng was in power[18]. Whether the family feud exists or not, Xi undertook to overhaul China's policies by introducing larger Party control over economy and the PLA. In fact, this centralization of power, reflecting a new attempt at curiously combining Mao-Deng principles has its effects in social, economic and political dimensions of present day China[19] [20].

It is also to be recalled that within few days of assuming the mantle, Xi Jinping had called all higher officials to Tiananmen Square where he recalled to their memory the 'Hundred Years of Shame' (in the aftermath of the Opium Wars) and revival of China's historical glory.[21] President Xi's vision for China can be summarized as:

- Reclaiming China's past glory, which can be read as realizing the Mao's ideal of bringing the Five Fingers into Chinese control again.
- Reviving China's trade through a party controlled mechanism that will expand trade and economic relations through BRI, patently suitable to Chinese interests.

These two emerging perceptions coupled with Xi's consistent attempt at retaining power (he had already appropriated to himself the power to stay in power for life)[22], purging the Party and bureaucracy or even the PLA of elements not inclined to support his vision[23] [24] lead to a perceptible motive in China's PLA's bullying tactics in various points across the Sino-Indian border with an increasing frequency from 2013.

The changes in the dynamics of internal political power structure in China could be understood, more sharply, by this observation in a scholarly study by Dimitar D. Gueorguiev[25]:

> Elite politics under the Xi Jinping administration has been anything but dull. Former and rising leaders within the Party have been convicted of corruption and the top echelons of power have been thoroughly reconstituted, all while Xi Jinping has doubled his portfolio, enshrined his name in the CCP charter, expanded his anti-corruption campaign to the state and public sector, and abolished any legal impediments to holding on to power indefinitely.
>
> Even though we cannot predict Xi's intentions, we can observe the more subtle but systemic impact his power consolidation efforts have had on the Chinese political and administrative system. The impact is broad but concentrated in three areas. First, traditional divisions of power are being blurred, with party and state functions becoming increasingly indistinguishable. Second, with regards to leadership selection and elite decision-making, we are seeing a departure from intra-party democracy in favour of more top-heavy modes of consultation. The third concerns future cohorts of power, where bottlenecks in the leadership pipeline reveal potential shortages in qualified contenders for future transitions. While these changes do not directly impinge on party norms, they pose challenges to the institutional structure of the party-state and its ability to govern.

Apart from April 2013 in eastern Ladakh, PLA again returned in September 2014 on a three week-standoff in Demchok in Ladakh. A year later, in 2015, PLA again ventured into Burtse, northern Ladakh in which Indian troops eventually dismantled the watch tower built by Chinese troops.

After a year of comparative peace in 2016, PLA returned with a series of incursions in Ladakh and Sikkim in the following instances:

- **June 2017** - A military standoff occurs in the disputed territory of Doklam, near the Doka La pass along the Indian state of **Sikkim and Bhutan** border. China brings heavy road-building equipment to the Doklam region and begins constructing a road. This results in the Indian intervention of China's road construction on June 18, two days after the construction begins.
- **August 2017** - An incident occurs also at **Pangong Tso,** Ladakh. Several soldiers on both sides sustain injuries. Indian media reports that around 72 Indian soldiers are injured.
- **May 5, 2020** - Indian and Chinese soldiers clash at **Pangong Tso**, the lake that extends from Ladakh to the Tibetan Autonomous Region, China, with the LAC passing through it.
- **May 10, 2020** - Faceoff at the Muguthang Valley in **Sikkim**. Several troops numbering 11 men are left slightly injured in the encounter, of which seven are Chinese soldiers and four Indian ones, according to CNN-News18. Press Trust of India reported that the incident involved 150 soldiers; stones were also thrown.
- **May 21, 2020** - Chinese troops enter into the Galwan River valley in **Ladakh** region, citing objections to Indian road construction. The road under construction is said to branch off from the Darbuk–Shyok–Daulat Beg Oldi Road and lead into the Galwan valley.
- **May 24, 2020** - Chinese camp at three places around **Pangong Tso**: Hot Springs, Patrolling Point 14, and Patrolling Point 15. At each of these places, around 800-1000 Chinese soldiers pitch tents, deploying heavy vehicles and monitoring equipment.
- **June 15, 2020** - An Indian colonel and 19 soldiers killed in a "violent face-off" with the Chinese troops at the Galwan Valley, **Ladakh.**

India's Internal Situation: It is queer that a research paper leaves something to the imagination and understanding of a reader. However, assuming that liberty since 2013-2014 marked a substantial change in the political environment of India, the readers would be familiar with recent events. Balakot strikes need not be mentioned, which postulates as the watershed moment in India's thinking and the demonstrated change in the way government of India expresses its intent.

Part II: Inferences

The adventures of the PLA from 1962 till now can be tabulated as below:

Table 1: China's Incursions into Indian Territory

Year	Place of Intrusion or Clashes
1962	Aksai Chin, Ladakh & NEFA (Arunachal Pradesh)
1967	Nathu La and Cho La, Sikkim
1975	Tulung La, Tawang, Arunachal Pradesh
1986-87	Sumdorong Chu, Tawang, Arunachal Pradesh
2013	DBO, Ladakh
June 2017	Doklam, Sikkim-Bhutan
August 2017	Pangong Tso, Ladakh
May 2020	Pangong Tso, Ladakh
May 2020	Muguthang, Sikkim
May-June 2020	Pangong Tso & Galwan, Ladakh

Source: Compiled by Author

The tabulation shows that out of the eleven sector/region wise recorded standoff or clash between India and China, 03 are in Arunachal Pradesh (Tawang), 05 are in Ladakh and 03 are in Sikkim.

Statistical research has only one purpose: it leads to the most logical next question, why? In the tons of contemporary analysis available in public domain on China and its BRI program many obvious answers stand out.

1. Indian Ocean has become key to China's BRI program and its discernible ambition for "Two Oceans Policy". A stated investment of USD 60 billion in CPEC which is the largest single chunk of its BRI program; acquiring Hambantota in Sri Lanka; port facilities in Bangladesh; over USD 20 bn investment in Myanmar and acquisition of Djibouti - each of these demonstrate its commitment to what Xi calls as the glorious revival of China's past through trade.
2. With the internal stability of Pakistan perennially in question, especially the Baluch resistance to Chinese projects,[26] Pakistan being a reliable partner is a thorn that is pressing the skin of its dream balloon. The other alternatives are through Myanmar, which is under unprecedented internal uprising threatening an easier approach to Bay of Bengal through 'win-win partnership', a term that Xi is fond of using.
3. Sri Lanka and Djibouti are advantageous when the alternate route to Indian Ocean through Gwadar or Myanmar are securely in China's hold. The connectivity to Europe through Gwadar is likely to reduce transportation charges by over 50 percent.[27] However, the CPEC road passes through

Pakistan Occupied Kashmir and therefore subject to perceivable threats due to India's turbulent relations with Pakistan. The Indian decision to abrogate Article 370 and trifurcate Jammu & Kashmir was vociferously objected to by China owing to its own economic concerns than its concerns for its all-weather friend, Pakistan.

4. Predominant Chinese interest in securing more territories in Aksai Chin towards Galwan and Pangong Tso valley therefore could be read as its actions to protect its flanks. This in the foreseeable future may become more aggressive, subject only to Pakistan's ability to maintain law and order in its own territories.
5. Though laudable, the 16 rounds of Sino-Indian border negotiations merit mention only on the diplomatic score card. On ground, China's unwillingness to revert to its own stated '1959 positions' has seen much water flow below the bridge.

Part III: Theorizing China's Internal Dynamics in its Relations with India

Our brief survey of Chinese internal political dynamics brings forth two distinctive principles that appear to be guiding China's actions: **its historical-cultural ambitions and the prestige of ruling elite** (as reflected through PLA's actions in securing power to ruling elites). The contemporary history of China vis-à-vis its relations with India could be summarized as below:

1. In the Mao era spanning from 1949 to 1976, historic claims to territory and need to enhance PLA's prestige were used as a tool for appropriating power to Mao and obtaining internal political stability.
2. In the Deng era from 1978 to 1989, China went inwards to focus on negating some of Mao's ideals, opening its economy and facilitating foreign trade to bring in development. In the process, it remained focused on revamping its internal strength without, of course, giving up its historical claims to Indian territories. These policies generally appear to have been upheld by Hu Jintao and Jiang Jemin.
3. In the Xi Jinping era commencing 2012, China's historic claims appear to have been married to its economic development goals. In the process, China has become increasingly aggressive in utilizing PLA in its attempts to browbeat India, if not to give up its territories, at least to accommodate its interests through trade and other negotiations.

The grand visions that Xi has set forth for China are intertwined with its perception of cultural-historical superiority and the faith in the collective wisdom that Xi appears to be drawing from a combination of Mao-Deng philosophies. His hard stand on decentralized power structure or liberalization of trade against what he calls 'socialist economic system', for example, could be understood from his statements like:

> ...any point of view that wants to negate the public ownership economy or wants to negate the non-public economy, is not in accordance with the fundamental interests of the vast majority of the people. All of them are wrong because of their lack in conformity with the requirements of China's reform and development.[28]

Conclusion

To conclude this attempt at understanding China's internal political dynamics and its impact on India, the following are pertinent:

- China holds her historical imagination of tribute extracting state as central to her imagination of its political power. Any action by any other country that would ingress on this conception would be viewed as inimical to China's interests.
- China used the historical claims to borders with India in periods of its internal crisis to raise the prestige of PLA, divert national attention and use PLA to vanquish and purge people to secure power to the ruling elite.
- China's BRI dream is a combination of Mao's imagination of the cultural superiority of Chinese and its ambition to reclaim past economic glory, which it feels was lost during the Hundred Years of Shame. Xi's China acts on these constructs.

On India's part, it had neither territorial ambitions in the past nor is attempting to develop one now. The superiority of its culture has never clouded India's willingness to understand and reach out to other nations without any express self-interest. However, with reference to China, India needs to take its Look East-Act East; Middle East, Central Asia and West Asia Policies to the next level of constructive engagement so as to negate undesirable fall outs on its national interests. Energy security, human security and environmental security agenda apart, India must embark on, if one may say, security of democracy in the subcontinent and beyond through meaningful engagements to promote, consolidate and strengthen democratic frameworks in other nations.

In so far as physical aggressions are concerned, India must spell out the national concerns with reference to borders, develop a robust military infrastructure led by world class military leadership. The Sagat Singh-Manekshaw episodes provide adequate examples in drawing this conclusion. To this extent, apart from steps taken towards promoting indigenization in Defence production, India must fructify institutions like Indian National Defence University (INDU) which could become the bedrock of R&D in the intellectual dimension in assessing the nuts and bolts of international relations, theoretically or otherwise.

China will aggress again since its internal challenges are growing due to continuing Uygur, Tibetan and Hong Kong agitations. The internet highway, how much so ever China may control it, will bring in new ideas and aspirations for democracy, not necessarily in the western construct but more due to the aspirations of common Chinese citizens. Its compulsions and setbacks in trade wars could threaten the power elite again since they have huge personal stakes in it.

Its Debt Trap or Cheque Book diplomacy is increasingly creating misalignments in national economies, as is being witnessed in the recent Sri Lankan appeal for additional Chinese debt to service its economy,[29] which China cannot support in the long run. It is only a question of time before Pakistan and other countries in similar predicaments raise their borrowing/waiver hats too. These developments may push them more into China's camp in the short term, rending the South Asian or Asian stability into a predicament, but in the long term will be subjected to more rebellious response from their native populations. India needs to look at efficacious bilateral means to assist these countries to climb out of the economic collapse that they will eventually reach in the course of their current travel. Indo-Japanese joint offer to develop port infrastructure in Sri Lanka and India's cautious tone in Human Rights Council over war crimes in Sri Lanka indicate that the Indian polity is moving in the right direction. Such initiatives need to be evaluated with reference to Nepal, Bangladesh, Afghanistan, Mauritius and especially Myanmar. Positive engagement to assist in economic development of these countries and constructive mechanisms to promote democracy there are in India's long term interests.

India has a historic opportunity now to set the historical record right by perceptive analysis and prospective leadership.

2. China's Unilateral Withdrawal in 1962: Did China Have an Internal Compulsion?

Slap on the Face

India's first PM, Jawaharlal Nehru wrote to his daughter Indira Priyadarshini Gandhi-Nehru, a series of some 196 letters from his Nainital and Bareilly prisons from 1930 to 1933. These were published as The Glimpses of World History, first by Kitabistan, Allahabad, in two volumes and later as a single volume by the Jawaharlal Nehru Memorial Fund in 1982. In page 267 of the 1982 edition, Nehru (Nehru, 1982)[1] states that:

> For the eastern world, China is very much the elder brother, the clever, favoured and cultured one, very conscious of her superiority, but wishing well to the younger brothers and willing to teach them and share with them his own culture and civilization.

Nehru wrote at least eight letters spanning some 36 pages on China exclusively on her history, civilization, wars, turmoil during Opium Wars and the eventual forming of PRC. In the context of Japanese invasion of China, he again wrote:

> China has the philosophers' temperament, and philosophers do not act hastily. (P.663)[2]

With Nehru becoming the PM of India in 1947, relations with China were warmly established. But for consenting to allow Burma to become the first non-Soviet Bloc country to recognize the PRC in 1949, India may as well have been the first to do so. The period from 1949 to 1954 could be stated as the honeymoon era in Sino-Indian relations. Delhi's streets witnessed a beaming Nehru and his Chinese counterpart, Chou Enlai mouthing 'Hindi-Chini bhai, bhai' during this period. PM Chou Enlai visited India most regularly and eventually raised the border question with Nehru during his visit in 1955. A brief account of the events that led to 1962 conflict are below:

- 1949: India recognizes the People's Republic of China.

- 1950: India opposes UN resolutions branding China as an aggressor in the Korean War.
- 1954: China and India sign Panchsheel treaty
- 1955: India objects to the inclusion of a portion of northern frontier on the official map of China.
- 1956: Chou en Lai visits India for the second time. The border question is formally raised.
- 1958: India objects to inclusion of parts of Assam and NEFA as part of Chinese territories in its maps.
- 1959: Dalai Lama escapes from Tibet, India gives asylum. China refuses to accept the McMohan line. Chinese troops kill nine Indian soldiers and capture ten in Aksai Chin.
- 1960: Pushed by Khrushchev, Chou Enlai meets Nehru in Delhi. Talks end in a deadlock.
- 1961: Border skirmishes intensify.
- 1962: China captures Bomdila and then announces a unilateral ceasefire.
- 1962: Colombo proposals negotiated between Nehru and Chou en Lai.

Mountains of analyses have been written on the 1962 debacle that eventually dimmed Nehru's stature as a statesman. It would suffice to say that Nehru suffered more acutely from the 'slap' that Chinese successfully planted on Indian cheek for trusting them.

The general vein of tons of analyses on 1962 portray Chinese territorial ambitions, Nehru's ambivalent dealing with them, an unprepared army being stretched to indefensible positions, political interference in choice of commanders to oversee operations, Dalai lama's escape from Tibet and asylum in India, etc.

Objective

The intent in this paper is not to revisit well-known and widely discussed analyses or produce a critique on them. Instead, four questions mentioned below are examined to find answers to them:

1. Did China squander a victory and potential strategic advantage?
2. Were there compulsions for it to do so that have escaped the attention of India or the world, for that matter?
3. What advantages did it avail?
4. What can be learned from deciphering Chinese mind?

For doing so, an attempt to tease history is made to extract some lessons. Understanding China's methods and means by doing so, may reveal lessons to deal with or even anticipate its moves in the geopolitical maze of the contemporary world.

The nuts and bolts of 1962 war are found in tons of scholarly explorations, government reports like that of Henderson Brooks and the summary of personal experiences recorded by Brigadier Dalvi in his *Himalayan Blunder* or for that matter *The Untold Story* by Major General BM Kaul. These details are therefore passed over. The political instances concerning Sardar Patel's prophetic warning to Nehru in 1957 of Chinese incursions, Defence Minister Krishna Menon's fracas with the military top brass, the strength of relationship between Nehru & Krishna Menon, and, the temptation to visit Sardar KM Panikkar's *In Two Chinas: Memoirs of a Diplomat,* are also side-stepped. Instead, we step right into 1962, before taking a brief tour of China's internal political climate.

A Strange Way to Squander Victory

Credible inputs from all sources openly available on the war indicate that the Chinese first set foot into Indian Arunachal Pradesh on 20 October 1962. In the course of events thereafter, the Chinese forces reached the outskirts of Tezpur in Assam, a good 150 kilometers from their point of entry into Indian Territory. Panic set about in the town reached a crescendo when business men fled the city, mass fleeing of civilian families occurred and even the State bank of India went about burning currency notes to prevent them from falling into Chinese hands. To top it all, the District Commissioner (DC) at Tezpur, Dr PK Das, fled the town with his family in a military vehicle, leaving the administration to fall into a spiral of panic. Dr Das was perhaps the only case when a DC was dismissed by the President of India for dereliction of duty! [3, 4, 5]

Tezpur straddles the Brahmputra River and the highway that crosses the Siliguri Corridor into the heart of India itself. The general retreat that drove the Indian army across the Siliguri Corridor and the lack of political will rendered a rare opportunity to the Chinese to march into the heartlands of India. There was little in those times that would have stopped them from doing so or at least add to India's discomfiture in monumental terms. Yet, thirty one days after crossing into India, and slapping its pride where it hurts even today, Chinese declared unilateral ceasefire on 21 November and voluntarily withdrew to the pre-war positions, at least in Arunachal Pradesh.

Why did they do so? Even if we grant that India could not have been beaten into that kind of submission had the Chinese ventured up to the Siliguri Corridor, there is as yet no credible analysis as to why did they act so mysteriously?

What was happening in or about China to give up the victory?

To elicit an answer, it is necessary to cross into the Chinese border virtually and visit them in Peking (Beijing).

Soon after assuming power as Head of State in the Chinese Revolution of 1949, Mao Tse Tung visited Soviet Russia. In the longest recorded stay of a Head of State in a foreign country, Mao toured Soviet factories and industries. What he saw drove home a lesson – industrialization was essential to develop the economy. Returning back to China with a pact with Joseph Stalin by which Soviet Union extended USD 300 million and technical assistance, Mao set about rebuilding a civil war ravaged China. The Soviet assistance included 150 development projects financed and staffed by Soviet Union. However, by 1957-58, Mao and Nikita Khrushchev had developed ideological differences leading to the withdrawal of 15000 Soviet engineers and staff from China. Realizing how vulnerable China was without homegrown technical expertise, Mao turned to technological development. This resulted in drawing young and abled Chinese from peasantry into industrialization efforts. A predominantly agrarian China, in the process suffered food shortages that took the form of the most catastrophic famine in contemporary world history. The 'Great Leap Forward' which Mao had announced in 1958 resulted in more than 56 million deaths, including 3 million by suicide[6]. The people of China as well as the elites in Communist Party like Marshal Peng Dehuai[7] who commanded the Chinese troops in the Korean War, denounced the lack of foresight and over reliance on Soviet Model of development. Mao's regime was left with little option but to persecute the 'rebels' to save the great Chinese nation and their communist ideology.

In 1957, China had also marched into Tibet to claim its sovereignty over a people who have at best been tribute paying territories, with no more allegiance to China than religious affinity and the fear of armed conflict. In 1959, Dalai Lama fled to India, seeking political asylum.

Facing vociferous protest at home over the Great Leap Forward, suffering millions of death, an explosive environment for counter-communist revolt, and the tenuous hold on Tibet attracting international attention, China needed something that would enhance the prestige of the ruling echelon as well as unite the nation under the communist party.

Internally, it took to purging people like Marshal Peng, sending a lesson to all those who 'doubted' the communist regime. Externally, China turned to India. An ambivalent leadership in India, poorly defined and defended borders (in any case never ratified by China historically or otherwise) and the inadvertent moves made by the Indian political leadership to push ill-equipped troops to the far reaches of Arunachal Pradesh were sufficient reasons to take recourse to such a step to divert national attention.

The armed revolts against China in Tibet aided by CIA and Nehru's belief that moving troops to the border outposts will perhaps force Chinese into granting a semblance of autonomy to Tibet provided exceptional excuses to Mao to take recourse to the war.

Advantages to China

Whether the Chinese really intended or not, the war gave them three strategically important advantages for posterity:

1. Even by the wildest stretch of imagination, India would never ever contemplate annexing Tibetan territories into its own or establishing formal diplomatic ties with Dalai Lama led Tibetan Government (in spite of allowing them to establish a government in exile at Dharamshala). Contemporary history tells us that this indeed proved to be the case and even after decades of the Tibetan Government in Exile functioning from its soil, India has not even formally recognized it. On the contrary, India's action of accepting Chinese suzerainty over Tibet in the immediate aftermath of Dalai Lama's exile and the war (Sangay, 2003)[8], reinforces our view that the Chinese assessment of Indian psyche could indeed be correct, at least in so far as the top political leadership was concerned.
2. Aksai Chin having been overrun, a strategically important wedge across the only all-weather high altitude pass in western Himalayas will be in their control. This would allow them to pressurize India at will. Added to this, China had already successfully negotiated with Pakistan to have 22000 sq km territory ceded to them in PoK that remained with Pakistan after the premature cessation of Indo-Pak hostilities in 1948 (Wagner & Stanzel, 2020)[9].
3. A vague and ill-defined border in Aksai Chin coupled with physical occupation of vast swathes of it will always act as a pressure point on India. Any move that India may make to claim those Chinese occupied territories can always be played nationally and internationally to portray India as the aggressor, and that retaliatory actions by China could be portrayed as its genuine concerns over protecting sovereign rights. Foreign Minister Wang Yi's statement[10] on March 07, 2021 to Chinese Parliament reinforces our presumption in this regard.
4. More importantly, shaming India that was led by Nehru, acclaimed as the greatest statesman of the decolonized world at that time, helped reinforce the superiority of the ideals of People's Revolution that Mao so eloquently represented. Though the PLA was poorly equipped, that a British trained-battle proven-modern (in comparison) Indian Army could be beaten

raised the prestige of Mao and CCP in a time when ordinary citizens were beginning to have serious doubts about it. It may also be pertinent to recall Nehru's decision not to commit a far superior Indian Air Force to battle, inadvertently again helped in shaping such an aura around PLA in China. The advantages for shoring up domestic prestige in the chaotic aftermath of the Great Leap Forward were indeed tremendous.

India, alas, was merely a scapegoat rendered vulnerable by virtue of its own lack of appreciation of the power of geopolitics. In any case, another dimension that helped the Chinese was the distrust and highhanded treatment that had despoiled the relations between the Indian Army headed by an illustrious man, General Thimmayya, and a Nehru-Menon combine that was mired in its own false pride and lurking fears of a military takeover of India[11]. Krishna Menon's push to have officers of his choice rise to positions of command (BM Kaul particularly[12]) had crippled the operational, professional and battle proven army. Nehru's precipitous announcement in the Parliament after the Khenzemane and Longju incidents of the decision to construct National Highway G219 across the Aksai Chin and directions to the Army to move to forward posts in NEFA (Arunachal Pradesh) without adequate equipment and supplies in August 1959 had led to the tendering of resignation by the Chief of the Army in protest. Instead of understanding the strategic implications, Nehru-Menon combine played out a slander campaign against the man who was loved by the Army as 'the Soldier's General'.[13]

The resulting environment of these cumulative events played to the advantage of China. To presume that China's embassy at New Delhi was not aware of the ripening Indian atmosphere when these events made banner headlines in Indian newspapers of the time is not as presumptuous as it seems.

This inference is also supported by studies done on China's foreign policy published by Stanford University as an edited volume titled New Directions in the Study of Chinese Foreign Policy, in which John w. Garver (Garver (2006)[14] specifically states:

> The goal was to be achieved by inflicting a painful defeat on India, thus demonstrating the futility and danger of aggressing against borders defended by the PLA and forcing India to abandon the forward policy. Sharp military defeat also would also compel India to again sit down at the negotiating table and solve the Sino-Indian Border problem. This too would achieve peaceful stability along the western borders.

The purpose of any research is to validate a theory. The hypothesis that China undertook the 1962 adventure owing to internal compulsions therefore needs validation. Unlike the Post-Galwan disengagement, there is a long span of contemporary history for us to attempt such an examination. China's internal environment in 1961-65 period requires a visitation.

Internal Political Compulsions in China

By 1959, Mao had established a "first line" reform that was headed by Liu Shaoqi as Chairman of PRC (with Mao still as the Party Chairman) and Deng Xiaoping. Both these leaders set about reforming the economy in what by 1962 Mao came to view as 'Soviet style Revisionism' that was contrary to the revolutionary tradition with which he had set about restructuring China.

> Indeed, by 1962 in many areas of rural China, the collective system in agriculture had broken down completely, and individual farming was revived. Policy toward literature, art, and motion pictures permitted a "thaw" involving treatment of a far broader range of subjects and a revival of many older, prerevolutionary artistic forms. The new program in industry strengthened the hands of managers and made a worker's efforts more closely attuned to his rewards. Similar policies were adopted in other areas.[15]

Mao felt that these revisionist policies by Liu-Deng will undo the very ideals on which his peasant revolution was based. He therefore, by January 1962, moved to the 'second line' to concentrate "on dealing with questions of the direction, policy, and line of the party and the state."

> Mao took a number of initiatives in domestic and foreign policy during the period. At a major Central Committee plenum in September 1962, he insisted that "class struggle" remain high on the Chinese agenda, even as enormous efforts continued to be made to revive the economy. He also called for a campaign of "socialist education," aimed primarily at reviving the demoralized party apparatus in the countryside. [16]

In his drive towards revolutionization of China, Mao viewed PLA as an important tool. He and his trusted lieutenant Lin Biao who headed the Military, had set about re-building the PLA modeled on the cardinal Maoist ideal of a peasant army - consisting of high morale (perceived of as) sufficient to deal with technological superiority of western styled armies – a lesson that Mao sincerely believed from his days from the Long March when he successfully defeated Kuomintang armies that relied on American weapons to fight his revolutionaries. This also perhaps explains the 'wave technique' employed by the PLA comprising of unarmed Chinese soldiers repeatedly attacking Indian positions.

> **Events on the Sino-Indian border in the fall of 1962 helped the PLA reestablish discipline and its image.** From 1959 to 1962 both India and China, initially as a by-product of the uprising in Tibet, resorted to military force along their

> disputed border. On Oct. 12, 1962, a week before the Chinese moved troops into disputed border territories, Indian Prime Minister Jawaharlal Nehru stated that the army was to free all Indian Territory of "Chinese intruders." In the conflict that followed, Beijing's regiments defeated Indian forces in the border region, penetrating well beyond it. The Chinese then withdrew from most of the invaded area and established a demilitarized zone on either side of the line of control. **Most significantly, the leadership seized on the army's victory and began to experiment with the possibility of using army heroes as the ideal types for popular emulation.**

As the military forces under Lin increasingly showed that they could combine ideological purity with technical virtuosity, Mao tried to expand the PLA's organizational authority and its political role. Beginning in 1963, Mao called on all Chinese to "learn from the PLA." Then, starting in 1964, Mao insisted that political departments modeled on those in the PLA be established in all major government bureaucracies. In many cases, political workers from the PLA itself staffed these new bodies, thus effectively penetrating the civilian government apparatus. Other efforts, such as a national propaganda campaign to learn from a purported army hero, Lei Feng, also contributed to enhancement of the PLA's prestige. [17]

> The analysis therefore shows that Mao used the unilateral withdrawal in 1962 for consolidating his political power and also reinforce the image that his ideology was supreme over the Soviet model reforms that Li Shaoqi and Deng apparently attempted to enlarge. It is evident that the PLA was used as an effective to tool to stabilize the internal political struggle in China and also to demonstrate Mao's concept of peoples' war. In this view, we are supported by inferences drawn by Ranjana Kakkar (Kakkar, 1977)[18].

In the aftermath of 1962, China turned inward with Mao consolidating his power and eventually launching the Cultural Revolution of 1968-69 to purge the Party, Cadre and even the PLA of all those elements that went against the Maoist programs for reforms in China. However, **Mao's decision to turn PLA into an instrument of 'peacekeeping' in rural China in this period seriously affected its effectiveness as a professional military as witnessed in the 1969 Sino-Soviet war and 1979 Sino-Vietnamese War** (Andrew, 2009)[19].

Exploring the Intent

Placed in perspective, this appears as a plausible reason for abrupt, unilateral and voluntary withdrawal from Assam, when there was nothing to stop them in concretizing their claim over Arunachal Pradesh. After all, the strategic advantages of sabre rattling, as listed above, were too tempting to let go for the sake of international niceties. However, it appears that the Chinese had more pressing agenda back in Beijing towards consolidating their regime than to pursue the historical ambition for territorial expansion. India can be tested again at will when more opportune moments arrive.

The foregoing analysis therefore suggests that the internal events in China need to be factored into any appreciation as to its external actions or ambitions.

Lessons for Contemplation

Having teased history a bit, albeit briefly, the summary of lessons in understanding the Chinese mind could be stated as below:

- China, unlike Pakistan, has historical notions of ownership of lands that never really belonged to the Chinese. However, **their desire in this direction can be understood if we look at their history** which reveals tribute paying vassal states (kowtowing to the might of the Chinese sword) is a necessary construct in their scheme of political power.

In the history of Tibet, except for brief periods during two of the earlier Dalai Lamas (the 6th and the 13th), Tibet was autonomous and not a vassal state of China. Interestingly, both the 6th and 13th Dalai Lamas, HH Tsangyang Gyatso and HH Thubten Gyatso, died in Qinghai (China) and Lhasa held by China! While their death is not relevant to our study, the birth of 6th Dalai Lama in 1683 is quite relevant, for it is at the heart of Chinese claims over Arunachal Pradesh. The Chinese geopolitical mind works at best in mysterious ways – We are masters of Tibet – 6th Dalai Lama of Tibet was born in Tawang – so, Tawang and Arunachal Pradesh belongs to Tibet and therefore to us! (A research article is expected to avoid such statements. However, there is not another way that could quickly portray the way Chinese think!)

To refresh our memory on the border question, it is necessary for India to revisit its Colonial History. The claims made by China or for that matter Pakistan on territories in India are based on presumptions resting on vanity. In a paper on borders (Srinivasan, 2019)[20], it was stated that:

- They actually represent the ambiguous belief and ambitious extent of the sphere of each other's influences into the territories beyond their physical markings based on communal reasons and vaguely supported historical evidences. Scholarly studies reveal that the notion of sovereignty held by each of these states actually extends to the territories beyond their physical control (Gupta, 1966) (Berenice, 2013).
- China consistently seeks to understand political, economic and military weaknesses in its friends and adversaries alike. Chinese diplomatic, trade,

cultural and military delegations are important tools in developing such perceptions. More interestingly, China has also used its students (which it practically sends to every country in the world) to obtain local perceptions. The 'discovery' of a professor at Harvard (US Dept of Justice, January 28, 2020)[21] passing vital information and technology to China recently is just one of such indicators. **The lesson that must be learned is clear – constantly seek to understand and study their actions across all spheres of their national life**.

- Nehru was prophetic when he stated that China has a philosophers' temperament and philosophers do not act in haste. China's forays into Indian territories at moments of Indian national weakness or Chinese national compulsions is a portent lesson and proof of Nehru's prophecy, though it cannot be said that he himself anticipated it. The **inability to translate his historical understanding into the political dimension** perhaps was his greatest fault in the years leading to 1962. That is an important lesson we must hasten to learn.
- Nehru's statement that China's is willing to teach them (his younger brothers in Asia) and share with them his own culture and civilization' is prophetic again. When "*willing to*" is replaced with "***wanting to***", it is easy to appreciate in the current geopolitical scenario.
- Nehru has been blamed for many things. However, anyone who has ever studied Nehru cannot but accept that he had a tremendous sense of history. He was a scholar whose monumental works (especially the Glimpses of World History and Discovery of India) alas, are at best consigned to libraries. Students of history, international relations, strategic studies and geopolitics in India would avail great insights if these books are made compulsory reading and study. If this recommendation is extended, his writings are to be endorsed as compulsory reading to every aspirant in political arena. Such studies are not to be confused with political or ideological alignment of the student.
- Going back to China's history, granting that our deduction that the failures of Great Leap Forward induced the necessity for 1962 Sino-Indian conflict, the present scenario in China is not too different. Sanctions in the wake of 1989 Tiananmen Square still have their stings; Hong Kong has become a festering wound in Chinese flesh; despite a considerable military deployed in SCS, US and combined counter pressure on China is palpable; Uyghurs have shown no interest in succumbing to Sinification; Baluch are turning CPEC into a costlier dream than was perceived; Wuhan Virus has left even China licking its economic wounds, whether openly accepted or not, and

international manipulations (read WHO) have created counter issues. There are as much troubles at home as were historically present during Ch'ing and Manchu times or in the birth pangs of two Chinas. Cumulatively these indicate that China is not as invulnerable as it may imagine it to be. Rest of the world, particularly India, may have to simply recalibrate the way China is to be understood so as to predict its future actions.

Drawing from the sixty years of Sino-India relations and the incidents/ developments concerning disengagement in Ladakh, following recommendations can be made in conclusion:

- First, we need to have a concrete understanding of where the border is. Merely being content with LAC, LOAC, post-1962 or even pre-1993, or any such arrangements arrived at under compulsions of the times pertaining to them will always act to the advantage of China. In so far as Arunachal is concerned, a clearly defined McMohan Line (as drawn in 1914) should be categorically insisted, publicized, zealously and diplomatically driven.
- In so far Ladakh is concerned, it should be the pre-1962 positions, especially Macartney-Macdonald Line of 1899 proposed to the Chinese by the British (which in any case China neither accepted nor acknowledged)[22] or the Ardagh-Johnson Line of 1897, which the British decided to adopt at the time of India's independence.
- In the strategic discourses that ensued in the aftermath of Galwan, discussions on the above borders were either notionally referred to or were conspicuously absent. **Such ambiguity on our part enables the Chinese to use bluff and bluster to push the negotiations to accept ground positions. This is the primary cause of Chinese ability at nibbling away at Indian territories, while at the same time making the Indian establishment believe otherwise.** Therefore, it is strongly recommend that the position of the diplomatic, strategic and scholarly community in India and its friendly nations must be based on intense study and clearly stated positions.
- An army, especially Indian Army, will defend frontiers at all costs. However, it is necessary to appreciate that **the army does not define what or where the border is. That prerogative rests with the policy makers**. Therefore, sharp conceptual clarity on the subject is as much an inescapable pre-requisite as is consistency, irrespective of changes in our political climate. This is a lesson perhaps the contemporary world can learn from China.

China recognizes strength. On our part therefore, it is necessary to appreciate that strength in geopolitics comes from vision, ability and consistency. Closer scrutiny of China and evaluating it from a non-western approach is needed in order to predict it. That is not to say that western approach is inadequate. It is just to say, that the east is a bit different. Nehru, referring to considerable passage of time before China rose to glory again after each of the turmoil in its historical past, said, "Eastern culture is like an elephant. When an elephant falls, it takes time to get up". Extending his thought, when the elephant gets up and going, it needs watching. If its feet totter again, who knows which tree it will grab at to prevent a fall?

3. Flipside View of Sino-Indian Troop Disengagement: Victory or Lesson?

The Backdrop

The troop buildup in the wake of the Galwan clashes in June 2020 had culminated in both sides agreeing to withdraw to 'erstwhile' positions. The International community as well as Indian establishment had stood the test well. The 'pat-on-the-back' to all Indian actors on the stage including the military top brass liberally being handed by strategic analysts across the spectrum is understandable. With over 100000 troops on either side and at least 200 Chinese tanks, there was only one element needed for a catastrophic war - a trigger happy commander on either side to light the fuse in a momentary rush of adrenaline! Barring the Galwan clash, both the sides apparently held their head, kept their fists clenched, but withheld a punch. The diplomatic and political establishment in India went on a hyper drive soliciting international support and mobilizing counter show of strength through QUAD, PASSEX, MALABAR, and other exercises. A concerned world, more due to their own perceived threats from Chinese dominance in SCS than out of concern for protecting India's geographical integrity or international prestige, pitched in. In the 'who-will-blink-first' test of will, eventually both India and China agreed to pull back their troops. On January 11th, Hindustan Times reported that Chinese pulled out over 10000 troops from the area (Singh, January 10, 2021)[1].

Just about a month later, on February 12th, Hindustan Times (Gupta, February 12, 2021)[2] again reported that the Chinese withdrew 200 tanks and used over 100 heavy troop-carrying vehicles within 48 hours after reaching agreements with Indian authorities. The speed with which the disengagement was carried out took the Indian planners by surprise. Though approbation for diplomatic finesse and hard standing were handed to the Indian authorities, the speed of disengagement also sounded a note of caution as to Chinese capability for re-deployment.

The standoff had continued through harsh Himalayan winters, which some analysts of 1962 war had predicted as the reason for unilateral withdrawal back then. This time around, that theory did not hold any water! Also, Chinese had showed no signs of let up almost till the announcement – the offensive media attack alleging hegemonistic attitude by India continued in the same tone and tenor. Despite, many rounds of troop level to ministerial meetings, international facilitation and pressure, the mood on ground remained grim. And, suddenly, when the Himalayan snow showed similar signs, the standoff thawed, both sides blinked and troops started melting away.

The Hypothesis

Did the tough Indian stand do the magic by itself? Perhaps it did not. It may be hypothesized that China had more immediate concerns to be addressed a little farther east, in Myanmar. India could be handled later for there is nothing stopping them from coming back at a more suitable time. Hence, it set up the elaborate show of playing for peace, again successfully diverting the world attention from discovering its intent.

Having made this hypothesis, Sino-Myanmar relations needs to be examined in search of facts that may prove or negate the hypothesis.

Myanmar and Chinese Interests

History reveals that China's claim that Burma (Myanmar) has been a tribute paying vassal in a continuum is incorrect. Trager (Trager, 1964)[3] records many historical incidents that the relationship with China varied from conciliatory to contest predominantly owing to the trade interests between both the kingdoms that spanned Yunnan province of China. While the Chinese Emperors continued to pretend Myanmar as a tribute paying vassal state, Burmese kings continued to raise, unite and at times defeat the invading Chinese armies. However, these cat and mouse relations changed in the aftermath of the second Anglo-Burmese war. The British conquest ended up annexing the Northern areas into British India solely with the purpose of promoting trade with western China and Yunan. The British went to the extent of appeasing the Chinese Emperor (even after their singular victories in the two Opium Wars) by signing the 'O'Connor Convention Relating to Burma and Thibet' in 1886. Under the terms of this convention, Britain appropriated the right to do whatever was proper in Burma (Article II), in return for an apparently meaningless gesture of continuing to send decennial missions to the Chinese Court (tribute paying) that suited the Chinese sensibilities (Trager, 1964, P.38)[4]. Thus Burma came to be ingrained in Chinese psyche as an essentially tribute paying vassal.

When Burma, India and China attained their statehoods, Burmese anxiety over possible Chinese invasion of Burma remained credible. Thus, Burma even requested India to wait for the Burmese government to become the first nation to recognize PRC outside the Communist Bloc. India readily obliged. Burmese eagerness to please China was essentially out of the stated apprehension (FAN, 2012)[5]. That the Burmese question was of important to China as well as India from the early periods of their formation as nations could be seen from the recorded discussions between Mao and Nehru in 1954 cited below (Wilson Centre, n.d)[6]:

> **Mao**: *The Burmese government is the most suspicious of us, and that is because there is revolution in their country. They suspect that we will help the revolutionaries to overthrow the government* and that we will deliver weapons to the revolutionaries. When Premier Zhou visited Burma, he discussed this matter with Prime Minister U Nu. Prime Minister U Nu will be visiting China in one-month time. We will discuss [this] with him again. We will clarify this matter in accordance with the Five Principles. Now there are also Guomindang troops in Burma, and we have never used this as an excuse. We know that Burma faces difficulty, and this needs to be resolved gradually. But the existence of the Guomindang troops in Burma is disadvantageous to both China and Burma. But we will only tighten the defense of our borders and will not cross the border. As for how Burma will deal with the Guomindang troops, it is Burma's own business. We understand the difficulty that Burma is facing. There are two communist parties in Burma. One is the Red Flag, and the other one is the White Flag. This is also Burma's own business. *We do not even know who they are. The two parties all developed after Japan's occupation of Burma, and they belonged to the same alliance of which Prime Minister U Nu's party was also a member.*
>
> **Nehru**: In the past five to six years, it was the Karen people who have been making trouble. They have received support from American officers (but not necessarily the American government) and have also received weapons from America. American churches have also made the Karens Christians. The Karens have made troubles more than anyone else. As for the communist party, I also know that there is the difference of the Red Flag and the White Flag, but many of those who claim themselves to be communists actually know little about communism. They have no discipline and they are irresponsible. *But the main trouble has come from the Karens. In order to show their discontent with America's support to the Karens, Burma turned down America's technological support last year.*
>
> **Mao**: *The Guomindang troops in Burma have also been supported by the United States.* Aid has been delivered via Thailand. The Karens are not beneficial to Burma, and the Guomindang troops are not beneficial to Burma either, but they have received support from the United States. Probably, Britain also feels unhappy with these pro-American forces. As to the Burmese Communist Party, we have never given them a single gun, and we do not plan to give them help now. In the past, we supported Ho Chi Minh.

(Italics added for emphasis)

The instances covered bring out **three essential Chinese interests in Burma**: the alleged historical claim to sovereignty over Burmese territories (duly supported by O'Connor Convention); The Karen Question and the presence of Kuomintang in Burma that is seen as a potential security risk to western China.

China's foreign policy objectives of thwarting western imperialistic (read as capitalistic) influences in Asia at large that guided their policy options initially under Mao, also underwent a gradual but distinct change. In the next twenty years after 1949, its foreign policy tilted "toward efforts to win Asian neighbors away from alliances with the West through offers of peaceful coexistence" (Van Ness, 1970)[7]. Such a tilt could possibly have been the result of anti-Chinese revolt in Burma in 1967.

The period 1970-1990, however kept China focused inwards during which increasing US engagements in South Asia, especially of US partnerships with Thailand in SEATO and involvement in Vietnam were viewed as attempts at containment of China. However, these developments also led to recalibration in foreign policy by CCP. There are two specific instances of almost simultaneous occurrence in China and Burma that would perhaps call for critical revision of China's foreign policy approach towards Burma: the nationwide uprising against Ne Win regime in Burma in 1988 and the Tiananmen Square massacre in China in 1989 – both attracted swift international sanctions at the behest of USA on these countries. International whiplash perhaps set both the countries to re-evaluate their relations. As Hongwei (2012, P.24)[8] observes:

> With China's domestic rapid economic development and economic structure adjustment particularly after 1990s as well as western sanction on Myanmar, Beijing's perception on Burmese geo-strategic value changed once again. This new change was based on non-traditional strategic interests as well as longer-range traditional concerns over China's regional potential. These new concerns related particularly to its energy security, and expansion of trade and exports, and "Two Ocean Strategy". As a result, Myanmar has new and enhanced relevance to China due to its rich natural resources and geographic location of land bridge to the Indian Ocean. Now China is building China–Myanmar oil and gas pipelines and has China–Burma Geopolitical Relations in the Cold War planned to construct a railroad and a highway from Kyaukpyu, the Andaman Sea port in Myanmar's western Rakhine state to Ruili, the Yunnan's border town (which will extend to Kunming). Myanmar is becoming the gateway of China's access to the Indian Ocean.

Even before these developments occurred in China-Burma relations, the internal political climate had changed in Burma. Within two years of independence from British Rule, U Nu won the general elections to establish a democratic government in 1960. However, his tolerant policies towards separatists and attempts to introduce Buddhism as state religion was resented by the army. U Nu was overthrown in a coup and General Ne Win established a single party; military led socialist state in 1962. The Ne Win regime lasted till 1988, when riots broke out against the regime, thousands were killed or jailed and martial law was imposed. It was during these agitations that Aung San Suu Kyi heading National League for Democracy (NLD) was arrested.

NLD was reinstated to power after a prolonged international campaign though the military Junta retained their authority over parliament and imposed restrictions of all perceivable type to retain political oversight. Details of the events in Burma from 1997 till recently are of public knowledge. However, the visit of President Jiang Jemin of PRC to Burma in 2001 is of significance, when he stressed on economic reform[9]. The economic reform that he spoke off has been followed up by deeper engagement with the powers (irrespective of shades) in Burma. For example, even the NLD Chief Aung San Suu Kyi faced (perhaps still faces) a mortal dilemma over a single dam project in Rakine country on the Irrawaddy River where Chinese claim to have invested over USD 800 million. While she was not in power, Aung had spoken against the dam. However, after she came to power, she visited China and reversed her opinion by endorsing the project as a necessity for the economic revival of Burma. If NLD endorses the dam that Kachins oppose, she loses internal stability (which in any case is a tricky issue in Burma); if she scraps it, she has the indomitable prospect of paying a colossal debt that Burma apparently cannot service[10].

However, Aung San Suu Kyi is reportedly closer to the Chinese establishment than the west would like[11]. Yun Sun (Sun, February 19, 2021)[12] of the Stimson Centre summarized it in the following words:

> In comparison with the situation in Laos, Aung San Suu Kyi did a good job at managing the Chinese projects in the country. But at the same time, **because of how close Aung San Suu Kyi was to China, the Chinese used a lot of micro-projects to assert their influence in Myanmar**, through what they name as "welfare projects" (macrofinance, wind farms, etc.). To sum up, no megaproject in Myanmar does not mean that China's influence is smaller. It just means China is willing to adapt to the local demand and local approach.

It is also important to note that the power struggle between the military Junta and Aung San Suu Kyi is about control of the economy which apparently the military joysticks in many ways. Helen Reagan of CNN reported on the same in more crisp terms:

Other analysts have called the move a "preemptive strike" as the generals didn't like how powerful Suu Kyi had become.

"This is a coup to protect their interests," Mathieson said. "(They thought) she has a mandate now to dilute our economic power and our constitutional power, and our immunity from prosecution. There is no way that we're going to allow ourselves to be that vulnerable."[13]

There is also some truth behind the motive for the coup in Myanmar like the one inferred by Laura Edwards of UPenn[14]. She predicts that the most plausible reason is the aspiration for Presidency by General Min Aung Hlaing, the senior general of the military who is otherwise slated to retire. While personality clashes and power mongering are nothing new in politics that this alone led to the coup when a popular mass leader like Aung Suu Kyi with an international standing is leading the country, is unlikely. It would help rather subscribe to the theory that the military, however despotic they may have been, are alarmed by the proximity that China is gaining with Aung Suu Kyi since they have always dragged their feet about implementing the projects that China enticed them into in the past, in return for supporting them in UNSC by exercising its veto powers. This view is also supported by open source analysis like that of Joshua Cheetham (Cheetham, March 09, 2021)[15]

It is also pertinent to note that in the eight years between 2004 and 2011, 'with 21,000% increase in outward flows from China and a 9500% increase in outward stocks, Myanmar has developed into both a regional and global leader for Chinese FDI' (Mitchell, 2012)[16]. While the successive coups and alleged human rights violations kept the west busy in isolating Myanmar through stringent sanctions, as Mitchell observes, 'China took advantage of the lack of competitors and began to invest heavily in order to secure natural resources' (Mitchell, P.65).

China's current FDI in Myanmar, notwithstanding the internal/international political pressures, are reported as - "From 1988 to June 30, 2019, approved Chinese investment amounted to more than $20 billion—nearly 26 percent of total FDI in the country" (Lwin, 2019)[17]. With the political situation turning delicate again due to the coup, and the west reacting in the age-old predictable mode of stringent sanctions, China is yet again in the same advantageous position that it had in 1988.

That the Chinese official media have also been rather cautious on the coup in which no evidence of open support to the Military Junta nor any condemnation at least till now indicates the keen evaluation of newer opportunities for consolidation of its presence in Burma by the Chinese mind.

Deductions

Having dealt with Sino-Myanmar relations in a brief perspective, the analysis turns to the quintessential question: Is there a link between China's interests in Myanmar and the sudden reversal of the eight month stand-off leading to substantial troop reductions coupled with flow of warmth from China towards India? It may be presumed so, based on the following:

1. That the Indian establishment stood its grounds is a given factor. However, in the process of doing so, India had to shop for billions worth of military hardware, pump troops to inhospitable terrains and maintain them for months in a nerve racking who-blinks-first contest. The Finance Minister of India had to recast the Union Budget upping defense procurement as against other important economic spheres in a time when Covid19 had taken substantial toll on Indian economy. In economic terms, the cost-to-output ratio is disproportional (without taking the human costs into account). In tennis terms, it is Advantage China.
2. The aggressive postures China had adopted in SCS became secondary concerns to the world. America, even though locked in another who-blinks-first contest with Iran had to withdraw an entire carrier fleet to balance affairs in SCS. In the process, an indirect lesson was driven home to the west not to take Chinese maritime power lightly. Again, Advantage China.
3. The usurpation of power in Myanmar by the military lends the environment tenuous for Chinese long-term interests. The game could be gained or lost depending on international pressure succeeding in the release of Aung San Suu Kyi (who in any case is seen as friendly to the Chinese), or the Military Junta itself leaning over to China (as they did in 2007) and ratify its projects in an attempt to garner support at UNSC and elsewhere. Is this also Advantage China? The world have to wait for the counter serve.
4. In this scenario, it would perhaps be useful to beef up the troops at Sino-Myanmar border just to tempt either of the stake holders in Myanmar to make decisions suitable to China. To do so, diffuse the situation in Ladakh, withdraw in strength and simply relocate. Advantage China.
5. Geopolitical payouts of such actions are many: International community conveys its consent and 'sees' China as not being so expansionist after all – an angle that could be exploited by aggressive public relations exercises. The most telling evidence of this is the Chinese FM Wang Yi's statements in which he specifically said[18]:

"On many important issues, our positions are the same or close due to similar national realties, therefore China and India are each other's friends and partners, not threats or rivals...The two sides need to help each other to succeed instead of undercutting each other. We should intensify cooperation instead of harbouring suspicion at each other.... in the year ahead we hope India will work with China to truly deliver on the important common understanding reached by our leaders that the two countries are not threats to each other but opportunities for each other's development....Together we can bring greater benefits to the 2.7 billion people in China and India, make greater contributions to the advent of the Asian Century.... As two ancient civilisations, next door to each other and as two major emerging economies with each over one billion people, we have broad common interests and tremendous potential for cooperation". At home, both countries face the "historic mission" of bettering lives, accelerating growth, Wang added[19].

6. In the typical (by now predictable) Chinese manner, Wang Yi also stated: "the right and wrongs at what happened at the border area last year are clear, so are the stakes involved....We are committed to settling the boundary dispute through dialogue and consultation. **At the same time we are resolved to safeguard our sovereign rights**"[20] (emphasis added). Thus, it appears that China continues to keep the tirade about India aggressing into Chinese territories, just in case international observers think otherwise? In any case, Indian establishment will be under pressure to prove it otherwise. Advantage: China.

7. To garnish this portrait, in our opinion, Pakistan is encouraged to suddenly announce on 25th February that it will abide by ceasefire agreements of 2003, so that the attention of India and the world are suitably riveted to the possibilities of everlasting peace in South Asia. In a dramatic move,

   "Chief of Pakistan Army had talked "about mutual respect and peaceful coexistence in what was the first 'soft' stand on India since the Balakot air strike by the Indian Air Force two years ago. And a week later, Pakistani PM Pakistan, in yet another dramatic change, stuck to the topic of Covid-19 pandemic in a virtual SAARC meeting called by Prime Minister Narendra Modi. Pakistan did not make the usual rhetorical reference to the Kashmir issue at the meet (Dutta, February 26, 2021)[21].

   The timing of the announcement, just two weeks after Sino-Indian troop disengagement was agreed upon, is also an interesting pointer in the absence of credible and supporting developments in the immediate past across India's western front. If anything, the PM of Pakistan has been making diplomatically irresponsible statements, especially against Indian PM ever since the trifurcation of Jammu & Kashmir has been implemented and

Article 370 of the Indian Constitution was scrapped by due parliamentary process by India.

Reinforcing our perceptions as stated above are reports by the Freepress Journal, citing sources from ASPI[22] that 'Chinese soldiers were being transported into the country (Myanmar) on flights, or that 'Chinese-looking' troops have been spotted around Myanmar's cities'.

> According to a report published by a think tank -- Australian Strategic Policy Institute (ASPI), unregistered flights from China have been landing every night in Myanmar carrying unknown goods and personnel from China, for over a week now, despite a ban on international flights by the Myanmar military, which took over the country in a recent coup.

Conclusion

It is quite tempting to declare the result of geopolitical tennis as Game Set: China, so far! In the same breath, it is to be pointed out that in so far as China is concerned, to presume that it will buckle under diplomatic or military pressure is like believing that bloodletting can cure the wiliest of afflictions. Bloodletting does exactly what it does – it drains blood.

In the light of aforementioned discussions, the hypothesis that China accepted the disengagement formula to meet its more strategically important interests in Myanmar, is a more pragmatic assessment of Chinese intent. It took out troops and swung them into action in a theatre that is critical for addressing its energy needs as well as servicing its "Two Oceans" policy. The international isolation of Myanmar led by the west, which in any case is predictable, will act to China's advantage.

Having dealt with the attempt at understanding of Chinese intent behind the disengagement, following suggestions are put forth for contemplation by expert community:

- It may be necessary to revisit Look and Act East Policies to see how far the intended outreach is tempered by a comprehensive understanding of China and its regional ambitions in South and Southeast Asia. Such a pragmatic and holistic assessment will bolster India's strategic interests.
- China's actions on any one front should never be seen in stand-alone mode. A 360-degree appreciation of its desires, ambitions and demonstrated behaviour is necessary. This should become the agenda for setting up strategic analysts' groups, independently but into the Ministries of External Affairs and Defence.
- That India's armed forces remaining apolitical is the best insurance for continuing as a democracy. However, the best militaries in the world are

also fostered and groomed on the art of analysing history, diplomacy and geopolitics. This interface must be developed.

- Lastly, China understands power. It also understands when the power is consistent, focused and unwavering. Hence, preparing a strategic long-term vision and mission towards China is necessary. Such a vision cannot be obtained unless the military is integrated into the strategic dialogues at all levels of the policy establishment in its engagements with adversarial neighbours and distant friends alike.

There is a specific suggestion to western analysts too, especially those that guide policy frameworks: Sanctions in the contemporary world do not play out the same way gun boat diplomacies did in the colonial era. Perspective understanding and positive engagement are needed if good governance and human rights everywhere are to be obtained. This is expressly applicable in an environment where China has acquired the financial muscle to press through its political ambitions.

Note:

1. Burma and Myanmar have been interspersed in the paper. Officially, Myanmar is the appropriate name as written in English.
2. Italics and BOLD lettering have been used in paragraphs to highlight aspects from which our interpretations have been drawn.

4. Resolving Indo-Pak and Sino-Indian Border Disputes: Considerations and Prospects

Background

Borders across the world have evolved as a by-product of the historical experiences of countries concerned. While history tells us that the wars undertaken by ruling dispositions in countries have led to expansion or contraction of their physical borders, determination of borders through conflicts has ceased to be acceptable with the end of the colonial world order. In the post-World War II era, barring the determination of 36th Parallel as the boundary between North and South Korea, instances of military solutions to borders are indeed far and few. With United Nations Charter solemnly declaring war itself as illegal, negotiation and arbitration have gained acceptability as the credible means to settle disputes over contested territories.

South Asia in this regard, has a mixed story to reveal. Indo-Pak and Sino-Indian contestations using military means to address claims and counter claims are predominant themes in strategic discourses around the world. However, it also presents three compelling cases where the largest nation in the region, India, settled its maritime boundary questions with Myanmar, Sri Lanka and Bangladesh through negotiated settlement and arbitration. The willingness of the political leadership to arrive at amiable settlement bespeaks of the inclination of the leaderships to abide by international frameworks for peaceful resolution of disputes. While India seems to have displayed a standing commitment to international rule of law regime, its western neighbour Pakistan and the eastern neighbour China appear to be intent on invoking armed means, legally and illegally, to persist in their attempts to address border questions with India. After four wars with Pakistan and one war and numerous skirmishes with China, there appears to be a rigidity in the approach of the polity of both those countries to accept a reconciliatory approach to the issues at hand.

Pakistan on its part has consistently refused to abide by the Shimla Agreement 1972 that binds it to the bilateral negotiation mechanism to arrive at resolution. Every time India embarked on confidence building overtures to facilitate this process, Pakistan scuttled the initiatives by embarking upon abetting and aiding terrorist violence on Indian Territory that has only resulted in hardening of Indian stand. Indian PM Atal Bihari Vajpayee went to extraordinary lengths in commencing the rail and bus connectivity in 1998, only to be presented with Kargil intrusions in 1999. At the time of assuming office, PM Modi extended the invite to attend the Oath Taking ceremony to all SAARC Heads of State. Pakistan was conspicuous by its absence. By insisting on regionalising the Kashmir issue, Pakistan edged the SAARC nations to call of their summit in 2016 at Kathmandu. It has complicated the bilateral atmosphere further by first ceding substantial territories in Occupied Kashmir to China, even as the UN sponsored mandate of the time dictated maintenance of status quo till the dispute was resolved. In any case, with Shimla Agreement, Pakistan is obliged to resolve the differences through bilateral dialogue. Sensing the shift in geopolitical environment, Pakistan now sides with China so as to protect itself from the illegitimacies of its actions in this regard.

In so far China is concerned, the economic ambitions of emerging China perhaps compel it to claim sovereign rights over territories that have neither been part of historical China nor were acceded to it through sovereign will of the rulers of those territories. China's claims over Aksai Chin has no historical basis, evidence actually being contrary to it. In the case of Nepal, Bhutan and Sikkim too, these regions that abutted Tibet have neither been part of the kingdom of Tibet nor were historical tribute paying appendices to China except for certain discontinuous periods. The only claim that China has for Arunachal are as devious as only a rapacious imagination can admit. The birth of a Dalai Lama in Tawang and that Dalai Lama's Tibet being part of China (after forceful annexation) can only be connected through devious dialogues.

Considerations and Prospects

Pakistan

Pakistan's unresolved border issue with Afghnaistan dates before Pakistan was born. The Durand line that Afghnaistan recognises as legitimate border has not been accepted by Pakistan. There have been periodic reports of ingress by Pak forces across Durand Line and even the Taliban now in control of Kabul views Pakistan with suspicion on this issue[1]. Political instability in Afghanistan notwithstanding, the persistence of this issue points to the inability of Pakistani establishment to reconcile the same with a country over which it claims to have substantial influence.

In so far as India is concerned, whether Pakistan has a border issue or is dogged by an existential question is as yet unclear. Five issues had persisted between India and Pakistan as below:

a) Jammu & Kashmir

b) Rann of Kutch

c) Sir Creek

d) Wular Lake

e) Siachen Glacier

Jammu & Kashmir: Even though the political narratives behind Jammu & Kashmir label it as a clash of ideologies, a Hindu Raja's accession to India of a Muslim majority state, it is necessary to understand that Kashmir dispute has more than ideology behind. In a way, it is connected to the very survival of Pakistan since the Indus and its five tributaries originate and flow through Kashmir. The Pakistani incursions of 1948, the single minded action under Sardar Patel's foresight to bring Kashmir within Indian fold – both these revolve around the waters of the Indus. Even though Pakistan and India agreed to a ceasefire and Pakistan continued its occupation of northern portions of Kashmir (PoK), behind the scene negotiations from 1948 under the aegis of World Bank over 12 years resulted in the Indus Water Treaty 1960, a treaty hailed as a model for resolving water conflicts even today[2]. Under this treaty, the waters of three western rivers – Indus, Jhelum and Beas are given to Pakistan and the waters of the eastern rivers, Beas, Ravi and Sutlej are given to India. Despite the wars, both the countries have abided by the treaty till now.

Sir Creek issue that has persisted till date since both the countries, India to start with, discovered fossil fuel deposits and therefore are vying for larger control. Both the countries have availed arbitration but a solution is evading them, as AG Noorani points out 'the only obstacle to such an accord is the lack of political will'[3].

Siachen glacier is to the North-North East of Ladakh bordering Tibet and providing direct access to Xinjiang Province of China through Karakoram Pass. When India and Pakistan refereed their 1948 dispute to the United Nations, the Cease Fire Line agreed upon ended at point NJ9842, stopping short of the glacier. Both the countries paid little attention to the glacier till 1983. In 1983-84, India found credible evidence of Pakistani forces attempting to establish posts in the glacier, prompting it to send patrols and eventually establish its military firmly on the glacier frustrating Pakistan's surreptitious game plan. Thus the ambiguities of the 1949 Cease Fire Line appear to have been corrected, al beit through military means, by Indian planners after experiencing the duplicity and deceit that Pakistan appears to field in such matters. Today, Siachen and the areas adjoining are under ingress by Chinese forces too. The Galwan incidents of 2020 are the latest skirmish between Sino-Indian engagements in that general area.

Interestingly, Pakistan entered into an agreement with China in 1963 through which it claimed to have gained 2000 sq km while parting to China a little more. The legality of ceding territory is in contravention to the principles governing such issues, as observed by Abhishek Trivedi, a scholar from Pittsburg School of law[4]. Observers like Bruce Riedel[5] find that Pakistani planners and other forces within have never found common ground to work on issues with India, in the process losing credibility as a nation especially with India.

Even though eight decades of lack of trust have resulted in four wars, the resolution of Rann of Kutch issue through International Arbitration[6] and Indus Water Treaty demonstrate India's willingness to work within the framework of international law and settle issues through peaceable means. A similar commitment from Pakistan to enter into negotiations within the framework of Shimla Agreement has not been forthcoming. Especially after India unambiguously and firmly acted by revoking special status of Jammu & Kashmir (Art. 370), Pakistan appears to have sunk itself into ambiguity though political wisdom should have prevailed.

The way Pakistan has chosen to deal with its border questions amply demonstrates lack of political commitment to forge a pragmatic consensus to guide its policy towards its neighbours. It is also necessary to appreciate the hurdles Pakistan has created for itself in allowing such political wisdom from emerging, as explained briefly below.

Pakistan requires very little enumeration as a country that has become the hotbed and exporter of terrorism. The argument that extant factors were used by General Zia or his successors to devise a way to bleed India through a thousand cuts is too familiar as to warrant any explanation. That some of the most wanted heads of terrorist outfits are state sponsored and that terrorist funding has kept Pakistan consistently in FATF list[7] are realities. Even though religious ideology espoused by Pakistan is common factor with 56 other Muslim nations across the world, the other Muslim countries have time and again demonstrated their intent to keep away from allying with Pakistan on the religious fundamentalist note. In 2014, the OIC went to the extent of snubbing Pakistan when it attempted to bring up Kashmir for discussion[8]. In 2019, Indian Foreign Minister was invited to address OIC at Abu Dhabi. Pakistan's protests were rejected by OIC[9]. Countries like Saudi Arabia and UAE have taken extraordinary measures to strengthen their relations with India is an important pointer in this regard. Iran has maintained exceptional relations with India from historical times. North African nations like Egypt have also similarly maintained vibrant relations with India. That Pakistan has consistently been unsuccessful points to the realisation of its dubious and double standards by the international community.

Pakistan's current economic plight and the foreseeable quagmire into which the country is heading on account of CPEC should be important worries to the policy establishment there. The Baloch, Pashtun and Waziristan internal security situations further appear to drag that country towards a climate of potential implosion. Excessive exploitation of Indus river waters also indicates that water related issues are likely to impact the country in more ways than one[10]. India's largesse in allowing Pakistan to avail Indus waters beyond the scope of Indus Water Treaty is perhaps a major reason why agrarian crisis has not yet engulfed Pakistan. Obsessive involvement in Afghanistan from the time of Soviet invasion has had a potentially devastating impact in the form of drugs and drug money that is seen as one of the most important challenges Pakistan faces today[11]. The most compelling challenge that Pakistan faces today is to retrieve itself from the agenda of Islamization and how it chooses to address the same[12]. Bruce Riedel concisely states that tangible action by Pakistan against the LeT and other terrorists should be a priority, if it desires to arrive at settling issues with India[13].

China

China has had border disputes with all of its fourteen neighbours. Some of these disputes like those with Russia, Myanmar and Vietnam have hundreds of years of history behind them. Curiously, Myanmar and Vietnam also qualify as countries to whose territory China had pinned its 'tribute paying vassal' tag. However, commencing with Russia with whom it went to war on Zenbhao Island in 1969, China has remarkably settled its border questions with most of its neighbours through negotiation and reconciliation. Amongst the most persisting of its border disputes is with India and occasionally with Nepal and Bhutan. It is necessary to visit at least three instances briefly to perceive how Chinese approach the border question.

While dealing with how nations address their vexations over borders, Taylor Fravel had posited three strategies that they may adopt:

- A delaying strategy involves doing nothing except maintaining a state's claims through official maps and public declarations.
- An escalation strategy involves the threat or use of force over disputed territory.
- A cooperation strategy excludes the threat or use of force and involves instead an offer to compromise by dividing control of the contested land or dropping outstanding claims.[14]

Sino-Russian Dispute: Neville Maxwell[15] in his in-depth examination of the Sino-Russian border issue observes that China's strategy has traditionally been as under:

> With neighbors with whom there had been no boundary delimitation, China would carefully observe the status quo and, when both parties were ready, open negotiations to seek a mutually satisfactory territorial dispensation, based on the traditional and customary line or zone of separation. Burma was the outstanding instance.
>
> Where there had been formal delimitation, China would observe the boundary thus legitimized, without regard to the historical circumstances in which diplomatic settlement had been achieved or imposed. This fundamental decision expressed recognition that the bequeathed irredentist commitment to regain "lost lands" would, if pursued, embroil the PRC in intractable dispute and likely conflict with many of its neighbors, the USSR first among them, while putting the new China at odds with the international community. "Under modern international law, the validity of treaties signed prior to the Covenant of the League of Nations is not affected by whether or not they were negotiated under duress." Thus, the PRC determined to observe its treaty obligations, however "unequal" in origin they might be.
>
> When differences arose over treaty interpretation or implementation, again China would urge careful joint observance of the status quo pending negotiation to reconcile the differences. If there was a danger of patrol clashes that would envenom public attitudes, the parties should agree on mutual withdrawal of armed forces for an agreed reciprocal distance: such withdrawals would not involve civil administration nor have any bearing on the two sides' claims. Here, however, there was a crucial caveat. The negotiation, taking as its basis the relevant treaty, could not be piecemeal but must be comprehensive, covering the entire stretch of the boundary concerned; it should also issue a new treaty, not a revision of the old one (p53).

Even though Neville Maxwell ascribes such paramount clarity in Chinese perceptions, the resolution with Russia did not arise purely by Chinese commitment to observe treaty obligations however 'unequal' they may be in their origin. Michael Gerson[16], for example points to the selective 'leak' of Soviet intentions to use nuclear arsenal on China forcing leaders like Mao to even abandon Beijing and thus compelling China to adopt a more reconciliatory settlement. The realization that the nascent Chinese nuclear capabilities (set up with the help of USSR incidentally) in 1969 were no match for the Soviet capabilities was perhaps the most persuasive reason.

Sino-Vietnam Dispute: In contrast with their experience with Russia, China adopted the aggressive strategy with Vietnam[17]. Even though the border question was miniscule and resolvable through peaceable means, Vietnam aligning with USSR with whom China had started falling apart, the question of control over islands in the South China Sea and Vietnam's clashes with Cambodia whose Pol

Pot regime was supported by China prompted PLA to march into Vietnam. The 15 day clashes inflicted heavy casualties on both sides and eventually led to the withdrawal of Chinese troops. Even today CCP is averse to talk about this war as the PLA took severe casualties denting China's military image much against its desire[18]. An interesting similarity between Sino-Indian conflict of 1962 and Sino-Vietnamese conflict of 1979 is the decision not to use air power. India failed to deploy its battle proven air force in 1962 for reasons that remain shrouded in secrecy till date. The outcome of 1962 could have been substantially different had it chosen to do so. In 1979, China failed to deploy its airpower for a different reason. The Vietnamese had battle hardened pilots and the inexperienced PLAAF was perhaps no match for them, even though superior in number[19]. American analysis points to incapacity as the primary reason[20]. Notwithstanding the settlement of land border with Vietnam, the contest over Spratleys and other maritime boundaries have persisted till date.

Sino-Myanmar Dispute: As against both Russia and Vietnam, China resolved its border question with Myanmar rather peaceably. The historical claims that China had made to certain Burmese territories and the counter claims were affected by erstwhile British agreements with China. However, between 1948 and 1960, the two sides negotiated them without use of force and on 01 October 1960, both the governments finally inked their settlement to the satisfaction of each. In nutshell, both China and Burma accepted some compromises through negotiations[21]. Interestingly, China's interests in mining Lufang mines points to the continued Chinese involvement with Burma till date[22]. Even though this agreement has held for decades now, Chinese interference in Kachin territory on account of jade trade continues to provoke confrontations though not of military dimensions[23].

The instances where China is involved with its neighbours over border disputes bring out important lessons in so far as settling them is concerned. From Russia's experience to that of Burma, the following are evident:

1. China understands the power and the will to apply that power of the nation concerned. The inferred Soviet threat to use nuclear attack and China's lack of capacity to counter it apparently resulted in a compromise.
2. The lack of battle experience of the PLA and PLAAF played a significant role in Chinese retraction in the war with Vietnam. It also perhaps explains the Chinese all out intent to enhance their military power on par, if not more, with that of USA and Russia today. Extensive cooperation with UN and deployment in peace keeping missions perhaps is another manner in which China is attempting to battle inoculate its troops and develop its military leadership, apart from the obvious positive image as a nation in support of world peace.

3. Economic considerations appear to be paramount to China in arriving at compromises with non-equals like Burma. In the current geo-economic scenario, China investing over $ 30 bn USD in Myanmar appear to be guided by two intents, reach Bay of Bengal by a shorter route and exploit the natural resources of a country that stands isolated internationally. Considering that ethics does not sit well with politics, China's actions to keep a patently undemocratic Myanmar in its sphere of influence is quite evident.

India's Options

Borders have always remained the most contentious of issues between neighbours to resolve. International scholarship points to three distinct requirements to address the question of borders: delineation, delimitation and demarcation. While delineation generally points to the topographic representation as a cartographic exercise, delimitation requires extensive surveys on ground to identify features, habitats and such other physical features in order to determine what, why, to whom they should belong. Cultural, ethnic, historical and even germane considerations like lands under tillage etc need to be taken into consideration before delimitation can be finalized. Such an exercise calls for expertise from all backgrounds especially geology, geography, history and culture. When delimitation has been achieved, physical demarcation begins and the means will be dictated by the climate of relations between the nations concerned. In Europe, the Maginot Line dominated the imagination of border between France and Germany. The Saar region that speaks French but lay in Bavarian control remained the bone of contention. Today, Germany and France together form the bedrock of European Union and Maginot Line remains a historical curiosity.

Whether such a climate can arise in South Asia, as for now, is merely an aspiration. Even should that not happen, resolving the existing boundary questions is a matter of considerable importance to India. Consideration of India's experiences with its neighbours provides lessons that could help bring the contestations to a logical end.

1. India's borders were drawn more on paper by Sir Cyril Radclife and McMohan with as little delimitation and virtually no demarcation in the contexts in which they were drawn. British compulsions of those times are now of mere historical value. In a similar manner, Ardgah-Johnson Line of 1868 and the MacDonald Line of 1899 and of Tibet-Kashmir prepared by the British, though involving fair amount of delineation on ground remain at the bone of contention between India and China.

However illegal the 1963 Sino-Pak agreement may be, the current disposition of China and India coupled with CPEC ambitions of China make it apparent that a lot more diligent study into the exact position of the borders is needed if a resolution is to be obtained.

India needs to therefore create a scholarly group consisting of historians, geographers and the military to sit with the diplomatic corps to evolve a clear and consensual picture of the demarcations that it desires with China. The in-house expertise thus composed must also be part of the Joint Working Group in order to maintain consistency and clarity. It is also necessary that political leaders of appropriate seniority must be involved in the process. Considering the democratic framework in which India functions, politicians of standing from at least the major parties must be involved.

The exercise is apparently time consuming. In the short term, this expert group must familiarise with the existing frameworks and their understandings so as to factor current scenarios into their future projection.

2. The Sino-Russian border resolution also points to an important lesson. Russia's military prowess played an important role in driving the talks without confrontations till it was finally resolved in 1989. India faces critical challenges in developing such a military might, though it has come a long way from 1962. Indigenization, robust aircraft and ship building industry and deliberate deployments around the world have conferred on China a lead status in military power. More importantly, the reformatting of military regions in 2015 in China points to the political elite's understanding of the need to change with times. In comparison, India's indigenization programs are fairly nascent and its intent to incorporate civil technical expertise in building military potential is only beginning. As on date, India depends heavily on foreign powers to shore up its military capacity.

   It may also be of interest to note that Chinese leadership have consciously built overseas deployment capacity. Bogged in its interest for bureaucratic control over its military, India falls far short of synergising the civil-military cooperation so as to effectively employ military power as an expression of political will. As evident from Fiji, Uganda, Iraq and now Ukraine crises, India's diplomatic corps and military lack the seamless coordination to work together in national interest. It is an aspect requiring serious consideration since each of India's missions abroad have Military Attaches and Indian navy or Air Force have demonstrated capacity to act in unison.

3. India needs to seriously work on intelligence coordination. Each of the instances of contests, specially Kargil, Mumbai Attacks, attack on

Parliament, Chinese incursions from 1962 till now have a ring of intelligence failure surrounding them. It is time India took this matter seriously to evaluate its capacity to obtain and process real time intelligence.

The 9/11 Commission Report by US government should serve as an important subject of study by the civil and military intelligence agencies in India. The turf war between FBI, CIA, Border Control & Immigration resulting in the terrorists arriving in USA in March, obtaining pilot training and carrying out 9/11 successfully was a wake-up call. USA reformatted the intelligence mechanism and unified their efforts under the Homeland Security umbrella. Interestingly, the 9/11 Commission did not go about finding faults with individuals. Instead it focused on systemic changes necessitated by the lapses. Broadly, the Commission's work pointed to changes needed in the following dimensions[24]:

a) Unsuccessful diplomacy
b) Lack of military options
c) Problems within intelligence community
d) Problems in the FBI
e) Permeable borders and immigration controls
f) Permeable aviation security
g) Financing
h) Impoverished homeland defence
i) Emergency response
j) The Congress

India has made its own reformatting and installed NSA at the apex of the intelligence community advising the PMO directly. However, these consistent indicators of failures to provide credible and timely inputs and response to threats necessitates a review and if needed, restructuring, especially in the current geopolitical atmosphere.

4. In so far as Pakistan is specifically concerned, in at least two cases viz., bowing to the UN mandated Cease Fire Line 1949 and the Rann of Kutch, India has demonstrated its commitment to upholding international law. In the case of river water sharing too, India has honoured its commitments to Indus Water Treaty though the Pakistani actions of 1999 specially could have prompted India to stranglehold Pakistan using water as a weapon.

   In contrast, Pakistan illegally ceded 2000+ sq km of territory to China in North Kashmir to which it does not have sovereign claim even today. Chinese acceptance of the terms of 1963 treaty indicates its willingness to adopt to illegitimate means to serve its interests. Pakistan using the climate of Sino-Indian war 1962 to enter into agreement with China also points to the level to which Pakistani establishment is ready to stoop. The manner in which Pakistan reciprocated Indian confidence building overtures in 1999, Mumbai attacks, the persistent use of ISI and LeT to foster terror in Kashmir and its immature rattling of nuclear sabre – all these factors cumulatively point to the following that India needs to adopt:

- India must step up its diplomatic offensive on Pakistan, untiringly pointing to the world nations the duplicity and deceit that it employs not only with India but also with countries like Afghanistan and other neighbours.
- Strengthening its ties further with Organisation of Islamic countries, India must engage with them politically and economically so as to discourage them from aligning with Pakistan's skewed religious agenda.
- The unofficial trade with Pakistan is nearly $ 2bn USD annually. India must step up measures to discourage this trade.
- Re-vitalising SAARC is an important step India must explore. SAARC currency, SAFTA and MFN status to smaller neighbours and liberal assistance to foster quality education, technical skill and infrastructure building as part of Neighborhood First policy must be pursued aggressively.
- After having abolished Art. 370, India must now specifically focus on building the three regions of Kashmir, Ladakh and Jammu. Re-patriation of Pandits to Jammu, infrastructure building in Ladakh must find priority.

5. History of which China appears to draw from extensively, is indicative of enormous possibilities to resolve existing and foreseeable disputes with China. Considering the substantial scholarship available on Sino-Indian disputes, the options for India could be stated without preliminaries:

   - Engage at political level discussions while encouraging tactical level meetings to keep control of ground position. Questions on borders are beyond the scope of military to resolve. Hence the clarity of perception and purpose in policy circles is critical to arrive at solutions acceptable to both.
   - Engage with responsible big powers. With China's economic outreach through BRI and its consistent expansion of network across 90 countries, bringing China to the negotiating table calls for smart diplomacy backed by exceptional military capacity. In fact its own

RECP and BRI could be the Achilles heel in China's international posture, for it needs other countries to attain whatever ambitions it is working on. Engaging with ASEAN, Pacific nations and Central Asian countries more constructively therefore is the need of the hour. India has made great strides in this direction with Look East and Act East Policies. It is time that these outreaches are converted to substantial working relationships.

- China's recent attempts to build bridge at Pangong lake and name places in Arunachal must be protested in no uncertain words. China has a history of utilising historical ambiguities to support its claims over territories. It is also unfortunate that the international law on the subject is sufficiently vague to permit manipulating ground realities[25]. India must flag the issue to international community to draw adverse observations to desist China from advancing its designs.

6. India resolved its border questions with Sri Lanka, Myanmar and Bangladesh. However, it needs to formalise the border questions with Nepal and Bhutan too. Considering the historic relations with both of them, constructive dialogues must be set in motion to demarcate and formalize them to negate the possibility of these questions from being exploited by China to its advantage.

5. Implications of Recent Border Dispute between India and China Through the lens of a Military Personnel

(Note: This is the text of a talk delivered in a national webinar)

Historical background about Sino-Indian border

There are competing claims about the Sino-Indian border by both the countries. However, history apparently supports the Indian claim since the Province of Xinjiang (earlier East Turkestan) came under Chinese (Ming Empire) only in 1897. By then, circumstances surrounding the Great Game between Russia and Great Britain had already defined the issue of the border to a great extent.

The pattern of boundaries in the northwest became clearer in the last decade of the 19th century, when Britain, in negotiations with Afghanistan and Russia, delimited boundaries in the Pamirs region. At that time Gilgit, always understood to be part of Kashmir, was for strategic reasons constituted as a special agency in 1889 under a British agent[1]. In about five years' time, the Pamir Commission was able to settle the issue of Badakshan province, apportioning the south of Panj River as Afghan Badakshan. This 186 mile long and 46 mile wide finger like slice shares the border with Xinjiang Province of China through Wakhjir Pass. The Gilgit Province in Pak occupied Kashmir shares a land border with Badakshan Province.

Let's now briefly visit the pre-independence attempts to define the Sino-Indian Border:

Ardagh-Johnson Line 1897

The Ardagh–Johnson Line is a proposed boundary of Kashmir abutting Chinese Turkestan and Tibet. It was formally proposed to the British Indian government by Major General John Ardagh, chief of military intelligence in London, in 1897, based on the surveys conducted by William Johnson in 1865.

The Ardagh–Johnson Line represented the "forward school" that wanted to advance the boundary as forward as possible as a defence against the growing Russian empire.

MaCartney-MacDonald Line 1899

The Macartney–MacDonald Line was also a proposed boundary in the disputed area of Aksai Chin. It was proposed by British Indian Government to China in 1899 via its envoy to China, Sir Claude MacDonald. The Chinese Government never gave any response to the proposal. Subsequently, the British Indian Government is said to have reverted to its traditional boundary, the Ardagh-Johnson Line, which was then inherited by the independent Republic of India.

The McMahon Line 1914[2]

In the South-South East, China's defeat in the war with French in 1884-85 had already defined its Southeast Asian Borders. To the West, the Chinese territory had been defined till the Uighur lands six centuries ago by Kublai Khan. With reference to Tibet, Lamaism had considerable influence on the Yuan dynasty and therefore Tibet remained autonomous and outside Chinese interest. The Ming dynasty that followed Yuan preferred Confucian Buddhism over Tibetan Lamaism. However, the events concerning Western Powers over Canton had kept the Chinese away from Tibet. In 1914, when McMahon outlined the border between British India and Tibet, Chinese had very little interest with the process. The challenging Himalayan landscape from strategic perspective and apparent lack of interest of the Chinese in Tibet or the subcontinent sufficed the McMahon line as the northeastern territorial limit of the Empire.

Sino-Indian Disputes over Border

However, Chinese perception of border began to change when Mao Zedong sprang to power on 01 October 1949, after a two year-bloody-civil-war between the Nationalists and Communists in China. In early 1950, Mao proclaimed his famous Five Finger Policy – Tibet as the palm of the right hand, and Arunachal Pradesh, Bhutan, Sikkim, Nepal and Ladakh as the five fingers. Mao considered that these territories must remain under the control of China.The root cause of the border dispute between India and China therefore pertain to three of the fingers.

Arunachal and Aksai Chin-1962 war

The Chinese occupation of Tibet from 1950 onwards eventually led to Dalai Lama seeking asylum in India. This has never been accepted by China since China views any issue connected to Tibet as its internal affairs. Even though India and China signed the Panchsheel in the aftermath of the Bandung Conference in 1957 and the Chinese Premier visited India several times even up to 1960, a cooperative framework could not be reached, resulting in the Chinese aggression of 1962. It is a matter of history that Indian Army suffered great casualties and continues to live with a sense of betrayal owing to its losses in the war. China entered, occupied and unilaterally declared ceasefire and withdrew to positions that do not necessarily confirm to the McMohan Line in Arunachal. It is important also to note that China has made not even an indication of its willingness to recognize Arunachal as integral to India till now.

After 1962, till Galwan, India and China have had incidents and skirmishes periodically, such as:

Tulung La – 1975[3]in which four Assam Rifles jawans were ambushed and killed; **Sumdorong Chu 1986-87**[4], north of Tawang, which is the biggest face-off after 1962; **Depsang 2013**[5]**,** when PLA troops intruded 19 km into India territory in Depsang Bulge area of the DBO sector in Ladakh; **Doklam 2017**[6]**,** a 73-day confrontation on Bhutanese territory of Doklam near the Sikkim-Bhutan-Tibet trijunction after Indian soldiers blocked Chinese troops from extending a road. Doklam is surrounded by the Chumbi Valley of Tibet, Bhutan's Ha Valley and Sikkim and, finally, **Galwan Valley 15 June 2020**[7]**,** in which the Chinese ingressed about 500 meters into the Indian Territory in a sector that is critically close to Shyok River Valley leading to Siachen Glacier.

Contexts leading to and pertaining to Galwan

It is necessary for us to understand that Chinese territorial ambitions are not merely linked to the Five Finger Policy. They have an intricate connection to the history of Chinese people – more specifically, the history of Han Chinese.

Xi Jinping became the President of China on 14 March 2013. Just four days after assuming office, he invited the top brass of his government to Tiananmen Square, where he reminded them of the Hundred Years of Shame. The only other aspect he talked about was, the Silk Route and its relevance to China's prosperity.

We must therefore take a brief look at both these at this juncture.

Hundered Years of Shame

In May, 1841, upset over the opium trade that was holding China in its vice like grip, the Qing Emperor ordered his Army to re-take Canton from British control. The Chinese army launched fire ships at the British ships parked in Canton harbor. The attack was successfully fended off by mighty British ships, thereby signaling the end of China's domination of East Asian affairs, which it had enjoyed for centuries. By October that year, the British had consolidated control over the coast, annihilated the Qing navy and took the cities of Chusan and Ningbo. By July 1842, the British sailed up the Yangtze River, and threatened to cut off vital supply lines to the imperial capital at Beijing. The Chinese sued for peace and the Treaty of Nanking was signed on August 29, 1842. Western powers forced China to open its ports to trade after decades of strict protectionism, pay the equivalent of £21 million in reparations, and grant Westerners extraterritorial rights within its territory.

This humiliating defeat in the First Opium War was followed in 1850 when Christian militants rose up in the bloody Taiping Rebellion, resulting in the deaths of 20 to 30 million civilians and soldiers. In the garb of assisting the Qing government, British and French forces intervened, extracting further trade concessions from China in the process. Again in 1856, in the pretext of non-compliance with the Nanking Treaty, Western Powers went to war with China, resulting in further trade concessions. By then, the anti-Western sentiments ran so high that in 1899, the Boxer Rebellion broke out. The infamous Eight Nation Alliance[8] took over Beijing and their occupation is painfully etched in Chinese conscience as "the Rape of Nanking" along with events such as the Battle of the Yalu River. In particular, the ravaging of China by the Japanese Forces in 1894 and 1937 are still afresh in collective Chinese memory[9].

Thus the "century of humiliation", a period from the end of the First Opium War to the establishment of the People's Republic of China in 1949 is an important chapter in its history. The Chinese government has even meticulously maintained the Yuan Ming Yuan in a ruined state, which was burned and looted by British and French forces during the Second Opium War. It serves as a warning against decadence and highlights the importance of military strength[10].

BRI Ambitions of China

China's BRI vision has three components: a Chinese trade and economic network across Central Asia, CPEC economic corridor and the new Maritime Silk Road. Together, these will become the bulwark of 'Belt and Road Initiative' (BRI). It could be construed as having four phases, as given below:

PHASE I – Securing Karakoram in the aftermath of 1948 Indo-Pak war. The rail-road-sea connectivity from Guangzou to Gwadar will cut the cost of transportation by 50%. PHASE II – Focused on Central Asia. Towards this, Shanghai Five Group was formed in 1996. This became the Shanghai Cooperation Organization in 2001. PHASE III – Building bridges across Middle East. China reversed its stand on Palestine by recognizing Israel in 1972. Continuous US-Russia engagement in Middle East appears to be the only factor holding back Chinese inroads. However, trade has considerably increased. Iran alone supplies $ 1.5 bn USD of oil to China every month. PHASE IV – The Maritime Silk Road. Chinese interest in Malaysia, Hambantota, Gwadar, and Djibouti are along the same ancient Maritime Silk Route.

Experts see the BRI as a bold Chinese statecraft under Xi, alongside the Made in China 2025 economic development strategy. For Xi, the BRI serves as pushback against the much-touted U.S. "pivot to Asia," as well as a way for China to develop new investment opportunities, cultivate export markets, and boost Chinese incomes and domestic consumption. "Under Xi, China now actively seeks to shape international norms and institutions and forcefully asserts its presence on the global stage," writes CFR's Elizabeth C. Economy.

CPEC and the relevance of Galwan Valley

The CPEC corridor that commences from the Karakoram Pass (in Xinjiang Province) is critically dependent on who controls the Siachen Glacier area. With over 60 billion USD committed to CPEC, China has a lot at stake Indian control over Siachen therefore leaves China's flanks exposed in and around the Karakorum.

Analysts estimate the largest commitment so far in BRI to be the $68 billion China-Pakistan Economic Corridor, a collection of projects connecting China to Pakistan's Gwadar Port on the Arabian Sea. In total, China has already spent an estimated $200 billion on such efforts. Morgan Stanley has predicted China's overall expenses over the life of the BRI could reach $1.2–1.3 trillion by 2027, though estimates on total investments vary.

BRI has the strategic advantage of connecting China to Arabian Sea and the Five Finger Policy. Together with Bangladesh, Myanmar and Sri Lanka, BRI would facilitate Chinese strategic control over Malacca Strait.

Five Finger Policy

In the light of the above, we must revert back to Mao's Five Finger Policy, for it will give greater understanding of the border disputes with China in the Himalayan Region.

Sikkim

Though Sikkim was not formally colonized, it remained under British 'Protection' which continued post-Indian Independence as a Special Status. In 1975, a Referendum was held in which an overwhelming 97 percent voted in favor of merger with India. Its merger with India was not accepted by China for nearly three decades. Eventually, in 2003, China acknowledged Sikkim as integral to India. Though there are no specific border disputes in Sikkim, in May 2020 both Indian and Chinese troops in Sikkim had a 'fist first' perhaps as a prelude to Galwan!

Bhutan

The fourth finger of the China Five Finger Policy is Bhutan. In 1996, China "wanted to exchange the valleys to the north, with an area of 495 square kilometres, with the pasture land to the west, totaling 269 square kilometres." The deal would have benefited Bhutan by giving it the larger chunk of land, and resolving its tensions with China. However, this was a big worry for India, as the Doklam swap would give the People's Liberation Army (PLA) access to the strategically sensitive "chicken neck" of the Siliguri corridor[11].

Arunachal Pradesh

We have already referred to the 1962 war. While India maintains McMahon Line as the international boundary line, China rejects it. Interestingly, Chinese claims on Arunachal are based on two planks: the 6th Dalai Lama of Tibet was born in Tawang on 01 March 1683, and Tibet belongs to China!!

Nepal

Nepal and Tibet had fought two rounds of war over coinage issue from 1789 to 1792. While the Nepalese won the first round and subjected Tibet to a tributary system, in the second round, Tibet was able to save itself from total defeat with Qing Emperor's help. The Treaty of Betravati of 1792 resulted in Nepal paying tribute to Chinese Empire. However, when Anglo-Nepal war resulted in British influence over Nepal, the tributes were discontinued. Though history does not support it, China still views Nepal as part of the Five Fingers.

Ladakh

Ladakh was won by Zorawar Singh of Maharaja Ranjit Singh's army of Kashmir in 1834. In 1842, Ladakh was added to the Dogra Kingdom. After 1850, the British interest in Ladakh became critical, eventually leading to the Ardagh-Johnson Line, which India recognizes as legitimate border. The border dispute at Ladakh needs greater understanding from this point of view. Such an understanding would also show how China illegitimately constructs bridges and villages to artificially create claims over lands that do not belong to it.

Implications of Galwan – For India and for South Asia

Border Disputes with South Asian Countries, particularly with India amply demonstrate the centrality of South Asia to BRI. Since India has categorically refused to join BRI bandwagon, keeping India under pressure and keeping Pakistan humored appears necessary for China. That being the case, the recent incidents in Nepal (cartographic aggression) and increased military activities near Bhutan and in Arunachal border appear to be part of a grand strategy.

Unstable political-economic scenario in South Asia and Central Asia adds advantage to China since many countries have challenges at home for which they do not have the economic muscle to handle. Countries like Pakistan are de-facto failed states and Afghanistan, Bangladesh and Myanmar need enormous aid packages to revive their violence torn domestic economies.

US Pullout from Afghanistan is going to create a vaccum that China would be too willing to fill. Resource rich Badakshan is already witnessing increasing Chinese presence.

Disarray in Regional Mechanism - specifically SAARC creates opportunities for expanding bilateral cooperation for China. Only threat to Chinese ambition in this dimension is the success of BIMSTEC.

Conclusion

The general background as sketched above presents a strategic challenge to India as well as other South Asian nations. While increased military spending becomes necessary to offset Chinese aggression, greater cooperation between nations in the region is necessary to give fillip to domestic economies. Unless regional economy becomes vibrant, the means to address challenges arising from Chinese interventions will elude South Asia.

To address territorial challenges by China, countries must also contemplate a joint framework for military cooperation, setting their internal political squabbles aside. It is important for them to realize that a strong India is the only option that will prevent them from falling into the net of debt diplomacy that China has already successfully cast over Pakistan, Sri Lanka and nearly over Maldives.

6. Bridges, Villages and Sovereign Claims: Playing the Chinese Way

On December 06, 2020, it was reported that China was building three villages near the border in Arunachal Pradesh[1]. On December 29, 2021, China went ahead and officially renamed 15 places in Arunachal Pradesh, claiming that it has sovereign right to do so[2]. On January 04, 2022, it was again reported that China was building a bridge to link the North and South banks of the Pangong Lake in Ladakh.

Each of these actions have been claimed by the Chinese government as acts in exercise of their sovereign right. It is apparent that Chinese government is vigorously pursuing a policy of assertion, duly backed by armed engagements to keep both India and the rest of the world guessing and at best, be on the defensive. Thus it becomes necessary to understand whether the concept of sovereign right is invoke-able or the Chinese are, in their usual manner, utilizing the ambiguities in international law to further their national agenda.

The Montevideo Convention 1933, still forms the bedrock of all learned discourses on questions of territory and territorial claims. While United nations General Assembly (UNGA) Resolutions and decisions of the ICJ, contribute to such discourses, the decision of individual states to recognize or not to recognize such claims plays an important role. Under the Montevideo Convention, a defined territory is a necessary condition for territorial claims. A careful examination of the case of Israel for its membership of the UN reveals that the UNGA considers *that the absence of delimitation or presence of disputes over territorial delimitation does not disqualify the claim to the status of a "State"*[3]. The ambiguity built into this considered view of UNGA resulted in grant of membership to Israel despite objections from Arab States.

The Case of Arunachal Pradesh

China's purportedly historical claims over Arunachal Pradesh and Ladakh are at best what they are – purported, without any real basis. For example, claim over Arunachal Pradesh is merely resting on the birth of the 6th HH Dalai Lama Tsangyang Gyatso who was born in Tawang in 1683. The Mon tribal areas of present day Arunachal were called the Zayul (South Tibet), Long before Dalai lamas came to rule Tibet from Lhasa. Zayul or Kingdom of sPO BO (as it was known in Tibetan) was a powerful kingdom that occupied most of Tibet itself. Inevitably, it had faced Chinese invasions and survived them without ever becoming a tribute paying territory of China. Even at the beginning of the 20th century, the kingdom was still reasonably strong and it enjoyed actual independence from Lhasa. The government of the Dalai Lama did not exercise any real political control over sPo Bo. The only payment that the sPo Bo were obliged to make was a yearly tax to the Lhasa government consisting of 100 ke of butter to be delivered to the official of the rTse la rDzong district, or rdzong dpon, in neighbouring Kong po[4]. With Tibet firmly under its control, China apparently is tweaking the history in a reverse order to lay claims to Arunachal Pradesh as a matter of sovereign right.

The Case of Ladakh

As an independent Kingdom, Ladakh had existed for over thousand years. In the 16th century, Ladakh was often at war with its neighbors i.e. the Muslim ruler of Kashmir (a vassal of the Mughal Emepror) and Tibet, apart from marauding Central Asian khans. In the war that broke out between Ladakh and Tibet in 1681, Ladakh sought help from the Kashmir ruler with whose assistance Tibetan armies were soundly defeated. Using this opportunity however, the Mughal Emperor encouraged Ladakh's king to embrace Islam. Though it was a token acceptance, Islam thus made its formal entry into Ladakh. Notwithstanding the loss of battle, prompted by the long standing cultural ties and fearing the onset of Islam in Ladakh, King of Tibet proposed a treaty with Ladakh. The terms included the return of Gughe* and Rudok** regions in Western Tibet to Lhasa, while retaining the region around Minsar near Lake Manasarovar. Minsar continued to pay taxes to Ladakh and then Kashmir until the 1950s. Lhasa also agreed to send 200 animal caravan of tea to Ladakh and in return, Ladakh agreed to triennial Lopchak (lo-phyag) trade/ tribute mission to Lhasa which was to present prescribed offerings to the Dalai Lama at the Monlam (smon-lam) great prayer festival[5].

The subsuming of Ladakh by the Dogra Kingdom of Jammu expressly permitted this Lopchak Missions to continue in its 1842 Dogra-Lhasa agreement. This system

* Gughe (in present-day Zanda County in far western Tibet, 50 kilometers from Xinjiang-Tibet Highway and 250 kilometers west of Mt Kailash) was an ancient kingdom founded by a branch of descendants of the last king of a unified Tibet in the 10th century.

** Rudok is the historical capital of the Rudok area in Western Tibet on the frontier with Ladakh. Rudok town is approximately 1140 km west North West of Lhasa.

of trade/tribute missions continued even during the British colonial rule since the British did not see it as political submission of Ladakh to Lhasa[6]. Eventually, after independence and accession of Kashmir into the Indian Union by Maharaja Hari Singh, India decided to stop the Lopchak mission in 1950 in view of Chinese activities in Tibet. In 1961 Chinese officials went so far as to claim the whole of Ladakh on the ground that the triennial Lopchak mission to Lhasa showed that Ladakh was subordinate to Tibet and was therefore part of China (Government of India 1961, p 131).

Mao and the Five Fingers Policy

It is important to understand how contemporary claims of China over Ladakh and Arunachal Pradesh are part of their political agenda. Mao Zedong, in Beijing's Tiananmen Square in the 1950s, talked about Tibet and the Himalayas in his Five Fingers Policy. He was explicit in saying: "Xizang (Tibet) is China's right hand's palm, which is detached from its five fingers — of Ladakh, Nepal, Sikkim, Bhutan and Arunachal (formerly NEFA). As all of these five are either occupied by, or under the influence of India, it is China's responsibility to 'liberate' the five to be rejoined with Xizang (Tibet)". Mao's description of the five fingers was not based on his vision for China's future; it was based on the historical perceptions that China developed about itself and in ample measure supported by the Tribute System[7].

The present Chinese leadership is giving shape to the Five Fingers policy by a skillful exploitation of the loopholes in international law concerning territories. The nibbling away of the territories in the borders adjoining Ladakh, Arunachal Pradesh and similar maneuvers with Nepal and Bhutan demonstrate the intent of the Chinese leadership for exploiting the ambivalence in international law. Combined with aggressive diplomacy and claims to sovereign rights, China has already flouted the Arbitration Award in favour of Phillipines in the South China Sea.

The renaming of locations in Arunachal Pradesh and the building of bridge in Pangong Lake therefore are not to be seen as mere exercises in pressurizing India or any of its neighbors to negotiate terms favourable to it in the dialogues on border issues. Historical evidence actually suggests that even the occupation of Aksai Chin in 1962 is a step forward in its Five Finger Policy. Therefore, the temporary progress obtained during border talks between military brasses, appropriately lauded by Chinese government officials should only be seen as buying-time-while-lulling-the-neighbour-into-confidence tactic.

Playing it the Chinese Way

Loopholes in international law are a matter of concern to the international community. However, it must also be reckoned that no law can ever be comprehensive to address all situations that may invite their application. Conversationally speaking, if the Chinese interpretation of the Montevideo Convention or even the UNGA interpretation on Israel is available to others to gain control over territories by adopting similar tactics, then no other country has better advantage on the Sino-Indian border issue than India.

Documented history reveals that Mon of Arunachal Pradesh had ruled vast territories in Tibet before the peaceable agreements with Dalai Lamas. Similarly, it is only in 1681 Ladakh conceded Gughe and Rudok to Tibet and continued to hold Minsar and Manasarovar Lake area till 1950. Thus the milder protestations and diplomatic conciliations that India registers on Chinese expansionist maneuvers actually help China in furthering its agenda.

It is time that the question of border is unambiguously spelt out to the Chinese government- that it stays in pre-1962 positions across all regions in the Himalayas and North East. No negotiation is possible until Chinese unilaterally dismantle all their constructions within the territories illegally under their occupation. Accepting the 1993 dialogues as the basis for border talks provides abundant scope to China for citing sovereign rights since this agreement technically allows China to maintain control over occupied areas till negotiated settlement is arrived at. By keeping the negotiations going for nearly two decades, it is apparent that the real intent to find a permanent solution is not the objective, at least in so far as China is concerned. The snail's pace of the talk has also allowed it to expand its military and civil infrastructure that could be tactfully used to exploit the ambiguity in international law.

India's Options

Spelling out India's own historical claims in unambiguous terms, after decades of negotiation will present only two options: One, China recognizes that negotiations on territorial issues is played at par and the balance cannot be upset by surreptitious exploitation of legal ambiguities; two, option to use force to claim territories will be to its greater disadvantage in a world that is compellingly inclusive due to forces of globalization.

It is also important to reckon that China's BRI dream largely rests on peaceable and reconciliatory approach. With a politically unstable Pakistan and Taliban ruled Afghanistan close to its own restive Xinjiang region, the reconciliatory approach would be in its favour. India must exploit this geopolitical situation to find a permanent solution to the Sino-Indian border issue before China's outreach into the Middle East compels india to accept terms that may be thrust upon it by Chinese BRI ambitions.

7. Fencing the Dragon Out: Cyber Security Challenges for India

"They (Non-Traditional Security Threats) are defined as challenges to the survival and well-being of peoples and states that arise primarily out of nonmilitary sources."

– Professor Mely Caballero-Anthony (Secretary General, Consortium on Non-Traditional Security Studies in Asia).

Non-Traditional threats to nations and societies have long been understood as emanating from sources that are outside the military frameworks. The advent and spread of information and communication technology, forming backbone of the financial system, economic and industrial infrastructure makes the cyber space especially vulnerable to interest groups as well as inimical groups. Social media riding on the IT highway has also demonstrated capabilities to affect the morale of large sections of society.

When USA went to war with Iraq in 1991, the world witnessed the power of this technological prowess in full play. The subsequent US-led global engagements in Serbia, Kosovo and the Estonian episode of 2007 indubitably established cyber space as an important element in the strategic calculus of any nation.

In the geopolitical scenario that has emerged in Indo-Pacific and SCS, the attention of scholars as well as strategic analysts has riveted itself to the capabilities that China has acquired or developed for itself over the past few decades. Such scholarly scrutiny has studied the cyber warfare capabilities too. Even before China began its ambitious engagement with the world through BRI, experts had begun to survey its cyber prowess. For example, Deepak Sharma (Sharma, 2011)[1] of IDSA who studied the cyber capabilities of China in 2011 summed it up in the following words.

> China has made major progress in synergising, combining, and coordinating its signal intelligence, EW, information security and computer network attack systems. These efforts have made the Chinese system more effective and secure.

In the same year, Desmond Ball (Ball, 2011)[2] from USA also studied these capabilities and came to the conclusion that "the extensive Chinese IW capabilities, and the possibilities for asymmetric strategies, are only potent if employed first". Ball was hinting at the potential disruption that China could cause to its adversaries **if** it carries out a preemptive strike. In his assessment China did not have the wherewithal to sustain or negate the counter capabilities of nations like US.

Even though these assessments conveyed mixed and sometimes misleading judgements on Chinese capabilities, in the years preceding and succeeding these assessments there was an increasing number of attempts to deploy those capabilities to the detriment of India. The reasons are obvious.

Dragon's footprints in Indian cyber sands

Below mentioned instances of Chinese cyber surveillance and attacks on Indian interests are not merely recent but are of considerable strategic importance:

- In 2015, a report by "Fire Eye" - a US based cyber security firm reported that China had been spying on Indian government and businesses for more than a decade without India being aware of it. It would be safe to assume that a spate of intrusions and attempted intrusions like the ones on NIC (National Informatics Centre) in 2009, Websites of MHA (Ministry of Home affairs) and MEA (Ministry of External affairs) in 2012, Northern Power Grid in 2012, Websites of DRDO and PMO in 2013 etc do draw a high level of suspicion against China. In 2017, there was also talk of Chinese hackers attempting to intrude into systems that controlled and monitored Sukhoi 30 fighters of the India Air force in order to forcefully down them.[3]
- In 2018, a report by Computer Emergency Response (CERT-In) documented that China carried out the highest number of attacks on the official websites of India. China was the host country for 35% of all intrusion activities recorded from across the globe targeting Indian websites. The companies widely targeted government industries like ONGC and IRCTC and banks like SBI with a specific targeting of state data centres of banks across states[4].
- On 04th September 2019, India's largest nuclear power plant at Kudangulam suffered a cyber-attack purportedly by North Korean hackers. While the Nuclear Power Corporation of India Ltd (NPCIL) initially denied any such incident, it later admitted that Computer Emergency Response Team (CERT-In), had noticed a malware attack that breached India's largest nuclear power facility's administrative network on September 4th[5].
- On 12 October 2020, even as the stand-off in Eastern Ladakh continued, two thousand kilometers away, in Mumbai the financial capital of India,

the stock market shut down, local trains stopped and the city of 20 million came to a grinding halt. Hospitals battling Covid 19 had to switch over to generators and pray that the outage would be restored soon. The Chief Minister ordered an enquiry and central minister promised to send a special team to investigate[6]. Tata Power that supplies electricity to Mumbai said that the outage was triggered due to the simultaneous tripping of power transmissions lines[7]. The political leaders started blaming each other for letting the financial capital 'power-less' for over 2 hours.

- Fifteen weeks later, David E. Sanger and Emily Schmall (Schmall & Sanger, February 28, 2021)[8] reported in the New York Times that Recorded Future, a Somerville, Mass., company that studies the use of the internet by state actors, had investigated the Mumbai outage and found that the Chinese state-sponsored group, which the firm named Red Echo, "has been seen to systematically utilize advanced cyberintrusion techniques to quietly gain a foothold in nearly a dozen critical nodes across the Indian power generation and transmission infrastructure." Recorded Future reported the findings to Indian authorities for further investigation.
- Exploring further into the Mumbai outage case, Rezaul Laskar and Tanushree Venkatraman (Laskar & Venkatraman, 01 March 2021)[9] further report that the Red Echo had targeted 12 organisations viz., Power System Operation Corporation Limited, NTPC Limited, NTPC's Kudgi power plant, Western Regional Load Dispatch Centre, Southern Regional Load Dispatch Centre, North Eastern Regional Load Dispatch Centre, Eastern Regional Load Dispatch Centre, Telangana State Load Dispatch Centre, Delhi State Load Dispatch Centre, the DTL Tikri Kalan (Mundka) sub-station of Delhi Transco Ltd, VO Chidambaranar Port and Mumbai Port Trust. All these groups use ShadowPad, a modular backdoor tool that has been utilised by China-backed groups in network intrusion campaigns since 2017.

Cyber Security Framework in India

The Indian government has also been aggressively addressing the rising prevalence of cyber threats. **National Cyber Security Policy 2013** has been framed to create a secure cyber ecosystem, ensure compliance with global security systems and strengthen the regulatory framework. The union budget for 2017 included the formation of Computer Emergency Response Team (CERT) for the financial sector.

The government has also sought data security protocol details from several smart phone manufacturers insisting that mobile manufacturing units be security-compliant. The Technology Development Board and Data Security Council of India (DSCI) have jointly decided to promote cyber security startups in India.

NASSCOM and DSCI Cyber security Task Force have also launched a roadmap to develop the cyber security ecosystem to $35 USD billion by 2025.

Information Technology Act, 2000

- The act regulates use of computers, computer systems, computer networks and also data and information in electronic format. It lists down among other things, following as offences:
  - Tampering with computer source documents.
  - Hacking with computer system
  - Act of cyber terrorism i.e. accessing a protected system with the intention of threatening the unity, integrity, sovereignty or security of country.
  - Cheating using computer resource etc.

Strategies under National Cyber Policy, 2013

- Creating a secure cyber ecosystem.
- Creating mechanisms for security threats and responses to the same through national systems and processes.
- National Computer Emergency Response Team (CERT-in) functions as the nodal agency for coordination of all cyber security efforts, emergency responses, and crisis management.
- Securing e-governance by implementing global best practices, and wider use of Public Key Infrastructure.
- Protection and resilience of critical information infrastructure with the **National Critical Information Infrastructure Protection Centre** (NCIIPC) operating as the nodal agency.
  - NCIIPC has been created under Information Technology Act, 2000 to secure India's critical information infrastructure. It is based in New Delhi.
- Promoting cutting edge research and development of cyber security technology.
- Human Resource Development through education and training programs to build capacity.

Recent Steps by Government of India

- **National Cyber security Coordination Centre (NCCC):** Created in 2017, its mandate is to scan internet traffic and communication metadata (which are little snippets of information hidden inside each communication) coming into the country to detect real-time cyber threats.
- **Cyber Swachhta Kendra:** Launched in 2017, this platform is meant for internet users to clean their computers and devices by wiping out viruses and malware.
- **Cyber Surakshit Bharat Initiative:** It was launched in 2018 with an aim to spread awareness about cybercrime and building capacity for safety measures for Chief Information Security Officers (CISOs) and frontline IT staff across all government departments.
- Training of 1.14 Lakh persons through 52 institutions under the **Information Security Education and Awareness Project (ISEA)** – a project to raise awareness and to provide research, education and training in the field of Information Security.
- **International cooperation:** Looking forward to becoming a secure cyber ecosystem, India has joined hands with several developed countries like the United States, Singapore, Japan, etc, towards establishing a secure cyber ecosystem. Agreements with these countries will help India to challenge even more sophisticated cyber threats.

Understanding China's Cyber Policy

Cyber capabilities are as difficult to compare as normal military hardware capabilities. In any case, both depend on the strategic framework or operational philosophy of the employer. Commencing from 1991, China seems to have studied the Desert Storm and Desert Shield operations by USA with great interest. The use of social media as a powerful tool during Arab Spring also appears to have given substantial lessons in managing social media to the Chinese Communist Party and PLA. China's actions to curtail Hong Kong pro-democracy movement provides adequate clarity as to the 'conceptual' policy clarity that China has arrived at in this dimension. The importance given to cyber space in Chinese strategic thinking is highlighted in a White paper published by Ministry of National Defence of PRC dated 24th July 2019[10]:

- Cyberspace is a key area for national security, economic growth and social development. Cyber security remains a global challenge and poses a severe threat to China. China's armed forces accelerate the building of their cyberspace capabilities, develop cyber security and defense means, and build cyber defense capabilities consistent with China's international standing and its status as a major cyber country. They reinforce national cyber border defense, and promptly detect and counter network intrusions. They safeguard information and cyber security, and resolutely maintain national cyber sovereignty, information security and social stability.

- ➢ The PLASSF is a new type of combat force for safeguarding national security and an important driver for the growth of new combat capabilities. It comprises supporting forces for battlefield environment, information, communications, information security, and new technology testing. In line with the strategic requirements of integrating existing systems and aligning civil and military endeavors, the PLASSF is seeking to achieve big development strides in key areas and accelerate the integrated development of new-type combat forces, so as to build a strong and modernized strategic support force.
- ➢ Promoting innovation in defense S&T and military theory. China's armed forces are accelerating the implementation of the strategy to develop the military through S&T in a bid to maintain and enhance the strength of the areas where they lead, and intensify innovation in emerging areas. They have made great progress in independent innovation in some strategic, cutting-edge and disruptive technologies, and succeeded in developing strategic hi-tech products such as the Tianhe-2 supercomputer. Focusing on war and fighting wars, China's armed forces have innovated in military doctrines and delivered outcomes in military strategy, joint operations and informationization, which have provided a theoretical support to defense and military development.

Concluding Thoughts

It is evident that China has understood the importance of cyber space and laid out its policies and programs in tune with its national and international aspirations. Use of the term *consistent with China's international standing and its status as a major cyber country* in its ministerial policy document is ample evidence of such an understanding as well as its aspirations. Even though the cited studies and an appreciation by Carnegie as recently in 2019 (Jinghua, 2019)[11] point to critical technological insufficiencies that China still suffers from, especially the language handicap, Jinghua's recommendation that "a more comprehensive and objective assessment of China's cyber power is in urgent need" should serve as a warning to policy and strategic planners in India.

ICT Development Index which rates a country's cyber capabilities on an 11 point technology/capacity scale, places China at world no. 80, much behind United

States (16), UK (5) and Germany (12). Interestingly, it places Hong Kong (China) at No. 06!! The common understanding that we derive from earlier studies and these assessments could be seen as though China has miles to catch up, provided we close our eyes on the capacity available to it at Hong Kong. The demonstrated behavior the world has evidenced from China thus far, duly underlined by the cyber-attack incidents on critical infrastructure in India should actually provide substantial impetus for India to revamp its cyber policy, duly integrating armed forces into its national counter cyber-attack grid. It may also be worthwhile to note that in spite of the policy frameworks brought about by India, it is ranked at No.134 by ICT.

It would be fruitful to visit and contemplate over some of the insightful and 'doctrinal' precepts that Martin Libicki spelt out in the Rand Air Force Project study on Cyber deterrence and Cyber War[12]:

- The basic message is simple: Cyberspace is its own medium with its own rules. Cyber-attacks, for instance, are enabled not through the generation of force but by the exploitation of the enemy's vulnerabilities. (p-iii)
- Deterrence and war fighting tenets established in other media do not necessarily translate reliably into cyberspace. Such tenets must be rethought. (P-iii)
- The establishment of the 24th Air Force and U.S. Cyber Command marks the ascent of cyberspace as a military domain. As such, it joins the historic domains of land, sea, air, and space. All this might lead to a belief that the historic constructs of war—force, offense, defense, deterrence—can be applied to cyberspace with little modification. Not so. Instead, cyberspace must be understood in its own terms, and policy decisions being made for these and other new commands must reflect such understanding. Attempts to transfer policy constructs from other forms of warfare will not only fail but also hinder policy and planning. (P-xiii)
- Cyber-attacks Are Possible Only Because Systems Have Flaws (P-xiii)
- It is only a modest exaggeration to say that organizations are vulnerable to cyber-attack only to the extent they want to be. In no other domain of warfare can such a statement be made. (P-xiv)

While evaluating the recent Nagrono-Karabakh conflict, it was observed that the extensive use of unmanned platforms could have been the test-bed for such a strategy envisaged in Taiwan's revised ODC (Srinivasan, February 11, 2021)[13]. In eastern Ladakh stand-off, the probability of China employing unmanned platforms remained at the core of many strategic discourses. Instead, Chinese successful attempt to disrupt power supply in the financial capital of India yet again appears to be a testing-bed for their cyber warfare theories, particularly when read with the Ministerial statement that, "*They have made great progress in independent innovation in some strategic, cutting-edge and disruptive technologies, and succeeded in developing strategic hi-tech products such as the Tianhe-2 supercomputer*".

With Sagarmala, Bharatmala, dedicated initiative for expanding indigenized capacity for defence production through Atmanirbhar philosophy, India's reliance on cyber space to run its economic and strategic enterprises will only increase. Therefore, a credible counter cyber-attack capability is critical for India. Having started with well-conceived cyber policies in the preceding decade and having experienced the increasingly belligerent Chinese footprints in South Asia and Indian Ocean Region, a concerted attempt to re-define cyber policies and frameworks for safeguarding national assets appears to be need of the hour. Towards this, the following measures are suggested:

- India has the largest pool of skilled manpower in information technology domain which is acknowledged across the world. Suitable number of brilliant young minds from credible backgrounds could be pooled to work with CERT-In with a preventive task envelope.
- Create an interface between civilian entities and military institutional frameworks for preventing and combating cyber intrusions that could affect dual use infrastructure like airports, railways, ports and ordinance/ military hardware manufacturing hubs.
- The ability to restore normalcy and full functional capacity in the shortest possible time frame after an attack is the fundamental principle that defines operational readiness of armed forces. The same principle needs to be incorporated, tested and evaluated in so for as the agencies responsible for preventing and countering cyber-attacks in civilian and military dimensions.
- The above would be of extreme criticality to the Air Force and the Navy since they are critically dependent on technology.

What India therefore needs is the recalibration of its strategic thinking that duly recognizes emerging trends in cyber security space with particular emphasis on its growing infrastructure.

8. Pawns in a Board Game: China, India and Prisoners of War

India returns Chinese soldier

On 18 October 2020, Corporal Wang Ya Long of the Chinese PLA strayed across the LAC in Demchok sector and was apprehended by Indian Army. Army sources confirmed the apprehension and also issued a statement that he would be released after completing specified formalities[1]. Forty eight hours later, Corporal Wang Ya Long was handed over to PLA front line troops at Chushul-Moldo meeting point, which was corroborated by Chinese media in their press releases[2].

Though the above incident did not cause any stir in public minds, not to say scholarly discussions, it is an important of dimension to be looked at in the light of Sino-Indian skirmish at Galwan in May this year. The board game of chess that commenced at that time remains in spotlight what with both the countries moving their pawns in manners that are testing each other's will.

India and China are both signatories to the Geneva Conventions 1949. While India ratified the Conventions in 1950, China ratified them in 1956[3]. Under Article 118, first paragraph, of the 1949 **Geneva Convention** III (GC III): "**Prisoners of war** shall be released and repatriated without delay after the cessation of active hostilities." Being signatories to the Convention, both India and China have an International legal obligation to repatriate PsOW, should and whenever conflicts between the countries occur. Interestingly, GC III applies only in conflicts that are declared as war.

Technically speaking, a soldier in uniform (with or without weapons) straying into another country is deemed as a mercenary and is liable for criminal prosecution in the country where he is apprehended. Should that person be not in uniform, he is deemed as a spy and is likely to be prosecuted accordingly. Both these conditions could apply in situations where armed conflicts not declared as war by respective countries prevail. ICRC and the larger international community of scholars have always advocated fair treatment and return of soldiers even under these circumstances, though such opinions are at best looked upon as humanitarian appeals rather than mandates of GC III.

China and Indian PsOW

Immediately after the 1962 Sino-Indian operations, the Indian Red Cross handed over a list of 3968 names of Indian soldiers as having been wounded, killed or captured, to the Chinese Red Cross. China refuted the claims and delayed its responses till 1963. After an intensive diplomatic and international intervention, courtesy Rajkumari Amrit Kaur and Maj Gen CK Lakshmanan, China accepted that it held 1132 POW and returned 715 wounded with 13 dead bodies. On January 25, 1963, the ICRC's executive director wrote to General Lakshmanan to draw the IRC's attention to the announcements of the China News Agency that 2,156, (or 3,350) Indian POWs were still in Chinese hands.

On 6th February 1963, President ICRC himself took up the matter with Marshal Chen Yi, the then Chinese Minister of Foreign Affairs. Marshal Chen intimated ICRC two weeks later that "Since the Sino-Indian border clashes, the Chinese government has all along given good treatment in every respect to the Indian military personnel who were captured in the course of their attacks on the Chinese frontier guards."[4] China maintained that it was Indian troops that had attacked 'unsuspecting' border guards of the Chinese Army in Tibet and Sinkiang!!

Importantly, as Claude Arpi noted in his report, China found it "most regrettable that the India PoWs 'captured in the course of the Chinese frontier guards' counterattacks in self-defense' were equated with the 'law-abiding overseas Chinese illegally detained by the Indian authorities.' On 27th February 1963, the ICRC confirmed to General Lakshmanan that the total number of Indian prisoners of war still in Chinese hands was 3,319, excluding the 716 wounded and sick who have been repatriated and the 13 bodies returned by the Chinese Red Cross." [5] From 1963 onwards, China announced that it will release PsOW in batches. As of now, there does not appear to be any clear document or report by either governments whether all PsOW have been repatriated. Such an action by Chinese took nearly eighteen months after considerable international pressure.

India and PsOW

India's actions to repatriate 93000 Pakistani soldiers who surrendered at Dacca after 1971 Indo-Pak war stands testimony to the commitment to International Law and Humanitarian Principles that India stands by. Repatriating Wang Ya Long now reiterates India's position on such issues.

In contrast, during 1962, the Chinese had even pointed out that there was no 'Declaration of War' between India and China. They used this line of international legal logic to deny ICRC the right to visit China and inspect their internment facilities. Initiatives taken by President ICRC, Rajkumari Amrit Kaur as President of Indian Red Cross and Maj Gen Lakshmanan eventually melted down their cold denial.

Conclusion

Clauswitz famously said, "*War is not an independent phenomenon, but the continuation of politics by different means*"[6]. While the common perception is politics sans morality, war is not fought on barbaric terms. The soldiers partaking in war are merely executing the will of the polity. They have neither personal enmity nor do they entertain culturally induced hatred. Therefore, a polity when it chooses to defy international norms such as laid down in Geneva Conventions, indulges in acts that humanity has always held as abhorrent.

India's action to return Wang stands as a testimony to the nation's vibrant culture that upholds non-violence and forgiveness as core principles even in international relations where geopolitical compulsions give rise to temptations and vanity resulting in irresponsible acts by political actors.

Section II

China's Quest for Maritime Power

9. Postcolonial Approach to Understanding China's Quest for Maritime Power

Introduction

Nations as entities are organic beings and in that sense subject to the same laws of nature that individual species are subjected to. Herbert Spencer (1820-1903), perhaps the most notable but little read and much less studied sociologist far ahead of his times, is credited with the phrase "survival of the fittest" in discourses on theories of evolution. Spencer apparently developed an extraordinary theory of geopolitical and dialectical dynamics in his monumental works – *Descriptive Sociology* and *The Principles of Sociology* (Turner, et.al, 2002)[1].

In contrast, well adored Charles Darwin did not consider the process of evolution as the survival of the fittest; he regarded it as survival of the fitter, because the "struggle for existence" (a term he took from English economist and demographer Thomas Malthus) is relative and thus, not absolute. Instead, the winners with respect to species within ecosystems could become losers with a change of circumstances (Brittanica, n.d.)[2].

Deriving from Spencer and Darwin, however, is a quintessential lesson that applies to species as well as nations which may be stated in these terms: Nations that learn from their history lessons that have endangered their very survival, attain those capabilities that are essential to outlive similar environments.

Objective and Methodology

This paper attempts to examine Chinese history briefly, albeit in just the navy dimension, to see whether it has made an attempt to learn from it. To do so, a post-colonial approach to geopolitics has been adopted by consulting Oxford History of China which, believably, will reflect the western perception on Chinese capabilities and PLAN document published by Ministry of Defence of PRC which conveys the perceptions and philosophies that have guided them in building their naval capabilities.

China and the Opium War 1839-1842

Following instances from the Opium War to assess China's experiences vis-à-vis the British naval power are visited below before attempting to draw lessons from them. The Cambridge History of China, Vol 10, Late Ch'ing 1800-1911, Part-1(Twitchett & Fairbank, 2008)[3] has been relied upon to draw up these instances:

- (On) 21 June 1840, **sixteen British ships of war, four armed steamers and twenty eight transports carrying four thousand soldiers** had assembled off Macao. On 05 July, British ships bombarded Chusan which routed the garrison after which the British looted the city. (British Prime Minister) Palmerston had expected the capture of Chusan to shock the Chinese into immediate surrender. This did not happen. Since Chusan's garrison had been routed by naval artillery, the loss of the island did not destroy the myth that Englishmen could not fight ashore. (P-195)
- On 21 May 1841, I-shan (Emperor's cousin), sent flaming rafts downriver toward the English fleet anchored at Whampoa. In the ensuing battle, **seventy-one Chinese war junks were destroyed and sixty shore batteries seized**. Then, protected by the Nemesis, troopships moved around the city to land forces which occupied the northern heights just outside Canton's old walls. (P 202)
- Pottinger reached Hong Kong on 10 August 1841 to direct an expeditionary force ... that, by the end of the war, would include twenty-five ships of the line, fourteen steamers, nine support vessels and troopships carrying ten thousand infantry. He soon led the first two thousand men and part of the fleet north to the important Fukien port of Amoy. The commander of that region, Yen Po-shou, should have been eager to see them, because he had already persuaded the emperor to spend two million taels on defences there. **Fifty large junks, three 'impregnable' forts and nine thousand infantry were supposed to shatter the English forces** as soon as they approached. When the expeditionary fleet anchored off Amoy's approaches on 26 August, Admiral Parker did find the granite ramparts impenetrable to his shells, but the Chinese gunners could not keep a concerted fire going long enough. Amoy was taken the next day at a cost of two British dead and 15 wounded. (The city was looted, women raped and defenders massacred). (P-204)
- The British then moved on to Chusan, Ningpo and Chin-hai. **The long-held myth that British could not fight on land was literally blown to smithereens during the counter-attack on Ningpo in which the British field artillery got sick of killing the Chinese**! The Yangtze Campaign that followed lasted from 07 May to 20 August 1841. Having taken virtually

undefended Shanghai and Chinkiang, by August, British guns and ships had sliced China into half. (P-206)

- Treaty of Nanking was signed on board Pottinger's vessel, HMS Cornwallis, on 29 August 1842. Its main provisions were: (i) an indemnity of $21,000,000 to be paid in instalments: (ii) the opening for trade of the five ports of Canton, Amoy, Foochow, Ningpo and Shanghai; (iii) equal intercourse between officials of corresponding rank; (iv) British consuls at each port; (v) abolition of the Cohong monopoly; (vi) a uniformly moderate tariff to be imposed on both imports and exports; and (vii) cession of the island of Hong Kong to be British territory. China's door had finally been opened but the negotiators had still to arrange the terms on which the British could move in. (Pp 211-212)

  In short, it took 25 British ships of the line, 14 steamers, nine support vessels and troopships carrying ten thousand infantry to dispel the long held Chinese belief of the invincibility of their naval and ground troops. It is also important to note the following events precipitated by these military defeats shattered the Chinese empire, forcing China into what President Xi Jinping referred to as the Century of Humiliation (Ching, 2018)[4]:

- The May (1841) attack on Canton was not of immediate military significance for the English, but it was to carry great consequences for the Chinese. First, in the wake of the assault, with its looting and disorder, the normally rowdy local robbers and pirates of the delta became much bolder than before. Large portions of the Liang-Kuang - especially the hilly border area between the two provinces - were soon almost lost to bandit gangs. The years from 1841 to 1850 thus saw *a crescendo of social disorder that actually precipitated the Taiping Rebellion.* (P-202)
- Second, a tradition of anti-foreign resistance was created which profoundly affected China's later relations with the West. While the English and Indian troops north of Canton were waiting for the Chinese authorities to fulfil the conditions of the ransom agreement, they despoiled some of the local temples and raped several women in and around the rural marketing centre of San-yiian-li. Such specific incitements, together with pervasive popular anxieties about the war, *helped to transform relatively benign stereotypes about foreigners into xenophobic racism.* (P-202)

However, during the First and Second Opium Wars, not everything Chinese was as ineffective as one would presume about their ability and tactics. For Instance, American Commodore Josiah Tatnall, who was present and eventually got involved in rescuing the British from utter annihilation is reported to have penned exhaustive memoirs. Charles Jones (Jones, 1878)[5] who studied his life, presented the following observation:

> The Second Battle of the Dagu Forts is significant because it considerably extended the length and scope of the Opium War. The British loss not only caused a costly 13 month delay, but the fighting force went from 3,000-4,000 troops to a fleet of over 18,000 strong. Even if the Manchus could not defeat such a vast fleet, as was assembled in 1860, the cost to assemble the force alone is a loss for the invaders. The Qing didn't need sophisticated machinery or professional soldiers to win the battle, instead it was a basic tactic that had been around and perfected since the times of Sun Tzu: **deception**. The Manchus used the invaders misperceptions against them, as the British had seen Manchu soldiers flee fortresses countless times before invasions, and the British and French did not expect to be challenged at the Dagu Forts. The Manchu soldiers sprung their trap, defeated the British, and this one false move by the invaders cost them dearly.

The aftermath of these defeats and the Rape of Nanking by burning down the Yuan Ming Yuan (Winter Palace of the Emperor) in 1860 appear to have become living memories of the Chinese people (Bowlby, 2015)[6], influencing their special drive to rectify the weaknesses that led to their downfall.

Having visited Chinese experiences during and after the Opium War, a survey as to what China has done to imbibe these lessons into developing its PLA Navy is given below.

Growth Trajectory of Chinese Naval Capacity

In the years after the Treaty of Nanking, China went into a progressive decline. The Treaty System imposed by the British led to similar concessions granted to US, France and other foreign trading nations that took advantage of the clauses of the treaty to maximize profits from tea trading. Within two years of the Treaty of Nanking, US and France had even obtained the concession of Extra Territoriality by which citizens of these nations remained outside Chinese judicial powers for prosecution even for crimes committed on Chinese citizens. Such dilution of control as well as increasing abrasive behaviour by foreign merchants, troops and clergymen became the seeds of resentment against Manchu rule leading to successive rebellion. Taiping (1840-1868) in South East China, Nian (1851-1873) in Northeast China and Muslim Revolts (1855, 1868-1873) in West and Northwest China had weakened the Empire into a collapse. At the heart of the trouble was the outflow of silver due to opium trade which had exceeded nine million Taels (one Tael approximately weighs one ounce of silver), to cater to which the Empire had to exorbitantly tax the farmers and citizens. In this general economic scenario, Chinese navy received a little more than cursory attention for development.

However, between 1861 and 1875, Emperor Tongzhi attempted to revive Chinese power through what he called "self-strengthening" measures. Part of these measures under his minister Zeng Guofan was an attempt to obtain machinery for building new weapons and arsenal. Zeng commissioned Yung Wing (who had graduated from Yale in 1854) to the United States to buy machinery necessary for opening an arsenal in China capable of producing heavy weapons comparable with those of the western powers. The arsenal later became Jiangnan Shipyard[7]. Due to such measures[8], by 1868 China had begun to produce rifles and steam ships!

The reforms initiated by Emperor Tongzhi were not pursued when Cixi (Dowager Empress) ascended to power. Even then, Chinese Navy expanded into four distinct navies, Nothern, Southern, Foochow and Canton navies.

The realization of technological deficit vis-à-vis British, French, and American ships and farsighted initiatives like the one by Zeng Guofan translated into acquiring western technology and propelled innovation in China. Hsien-Ching Wang (Wang, 2009)[9] in studying this aspect notes in his abstract that:

> This article examines how China tackled the technological differences between itself and the West in the process of acquiring steam technology. It begins in the First Opium war (1839-1842), when the Chinese people witnessed British paddle-wheel steam warships. Having misunderstood the steam mechanism, they worked instead with the technology available to them in order to combat British naval forces. In the 1860s, they experimented with steam-powered ship technology again, but in a different environment in which foreign machine tools and knowledge of the steam mechanism were available. Through trial and error they realized the importance both of machine tools in turning the principle of steam power into a workable engine and of technical drawings in diffusing technical knowledge. Thereafter the Chinese government established arsenals and shipyards that used steam as their source of motive power. Along with foreign machine shops, they marked the beginning of radical changes in technology and society in China

However, Wang also found that "Chinese engineers lacked the requisite machine tools and technical drawing to replicate the steamship effectively" (P. 43-47). Scholars in Chinese history like Jenny Huangfu Day (Day, 2015)[10] even observed that this change in approach to adopt and innovate western technology had to face the challenge of deep rooted notions of cultural superiority and overcome it through innumerable observations and evaluations by Chinese diplomats, admirals and travelers. As Day notes, the initial Chinese belief was that the western "fire ships" (huo chuan) or "boats with cartwheels" (chelun chuan) could be easily sunk by using water which is fire's natural enemy!

Notwithstanding such cultural barriers and the eternal corruption in its elite bureaucracy, China under the Tongzhi and Cixi empires went on to build a formidable steam propelled navy from the 1860s onwards. In about three decades, Chinese had built four navies.

> Amongst them, The Northern (Beiyang) fleet was the best of the whole Empire of the late Qing dynasty. From 1880, China started to order ships abroad, modernize its training, with the aid of a few British Officers. The modernized Foochow fleet however was entirely sunk by the French Navy over Indochina in 1884, and it's later rebuilding was largely supported by British and Germans, while Japan was at that time purchasing ships from France. It should be noted also that the fleet lacked ammunitions and more modern ships, as funds were embezzled by corrupt officials (even during the war), the Empress Dowager Cixi even spending military funds on renovating the Summer Palace.

The Battle of the Yalu River (1894-95) or the First Sino-Japanese War again was to test the mettle of this modern navy, especially its Beiyang Northern Fleet. For comparison, the Beiyang Fleet was led by her flagship, Dingyuan, and her sister ship, Zhenyuan, which were the biggest in Asia; With German-built armoured turret ships, they were armed with four 12in guns and two 6in guns, plus six smaller guns and three torpedo tubes. The Japanese fleet, including the Matsushima and her sister ships Itsukushima and Hashidate, were each armed with a single 12.6in Canet gun and 11 or 12 4.7in guns, plus smaller guns and four torpedo tubes (Lai, 2019)[11]. The far superior Beiyang fleet was shot out of the waters on 17 September 1894 by a much smaller Japanese fleet, which forever changed the context of Sino-Japanese relations. While the superiority in ship size and weaponry favoured the Chinese, agility and leadership won the day for the Japanese. For example, knowing the iron hulls of Chinese battleships as impregnable, the Japanese concentrated on the super structures setting the battle ships and ammunition stores ablaze. This battle was to prove the superiority in tactics and leadership as crucial lessons. Ironically the Chinese had even employed British and American naval officers of rank to command or co-command their ships. The Japanese too had employed French naval officers in their ships.

The intervening years from the close of 19th century till the Mao led revolution in 1949, kept China preoccupied with Japanese aggression, leaving little room for improvements to its navy. Thus in 1949 when PRC came into being, the maritime capabilities of the Navy were rudimentary, confined as it was to its coastal protection. In the aftermath of World War II, Britain sought to sell a number of its war ships owing to the impracticality of maintaining them. China stepped in to buy nearly 26 British naval ships. Though in the emerging Cold War scenario, China was forbidden to buy the ships with complete weaponry, the arrival of these ships marked the beginning of the expansion of the fleet again. At the peak of the Cold War in 1976, China entered into an agreement with

USSR to buy 36 ships with necessary technical assistance for rebuilding/refitting them with Soviet assistance. By 1980's China set about forming the culturally important four navy format.

In parallel, China also drafted for itself a clearly spelt policy framework defining the purposes for which PLA (N) would be created and deployed. The Report of Ministry of National Defence, PRC, 2019, merits an analysis to understand these aspects. Relevant inputs are drawn below from Ministry of National Defence, PRC (Li, 2019)[12]:

> The PLAN has a very important standing in the overall configuration of China's national security and development. It comprises submarine, surface ship, aviation, marine, and coastal defense forces. Under the PLAN, there are the ETC Navy (Donghai Fleet), the STC Navy (Nanhai Fleet), the NTC Navy (Beihai Fleet), and the PLAN Marine Corps. Under the TC navies there are naval bases, submarine flotillas, surface ship flotillas and aviation brigades. In line with the strategic requirements of near seas defense and far seas protection, the PLAN is speeding up the transition of its tasks from defense on the near seas to protection missions on the far seas, and improving its capabilities for strategic deterrence and counterattack, maritime maneuver operations, maritime joint operations, comprehensive defense, and integrated support, so as to build a strong and modernized naval force.

The Ministerial document further goes on to explain how PLA and PLA (N) went about building 'mutual trust, mutual benefit and win-win cooperation in carrying out pragmatic exchanges and cooperation with foreign militaries'. The document amplifies how, beginning 2008, PLA (N) task groups achieved cooperation with multiple naval forces across the globe, especially in the Sea of Aden to safeguard international SLOCs. It further provides instances of China's armed forces taking an active part in the international efforts for HADR.

The Ministry's Document also lays down the undermentioned principles for promoting 'Defence and military developments' in all respects:

- **Promoting innovation in defense S&T and military theory**. China's armed forces are accelerating the implementation of the strategy to develop the military through S&T in a bid to maintain and enhance the strength of the areas where they lead, and intensify innovation in emerging areas. *They have made great progress in independent innovation in some strategic, cutting-edge and disruptive technologies, and succeeded in developing strategic hi-tech products such as the Tianhe-2 supercomputer. Focusing on war and fighting wars, China's armed forces have innovated in military doctrines and delivered outcomes in military strategy, joint operations and* *informationization*, which have provided a theoretical support to defense and military development.

- **Establishing a modernized weaponry and equipment system**. China's armed forces are optimizing the overall composition of weaponry and equipment, coordinating the efforts of all services and arms in this regard, *promoting the balanced development of main battle equipment, information systems, and support equipment, with a view to comprehensively raising standardization, serial development and interoperability.* Old equipment is being phased out, and a system created that mainly comprises new and high-tech weaponry and equipment. Type 15 tanks, type 052D destroyers, J-20 fighters, and DF-26 intermediate and long-range ballistic missiles have been commissioned.
- **Building a combat-oriented modern logistics system**. China's armed forces are putting in place a support mechanism combining centralized and decentralized support, as well as general and special-purpose supplies, with *PLAJLSF as the backbone force and service logistics units as supplements.* They are also building a joint, lean and efficient logistic support system with the strategic and campaign level forces as the main force, the affiliated forces as the support, and the civil sectors as supplements. Logistics units have been incorporated into TC-level joint training, trans-theater training by services and arms, and joint exercises and training with foreign militaries to strengthen the integrated training of logistical and operational forces. *China's armed forces have acquired a rapid, multi-dimensional and precise support capability.*
- **Strengthening strategic management**. Adopting demand-oriented planning and planning-led resource allocation, China's armed forces have established and improved the *strategic management procedures of demand-planning-budgeting-execution-evaluation.* They have completed a system of strategic plans and programs composed of the development strategies of the military as a whole, and its key areas, branches, and the PAP. They have regulated military strategic planning, promulgated and implemented the *Outline of the 13th Five-Year Plan for Military Development*, and optimized the mechanisms for evaluation, supervision and control.

In order to appreciate whether Chinese policies and programs have bequeathed to them a credible maritime power based on their experiences through stated historical narratives, it is necessary to revert to contemporary western perceptions and analyses which may not fully portray the capabilities[13] but still afford greater understanding.

Western Conceptions about Contemporary Chinese Naval Capabilities

United States has had an abiding strategic interest in the Pacific and specifically with reference to China in a pronounced manner after the infamous Japanese attack on Pearl Harbor. The fortuitous absence of the US carrier fleets in Pearl Harbor on 07 December 1941 helped America to declare war and launch counter attacks, eventually culminating in the Japanese surrender in 1945. While mounting the counter offensive in the Pacific Theatre against Japan, United States also mounted a mammoth operation known as the Hump to assist Chiang Kai Sheikh in countering Japanese land forces which had practically over run Han China. It had built innumerous airfields in the northeast of British India and deployed hundreds of aircraft that flew thousands of sorties across the Himalayas providing military hardware and supplies to Chiang. In the aftermath of the Japanese surrender, US also undertook to protect Chiang's Nationalist Forces and eventually helped in establishing Taiwan as Republic of China. When Mao emerged as the strongman of continental China and established the PRC, US assistance to Taiwan became the impediment in establishing normal ties with PRC that persists till date. The Korean and Vietnam Wars as a result of Cold War perceptions contributed in furthering mutual distrust and suspicions, initially on ideological basis and subsequently in no small measure by the increasing bonhomie between USSR/Russia and PRC. China's overtures to Pakistan specifically from the late 1980's are also essential to be kept in mind owing to the developments concerning Afghanistan in the pre-and-post 9/11 era. China's economic growth and outreach under Deng and Hu Jintao during these periods and now Xi Jinping, are a matter of contemporary history on which volumes of scholarly studies are available.

This brief narrative linking the past to the present is relevant and is to be viewed in perspective. In order to study developments concerning PLA (N) in the post-Mao era, relevant inputs drawn from a 2009 document published by United States Office of Naval Intelligence (ONI, 2009) [14] are listed below:

> From its inception in 1949 until the mid-1980s, the PLA (N)'s primary strategic concept was one of *"coastal defense."* This strategy focused the PLA (N) on defending China's coast from the Soviet Pacific Fleet as a small component of what would primarily be a land war. By 1982, despite the lack of resources and continued focus on continental threats, PLA (N) Commander Admiral Liu Huaqing directed the PLA (N)'s naval research toward *"offshore defense." (P-5)*
>
> Offshore defense is a regional strategy that does not advocate replicating U.S. or Soviet "blue-water" naval capabilities. Instead, it calls for naval capabilities suited for China's specific regional maritime interests. While offshore defense has often

been generically described as operations within China's 200 nautical mile (nm) Exclusive Economic Zone, Admiral Liu defined China's offshore areas as the Yellow Sea, East China Sea, South China Sea, the seas around the Spratly Islands and Taiwan, the areas inside and outside the Okinawa island chain as well as the northern part of the Pacific Ocean. This includes areas outside of the "First Island Chain" as well as the more traditional coastal waters. (P-5)

Events of the 1990s, including the U.S.-led operations against Iraq and Serbia, U.S. intervention in the Taiwan Strait crisis of 1996 and the ongoing modernization of both Japan's and Taiwan's navies, highlighted to Chinese strategists both the weakness of China's maritime flank and China's vulnerability to long-range precision strike weapons. Specifically, *the success of U.S. weapons combined with the willingness of the United States to intervene in regional conflicts made it clear to Beijing that China was not prepared for the realities of modern warfare.* (P5)

The CMC charged the PLA with developing the ability to fight "local wars under modern high-tech conditions." In order to do so, the PLA introduced two key concepts to help guide its modernization: "informationization" and "non-contact warfare." (P-6)

Chinese scholars and PLA (N) strategists now advocate a new strategy for the 21't century, termed "distant sea defense." This new strategy would not bound operations geographically, but rather be defined according to China's maritime needs. In addition to the continued protection of maritime interests, advocates of distant sea defense see a respected modern navy as a necessary component of China's rising international status. (P-6)

Concepts behind Chinese Naval Strategy

The ONI document also delves on the doctrinal concepts that in its assessment the Chinese Communist Party leadership had mandated to PLA (N). ONI (2009, p.7)[15] lists three concepts that appear to be the foundational doctrines on which PLA (N) would be developed viz., Informationization, Non-Contact Warfare and Distant Sea Defence:

"**Informationization**" describes China's military effort to incorporate modern technology into all aspects of operations. It recognizes that modern, long-range weapons require fast and accurate means for coordinating data over long distances. A military adept in informationized warfare would be able to effectively control and coordinate forces with speed and precision, while inhibiting the enemy's ability to do the same. Thus informationization includes means to protect one's own information, such as modern command and control systems, as well as means to disrupt the information of the adversary, such as cyber-attacks and electronic jamming. The greater coordination between multiple naval units and "smarter"

> weapons enabled by informationization gives rise to a key element of modern warfare referred to in the PLA as non-contact warfare.
>
> "**Non-contact warfare**" involves employing platforms and weapons in precision strikes from outside of an enemy's "defended zone," reducing the risk to friendly platforms. Similar to U.S. doctrine that emphasize s parallel attacks against key node s with in an enemy's system, Chinese writings on non-contact warfare stress non-linear attacks against the entirety of an enemy's operational and strategic depth, causing an opponent to lose the ability and will to resist. From a naval perspective, non-contact warfare is demonstrated by the PLA (N)'s development and acquisition of long-range weapons to be launched from ships, submarines, aircraft, or shore-based platforms as well as the associated detection and targeting capabilities required to employ these weapons to their fullest capacity.
>
> "**Distant sea defense**" While coastal defense and to a certain extent offshore defense have either an explicit or implied geographical limitation (that the PLA (N) would only operate a certain distance from China), distant sea defense has no such limitations regarding distance from the mainland. The PLA (N) would be required to be able to defend China's maritime interests whether they were close to home or on the other side of the world. This is not to say China will develop a global navy like the United States, but that the PLA (N) would be required to have a basic global reach to defend China's specific needs, such as the anti-piracy patrols in the Gulf of Aden.

A decade later, in 2019 James Fanell (Fanell, 2019) [16] cited ONI of US extensively to draw up the below given perceptions:

> The PLAN's expansion from 2000 to 2018 far exceeds the buildup in any other nation's navy in the post–World War II era, save for the U.S. Navy under President Ronald W. Reagan during the 1980s. *For China's leaders to achieve their vision of a rejuvenated and restored China, they need a fleet that can expand China's interior lines out into the maritime domain. In other words, they need naval, air, missile, and expeditionary forces that can take China's regional military dominance and intimidation to the global realm.* Because of atrophy of U.S. naval forces over the last decade, Beijing's goal is expected to be realized by 2020. Concurrent with the PLAN modernization has been the changing pattern of its operations. Instead of continuing its role as a coastal naval force operating within fifty nautical miles (nm) of China's coast, today the PLAN has pushed out into the blue water of the Pacific Ocean and beyond. An examination of PLAN blue-water operations during the past fifteen years reveals that "*China's ambitious naval modernization has produced a more technologically advanced and flexible force.*" This evolving naval force will provide Beijing with the capability to conduct a military campaign successfully within the first island chain (for instance, to take Taiwan or the Senkaku Islands).

Survey of Lessons and Their Practice

Having surveyed the Chinese historical experiences till 1949, China's stated policy objectives and the contemporary western assessment of China in maritime power dimensions, a list of lessons the Chinese are perceived to have learnt are listed first. Thereafter, an attempt to evolve some lessons to facilitate greater understanding of the Chinese mind, is also made.

Survey of the Opium Wars and the Yalu Campaign appear to be giving forth the following lessons to the Chinese:

- The importance of a powerful navy (commensurate if not above the capacity of foreseeable opponents,
- The importance of amphibious capability, and
- The need to acquire extra-regional or even global operational capacity which is independent of homeland, if China were to meet challenges to its aspirations.

There are also certain other lessons available through these narratives that are useful in understanding the Chinese mind in the contemporary world. These could indicate strengths as well as inherent weaknesses:

- **A powerful and centralized government that is focused on increasing military capacity is necessary**. Manchu dynasty's failure to have a centralized military equipped with contemporary weapons and tactics was the single most reason why the Opium Wars resulted in 'shaming' China. Reliance on sword wielding troops, relying on fixed battlements with aging cannons that could only take on massed frontal attacks, mobilizing regional overlords to supplement troops hastily drawn from peasant population, and disjointed attacks without realistically assessing enemy capacity, for example, are some of the portent lessons that come from the Opium episode.
- **Underestimating the foreign powers** – The cultural perceptions, notions of superiority (Heavenly Mandate) and lack of battle proven leadership were serious pitfalls. This is not to say that Manchu army was not battle worthy. At least some elements of the army were professional soldiers with theatre experience. However, their critical strength was advantageous in land battles. With the vast hinterland where home troops were more proficient, had the Manchu drawn the British into running battles across Han China, the story of Opium War could have been different. This view was also held by avid Chinese scholars including an advisor to Mike Pampeo (Yu, 2018)[17]. Instead Chinese decided to use fixed batteries to take on British frigates and anticipated classical frontal attacks (them being

masters of siege warfare) from their enemies. In other words, they expected the British to play the war by the Chinese book!!

- **Over reliance on cultural perceptions** – for example, believing that Taoist tantric divers could stay under water to place mines on British battle ships; the invincibility of Manchu army based on victories in battles with tribes and marauding armies who had similar weapons and tactics, perhaps far inferior; the belief that "Heavenly Mandate" of the Emperor by itself could dispel British guns; tactics based on cultural beliefs like 'water is the nemesis of fire'. Hence fire spewing British ships could be sunk by flaming rafts; etc. It is important to note that the Ministry of National Defence document refers to the cultural superiority of Chinese society, while carefully tempering it with the necessities of adopting to prevalent technological environments.
- **Mandate of Heaven in a new format** – Universal peace, order and framework of values based on Chinese beliefs is the underlying theme of every policy and program that the Ministerial document states.
- **Acquiring Knowledge and Innovation** – the building of navy and arsenal as evidenced from Yung Wing Biography, writings of Jenny Huangfu Day and other scholars cited gives ample evidence to the inherent understanding about importance of credible maritime power derived from their experiences. More importantly, sending students across to study in western universities, utilizing diplomatic and civilian voyages as opportunities to acquire contacts, information and technology – these appear to have been done systematically rather than incidentally. Chinese ability to replicate and improvise Soviet designs for their aircraft and ships is a matter of public knowledge. It is well known that Chinese students and scholars of Chinese origin are part and parcel of the scientific community in any nation that claims an iota of technical knowhow.
- **Loss of Tribute paying neighbors** – The events and weakening of the Empire in the course of the stated wars and Treaty System imposed by western powers (resulting in reversal of fortunes by which wealth started flowing out), led to the loss of Tribute paying neighbors viz., Korea, Vietnam and Burma. This rendered the Manchu Rule hollow, resulted in even their successor, the Qing Empire finally dissolving in 1912 and rise of nationalist and communist forces in China. These again point to the constant Chinese attempts towards territorial aggressions and expansions like annexation of Tibet, Xinjiang, acquiring Karakoram/Aksai Chin and bullying India over Arunachal Pradesh. China's engagement with North Korea and ill-fought war with Vietnam in 1987 are also to be seen in this

light. Mao's famous Five Finger Policy, when seen from this assessment, lends greater appreciation of Chinese intent.

Has US been a great source of learning for China?

The short answer is 'Yes'. However the answer needs to be qualified a little more.

The interest with which United States views developments concerning Chinese can be assessed by the volume of studies that US institutions publish about things concerning China – Naval War College, Universities, Departments of Government, Think Tanks, individual analysts, authors…the list is endless. Curiously, Chinese interest on US is reciprocal. It would be easy to say that this interest is because they are the only contestants for domination of the world order. This view cannot be subscribed to entirely. China's actions are driven by an urge for redemption through domination and restoration of the glory of Chinese culture. The redemption aspect has two components – redeem what is perceived as 'lost prestige' and redeem the prosperity that China enjoyed through trade that was lost in the aftermath of Opium Wars.

It may be of interest to note that when the initial hostilities in the Opium War appeared in the horizon, especially when Commissioner Lin succeeded in pushing the British to Macau in an attempt to isolate them, the American traders were spared. When Elliot (Factor of Canton) appealed to Americans to join the British, he was rebuffed in these words:

> Robert Bennett Forbes, the leading North American trader, had answered in turn that, 'I had not come to China for health or pleasure, and that I should remain at my post as long as I could sell a yard of goods or buy a pound of tea. . . . We Yankees had no Queen to guarantee our losses.'(Twitchett & Fairbank, 2008, P191)[18]

As a matter of fact, the Elliot himself had realized from the beginning that *the mere principle of extraterritoriality might seem less important to merchants than their profits* - especially if their competitors, the Americans, picked up their annual tea contracts. (P 191). As a record of history, Gladstone who was a Tory MP at that time, had condemned Palmerstone's appeal to the British Parliament to approve of a war on China in the following words:

> A war more unjust in its origin, a war more calculated to cover this country with permanent disgrace, I do not know and I have not read of. The right honourable gentleman opposite spoke of the British flag waving in glory at Canton. That flag is hoisted to protect an infamous contraband traffic; and if it were never hoisted except as it is now hoisted on the coast of China, we should recoil from its sight with horror. (Ibid, p.195)[19]

To the Chinese mind, this would (should) be an important lesson in understanding the western mind – that behind the veneer of principles of their national or international laws, western governments were driven by their merchant class which in their turn were driven by no greater motive than profiteering. This lesson about western minds should have been absorbed by the Chinese since the same principles are manifesting in the actions of the Chinese in developments concerning RCEP. Despite vociferous demands for investigations into the origin of Corona virus and joining the QUAD, Australia enlisted itself with RCEP in its 'national interest' (Srinivasan, 2020)[20].

That America stood behind Taiwan right from 1949, but continued expanding its trade ties with China in the post-1991 in spite of the ideological difference and growing evidence of Chinese footprints in SE Asia, Africa, Pakistan, Middle and East, Central Asia and Africa could perhaps serve well to reinforce the surmise that Chinese indeed have made a probing analysis of the western mind. Our surmise is also based on statements like "We already have slipped. If we fall any further, we may not recover" by Fanell[21]

Apart from these understandings of the western mind with reference to mercantilism, America's resounding victory against Japan in World War II was brought about by its navy in the Pacific. In the Cold War era, US spread its naval presence in the oceans of the world through its carrier groups. Moving the 5th Fleet to Indian Ocean forcing India to warm up to USSR in 1971, The Libyan War, Yugoslav-Serbian episode, Iraq 1991, hounding Osama by sea based attacks, blockade of Iran, and other such instances where US Navy and its carrier fleet played the clinching role are not merely a fact of history. They are of immense interest to strategic analysts everywhere else, including China in view of its policy commitment to protect its interests beyond domestic seas.

Carrier Fleets and China

The lesson that again stands out from these contemporary instances is the importance that maritime capabilities, especially of the aircraft carrier class, play a crucial role in furthering 'national interest'. To presume that this lesson has not been of interest to China would amount to the proverbial cat closing its eyes to drown the world in darkness. Again, the Chinese attempts to acquire blue water capabilities in terms of a carrier fleet is an important dimension to understanding Chinese mind. In overall analysis of the Chinese aircraft carrier program, following lessons were found (Srinivasan, December 28, 2020)[22] :

Lesson 1:

With two US carrier groups standing at its doorstep, especially of the Nimitz class, relying only on the Second Artillery Corps and fleet of J-7s would only repeat what happened at Canton in 1841 which President Xi Jinping specifically calls as the Century of Humiliation. Adventurism tempered with wisdom. So, lesson number one is: **Learn from your history**.

Lesson 2:

It took Chinese ten years to refit and induct Riga as their own Liaoning. The point to note is the rusting old float that was towed 28000 km over two years, became China's credible aircraft carrier through their own technical, homegrown expertise at the port of Dalian (Vavasseur, 2019)[23]. Lesson number two: **Grow your technical expertise to cater to FUTURE needs, before the future arrives**.

Lesson 3:

Liaoning even went through a refit after six years of service bringing new lessons. The third Chinese aircraft carrier is being developed now reportedly will come with CATOBAR (Catapult Assisted Take-Off But Arrested Recovery) design equipped with electromagnetic catapults). Lesson number three: **Learn again from your weapon system and involve R&D in improvising them**.

Interestingly, India's story of procuring INS Vikramaditya runs on a similar dateline to Liaoning. Rest is open to deductions.

Lesson 4:

The second carrier, Shandong, was launched in less than six years after the first, from the scratch. An ability to assimilate and focus research to produce what the country needs. Lesson number four: **Remain focused and constantly upgrade skills**.

Lesson 5:

The political scenario in China through the late 1990s to 2012 went through as many incidents and events as could draw parallel from India. Just to mention few events: in 1996, China launches Shanghai Five that became SCO later; in 1997, death of Deng Xiaoping witnesses riots, bombings and killings; in 1998, Zhu Rongji launches reforms, creating economic turmoil in and outside Party lines; in 1999, NATO bombs Chinese Embassy in Belgrade; in 2000, the purging of corrupt officials starts; in 2003+ SARS hits China and the Hong Kong rebellion breaks out; in 2005, China adopts new law that calls for use of force should Taipei declare independence from mainland China; 2005-06 witnessed rising tensions with Japan; in 2007-08, new Bishop chosen by China is approved by the Pope in Rome and the worst ever snowstorms kill over 100 million people; 2008-09 mark the global financial crisis impacting China too; 2010-12, notwithstanding allegation of Chinese cyber hacks and resultant trade issues with the US, it emerges as the world's no.2 economy; in 2012, the Bo Xilai scandal rocks China... (BBC, 2019)[24]. Lesson number five, and most important of all: **Internal or even externally assisted turmoil will come and pass over. As they say-Even This Shall Pass. The country's political, and bureaucratic institutions must be proofed against such vagaries of the times.**

Conclusion

Robert Dahl has an interesting perspective on the concept of power. Dahl (Dahl, 1957)[25]observed, "Unfortunately, in the English language power is an awkward word, for unlike 'influence' and 'control' it has no convenient verb form, nor can the subject and object of the relation be supplied with noun forms without resort to barbaric neologisms".

China's experiences during the Opium War underwrote the necessity to acquire power by whatever means which would force likely opponents to look for conciliatory approach in settling bilateral or multilateral issues on terms that China desires. That the Chinese navy today has grown to be a credible instrument of national power has been accepted by experts even avowedly critical of China. That deployment of such a 'power' would be seen as hegemonistic does not appear to be a concern to the Chinese mind. Its actions in bringing Sri Lanka, Pakistan, Bangladesh, and Djibouti to cede important concessions in maritime dimensions in Indian Ocean region through debt-trap diplomacy appear to support such a conclusion.

In its own domestic waters (SCS and beyond that China claims as its own), creation of militarized islands, deployment of PLAAF and PLA (N) in force to a level that has come to be of strategic concern to all nations of the world is yet again an indication that the lessons of history are being learnt, revised and improved upon with a consistency unaffected by domestic or international pressures. In the most recent instance when sabre rattling reached a high pitch compelling the US to pull out USS Nimitz from the Gulf to SCS, commander of USS Theodore Roosevelt made a pertinent remark:

> "We're seeing larger number of aircraft, larger number of ships available to the Chinese military being utilised on a daily basis. So the capacity has clearly increased," Verissimo told reporters via phone from aboard the USS Theodore Roosevelt (Sevastopulo & Hille, 2021)[26].

When read again, the underlying meaning of the statement by Admiral Verissimo indicates that due cognizance is to be taken of the demonstrable capabilities that Chinese have acquired in the maritime dimension. In addition, the power that they display now makes the most powerful navy in the world take caution!

Apart from expanding physical assets including a carrier group, considerable attention appears to have been paid to enhance leadership and operational philosophies through extensive frameworks with other countries. It is to be noted that the cooperative frameworks were achieved through internationally accepted best practices in military/naval diplomacy. To recall the activities in multifarious dimensions of maritime diplomacy, the report of the Ministry of National Defence (PRC) (Li, 2019)[27], lists:

- Since 2012, China has held over 100 joint exercises and training with more than 30 countries. These engagements have covered traditional and non-traditional security fields, in locations extending from China's periphery to the far seas, and the participating forces have expanded from land forces to multiple branches including the army, navy and air force. Cooperation and exchanges in personnel training have intensified. Since 2012, *the PLA has sent over 1,700 military personnel to study in more than 50 countries. Over 20 Chinese military educational institutions have established and maintained inter-collegiate exchanges with their counterparts from more than 40 countries. Meanwhile, more than 10,000 foreign military personnel from over 130 countries have studied in Chinese military universities and colleges.* (Italics supplied)
- In line with relevant UNSC resolutions, since December 2008, the Chinese government has dispatched naval ships to carry out regular vessel protection operations in the Gulf of Aden and the waters off the coast of Somalia. Chinese *PLAN task groups cooperate with multiple naval forces in the area to safeguard international SLOCs. In the past decade, over 100 vessels and 26,000 officers and sailors have been regularly deployed in 31 convoys, each consisting of three to four ships, in vessel protection operations. They have provided security protection for over 6,600 Chinese and foreign ships, and rescued, protected or assisted over 70 ships in distress.*
- China's armed forces take an active part in the international efforts for HADR. Military professionals are dispatched to conduct disaster relief operations in affected countries, provide relief materials and medical aid, and strengthen international exchanges in this respect. Since 2012, *China's armed forces have participated in the search for the missing Malaysian Airliner MH370, and in the relief operations for Typhoon Haiyan in the*

Philippines, the Ebola epidemic in West Africa, the water scarcity in Maldives, the earthquake in Nepal, and the flood caused by a dam collapse in Laos. Since it entered service a decade ago, the PLAN's hospital ship Ark Peace has fulfilled 7 voyages coded as Mission Harmony and visited 43 countries. During these visits, it provided medical services to the local communities, organized medical exchanges, and helped over 230,000 people.

That the Chinese have taken to diplomatic, military and personal engagements to appropriate knowledge and technology is a lesson that stands out through the threads of history as well as contemporary affairs.

There is something distinctly Chinese about learning from history. While CCP leadership repeatedly calls for reinforcing their culture as the basis of nation building, it appears that they have drawn extensively from that very culture an ability to remain committed to learning from history.

Chinese scholars like Chan (Chan, 2014) also observe that "The importance of understanding China's historical approaches to international law cannot be understated" (Chan, 2014)[28]. It is easy to infer that Chan's observation is valid in other dimensions too.

That as a matter of opinion, could also be China's Achilles heel!

Postscript

While it is unusual for essays and research papers to carry a postscript, it is necessary to append one owing to the peculiar methodology that was adopted to write this paper. It was stated in the beginning that a postcolonial approach would be adopted for this paper. To phrase it correctly, the paper is an attempt at adopting a postcolonial approach to history in order to draw lessons in geopolitics!

Having taken this approach, it is necessary to define 'postcolonial' approach. John McLeod in his *Beginning: Postcolonialism* makes the distinction between post-colonialism and Postcolonialism as the previous marking a study pertaining to a subject in the era after colonialism ended, while in the latter case, as 'postcolonialism recognizes both historical continuity and change' (McLeod, 2012)[29]. While colonial discourses 'explored the ways the representations and modes of perceptions are used as fundamental weapons of colonial power' (Ibid, p.17), postcolonial school led by Edward Said-Gayatri Spivak-Homi Bhabha explored the ways in which the colonized perceived their colonial masters.

Postcolonialism therefore, in our interpretation, is an approach that studies how the oppressed or beaten views and understands the oppressor. In the context of the Opium Wars, China was unequivocally beaten and subjugated by British and other western powers, so much so that the resultant environment eventually led to a political implosion in China overthrowing the 'Heavenly Mandate' of dynastic rule, only to be replaced with communist rule.

We have also seen that the British and other foreign powers could not have subjugated China to unfair treaties, unless they had held themselves in the classical mold of racially and culturally superior nations. The Cambridge History cited in this paper, in adequate terms, explains how sincerely the British led alliances believed in such constructs as evidenced from Palmerston's statements in the parliament exhorting the superiority of English race and English arms (P.195). The Cambridge History (P.185) also shows how the Chinese Emperor considered the foreigners, especially the British as nothing more than recalcitrant rebels who needed a bit of 'disciplining', if need be to bring them around to respect Chinese law. In fact, the mandate by the Emperor to Commissioner Lin in effect meant (Twitchett & Fairbank, 2008)[30]:

> They thought of the English more as recalcitrant rebels, whom Lin was going south to manage and pacify. If circumstances demanded it, he would resort to force, but this was not to be desired.
>
> Moral rectitude, decisive and unhesitating action, would awe the English as easily as it awed native opium dealers. 'War' was never the question.

An appropriate setting for postcolonial approach can be inferred that facilitates reading the contemporary geopolitical developments from this perspective.

10. From Macau, with Love: The Story of Chinese Aircraft Carrier

Sun Tzu said, "If you know the enemy and know yourself, you need not fear the result of a hundred battles. If you know yourself but not the enemy, for every victory gained you will also suffer a defeat. If you know neither the enemy nor yourself, you will succumb in every battle".

Strategic discourses across the globe have focused on China on account of the unprecedented militarization that has happened in the South China Sea. China's defiance of UNCLOS Arbitral Award to Philippines, building artificial islands in SCS and launching a series of military exercises close to Taiwan and Japan have been the theme of hundreds of strategic debates.

The Chinese actions in Galwan in June this year and the subsequent engagements and disengagements between India and China are also the themes of such discourses in India specially. India's action to hasten the arrival of five Rafale fighter from France, DRDO successfully testing improved Varunastra (torpedo), a ministerial announcement that billions of USD now are slated for upgrading defense equipment and such like news have been heartily discussed by experts almost to the point of hailing India's might and will to address Chinese ambitions on India's borders. It is to be recognized that such enthusiastic reading of the situation is good for national morale.

Experts agree that between equipment and morale, the latter is more important. There are a million battles in which this has been proved right too. However, experts also concede that morale is not a substitute for equipment. A poorly equipped army, however well motivated it may be, stands the risk humiliation in battle. Again, Sino-Indian conflict of 1961 provides ample lessons in this.

Taking the cue from Sun Tzu quoted above, an attempt is made first see how China balances this factor.

The Taiwan Crisis of 1996

In 1996, Taiwan announced its first ever democratic elections for its President. The sitting president, Lee Teng-hui of the Kuomintang party was voted to office in those elections. When the announcement for elections were made in 1995, as expected China protested and even mobilized its Second Artillery Corps (now designated as PLA Rocket Forces) and re-deployed its F-7 (MiG 21 Fishbed variant) fleet some 250 miles from Taiwan. Reportedly, hundreds of Chinese civilian fishing boats entered Taiwanese waters too. Chinese continued missile 'testing' and firing live missiles as part of the exercise even after March 1996 elections were over (Mizokami, 2019)[1]. With tensions rising, especially when two missiles fell within thirty five mile radius of Taipei, the beleaguered Taiwan turned to its staunchest ally, USA, fearing imminent invasion by PLA.

US responded quickly. Japan based carrier fleet led by USS Independence took position on the East of Taiwan. A bigger carrier group headed by USS Nimitz rushed from the Persian Gulf and took its position in Philippine Sea (Global Security, 2011)[2]. With two US Carrier Groups now flanking Taiwan, China called off its military exercises. A credible threat of invasion was averted.

While there were sighs of relief in Taiwan, US and its allies, China learnt a crucial lesson – the importance of aircraft carriers!

The PLAN as on that day had no carrier task force and its shore based missile corps or tin-pot naval ships were no match for the armada headed by Independence and Nimitz. It may not be out of place to say that historical memories of British-European battleships raining hellfire on Canton in 1839 may have flashed across the Chinese mind.

So what did the Chinese do?

In 1991 when USSR broke into 16 countries of Central Asia, Ukraine came in possession of Kuznetsov-class aircraft cruiser Riga which had been commissioned in 1988. Cash strapped Ukraine put the ship up for sale to Russia, India and China. In view of the diplomatic situation in the world in the aftermath of the collapse of USSR, China declined. India did not take interest and Russia was financially weak. So the fully constructed carrier, short of electronics and few other needs, was left to rust. In 1998 however, the rusting hulk was bought at auction for $20 million by Mr. Chong Lot for his company based in Macau. Chong Lot proposed that the ship would be converted into a $200 million floating hotel and casino (ARKIB, 1998)[3].

In a story that could become an international bestselling thriller, Riga commenced its journey in June 2000 and tugged around the Cape of Good Hope, reached Chinese waters in February 2002, a journey of 28200 km at a speed of

6 knots!! In 2012, after refits and modernization, now christened Liaoning, the aircraft carrier entered service with PLAN in September.

The entire exercise of obtaining its aircraft carrier was done in the typical Chinese way – bluff, divert and deny. For example, when reports started appearing in the news, the Chinese Navy official who master-minded the operation went 'missing'. Later it was reported that he was imprisoned for smuggling. In 2012, when reports of the carrier refit appeared, Chinese admitted candidly to refitting the ship for 'scientific and explorative purposes'. The consummate skill with which Chinese media puts out or denies information and misinformation makes it hard to discern the truths surrounding anything. Of course, what stands out undeniably is that China has its own aircraft carrier, the Liaoning. The second Liaoning class carrier, Shandong, was commissioned by the PLA Navy on December 17, 2019, in Sanya, South China's Hainan Province. What is important to note is the speed with which Shandong came into service, unlike Liaoning. Construction started in November 2013 and in December 2019, she was commissioned into PLAN (China Power Team, 2020)[4].

What do we learn?

Baku was built in 1987 and remained in Russian navy as a Gorshkov Class carrier till 1996. It was de-activated due to financial crisis in Russia. India's interest in the carrier began then. Eight years of negotiations later, India and Russia signed a deal for its purchase. It took nine more years before she entered service, now re-christened as INS Vikramaditya. Any diversion into the politico-bureaucratic delays and scandals that have racked defense procurement in India will take us away from what Sun Tzu taught us to do: "If you know the enemy and know yourself…". So the lessons that come out of the Chinese story is appropriate for a title in James Bond style – From Macau, with Love!

Lesson 1:

With two US carrier groups standing at its doorstep, especially of the Nimitz class, use of the entire Second Artillery Corps and fleet of J-7s would have only repeated what happened at Canton. President Xi Jinping specifically called it the Century of Humiliation. Adventurism tempered with wisdom. So, lesson number one is: Learn from your history.

Lesson 2:

It took Chinese ten years to refit and induct Riga as their own Liaoning. The point to note is the rusting old float that was towed 28000 km became China's credible aircraft carrier through their own technical, home grown expertise at the port of

Dalian (Vavasseur, 2019)[5]. Lesson number two: Grow your technical expertise to cater to FUTURE needs.

Lesson 3:

Liaoning even went through a refit after six years of service bringing new lessons. The third aircraft carrier the China is developing now reportedly will come with CATOBAR (Catapult Assisted Take-Off but Arrested Recovery) design equipped with electromagnetic catapults. Lesson number three: Learn again from your weapon system and involve R&D in improvising them.

Interestingly, India's story of procuring INS Vikramaditya runs on a similar dateline to Liaoning. Rest is open to deductions.

Lesson 4:

The second carrier, Shandong, was launched in less than six years from the scratch. An ability to assimilate and focus research to produce what the country needs. Lesson number four: Remain focused and constantly upgrade skills.

Lesson 5:

The political scenario in China through late 1990's to 2012 went through as many incidents and events as could draw parallel from India. Just to mention few events: in 1996, China launches Shanghai Five that became SCO later; in 1997, death of Deng Xiaoping witnesses riots, bombings and killings; in 1998, Zhu Rongji launches reforms, creating economic turmoil in and outside Party lines; in 1999, NATO bombs Chinese Embassy in Belgrade; in 2000, the purging of corrupt officials starts; in 2003+ SARS hits China and the Hong Kong rebellion breaks out; in 2005, China adopts new law that calls for use of force should Taipei declare independence from mainland China; 2005-06 witness rising tensions with Japan; in 2007-08, new Bishop chosen by China is approved by the Pope in Rome and the worst ever snow storms kill over a 100 million people; 2008-09 mark the global financial crisis impacting China too; 2010-12, notwithstanding allegation of Chinese cyber hacks and resultant acrimony with US, it emerges as the world's no.2 economy; in 2012. The Bo Xilai scandal rocks China… (BBC, 2019)[6]

Lesson number five, and most important of all: Internal or even externally assisted turmoil come and pass over. As they say-Even This Shall Pass. The country's political, bureaucratic mechanism must be proofed against such vagaries of the times.

Conclusion

The lessons that can be drawn from China's aircraft carrier acquisition may appear too big for the type of events introspected into. But then, the Tamil Saint-Philosopher Tiruvalluvar chastises us by saying (Sanskrit Roots, n.d)[7]:

எற்றுஎன்று இரங்குவ செய்யற்க செய்வானேல்
மற்றுஅன்ன செய்யாமை நன்று

"A person shall not undertake in the first place, any act which might force him to regret later. If by chance, he had done such an act by mistake due to ignorance or unavoidable circumstances, let him not repeat it"

Manu, the giver of law that even today forms the basis of Indian Civil law, also said the same:

अज्ञानाद् यदि वा ज्ञानात् कृत्वा कर्म विगर्हितम् ।
तस्माद् विमुक्तिमन्विच्छन् द्वितीयं न समाचरेत् ॥

"He who, having either unintentionally or intentionally committed a regrettable deed, desires to be freed from the guilt on it, must not commit it a second time".

We generally take these philosophers as having dealt with man's quest for spiritual realization. However, these lessons equally apply in all the spheres of life of a society.

Even Sun Tzu never wrote his treatise keeping only Generals and Commanders in mind!!

Section III

China, Pakistan, Afghanistan, Australia and the World

11. Regime Change in Pakistan and Chinese BRI Dream

Is China worried over Pakistan?

The New Indian Express (Coimbatore Edition)[1] reports today that a regime change is likely in Pakistan by Sunday. With parties pulling out support for PM Imran Khan, he is likely to face a 'no confidence' motion and may be out of power. The report says Chief of Pakistan Army, General Bajwa and the ISI Chief have already advised Imran Khan to step down or face the consequences.

Chinese Foreign Minister Wang Yi visited Pakistan for three days from 21st to 23rd March. While the apparent reason was to attend OIC Meeting (the first ever by Chinese FM), he stayed for three days in Pakistan. During the visit, he had talks with PM Imran Khan, his counterpart Pak FM Qureshi and Chief of Army General Bajwa.

While such interactions are quite routine in such high power visits, what was unusual was the Chinese Foreign Minister discussing CPEC, Afghanistan and the 3rd Meeting of Foreign Ministers on Afghan Issue, with the Chief of Army.

On the contrary, the Chinese FM discussed India's so-called human rights violation in India-occupied areas of Jammu and Kashmir and on a recent firing of missile from India into Pakistan, with Pak FM! These official discussions do raise some questions:

1. Is Pak holding out the same carrot implying its deep influence with Taliban, like it didi with USA?
2. Why discuss calling for China-Pak cooperation to build 'open and inclusive architecture…prudent domestic and foreign policy and resolutely comabating terrorism' with Chief of the Army?
3. Is China acknowledging Pak Army's capacity to train and export terrorism and its worries over Uyghur unrest? Is it getting blackmailed and falling into Pak trap, in the same way US did?

4. Does it indicate political instability in Pak and a possible regime change?

Interestingly, Chinese official foreign ministry release itself provides some indicative answers to these question[2].

> (While discussing with General Bajwa,) Wang Yi congratulated Pakistan ...saying that China appreciates the positive efforts and important contributions made by the Pakistani military over the years to consolidate and enhance the all-weather strategic cooperative partnership between China and Pakistan, ensure the safe and smooth development of the China-Pakistan Economic Corridor and safeguard the security of Chinese institutions and personnel in Pakistan. **Wang Yi said, the Pakistani military has played the role of a stabilizer and ballast stone in building a closer China-Pakistan community with a shared future in the new era**.
>
> Bajwa said, the Ukraine issue is very important, but the international community should not ignore the Afghan issue. **Pakistan appreciates** and supports China's hosting of the Third Foreign Ministers' Meeting on the Afghan Issue Among the Neighboring Countries of Afghanistan **and believes that the international community should pay more attention to and invest more in the people's wellbeing and security issues of Afghanistan.**
>
> Wang Yi said, the Afghan issue should not be solved by exerting pressure or imposing sanctions, but by drawing on the wisdom of the East to promote dialogue and communication. **Both China and Pakistan encourage the ruling authorities of Afghanistan to actively build an open and inclusive political architecture, implement moderate and prudent domestic and foreign policies and resolutely combat terrorism in all its forms**. Noting that Afghanistan enjoys favourable geographical advantages, resource endowment and development potential, he said that the international community should support Afghanistan in finding the right path of developing its economy, improving people's wellbeing, and realizing self-reliance and self-improvement.

Considering the timing of the visit amid political developments in Pakistan[3], it appears that China is indeed worried about CPEC that is critical to its BRI dream. Going by the official statements issued by China, it is evident that some guarantees were being sought from Pakistani Army to protect CPEC from the vulnerabilities of regime change in Pakistan.

It is also apparent that the role of Pak Army in securing China's interests by preventing the spill over of Islamic terror into Uyghur region (though not specifically mentioned) underwrote Chinese concerns. That perhaps explains the stopover visit to Kabul also where, in his discussions with Taliban FM Muttaqi, it was reported, that the talks included[4]:

- Political and economic ties, including starting work in the mining sector and Afghanistan's possible role in China's Belt and Road infrastructure initiative.
- To this, Minister Muttaqi added that the security brought about by the new (government) lays the foundation for foreign investment, including for China, in Afghanistan that ensures their interest besides cooperating with Afghans in economic growth & stability with the full support of the new government.

By its aggressive cheque book diplomacy, China has already enticed Pakistan into a debt trap that it can never aspire to service[5]. The political instability in Pakistan adds another dimension to Chinese concerns. At the same time considering that rampant corruption is a dominant feature in Pakistan, especially of the Army, it is rather obvious why the Chinese FM chose to discuss the issues that he did with Pak Chief of Army Staff. In Pakistan, the Army calls the shots is perhaps an understatement. The Army controls the nation and its economy[6], as is manifest from tons of evidences in public domain. As the Wire says, in Dumping Imran Khan, Pakistan Army Seeks Face-Saving, and Not Course-Correction. The army remains doggedly averse to cede its monopoly over defining the 'national interest' and formulating the national security and foreign policies[7]. [Text highlighted for emphasis]

12. Between the Devil and the Deep Sea: China's Options in Afghanistan

The Taliban have returned to power in Kabul. The developments in Afghanistan had held the breath of analysts all over the world in the past two months. The lightning speed with which the Taliban coursed through the provinces and the crippling blow it delivered to the semblance of counter action by Afghan forces is for all the world to see. Like an old man whose crutches were taken away in the middle of a hobble, the government fell and its top leaders have deserted the country. General Dostum and such like warlords now face the wrath of Taliban and there is little left for imagination as to the fate of groups that have stood with US-NATO Allies in their war initially on Al Qaeda and then with Taliban. The feverish pace with which the US-NATO allies are evacuating their Afghan sympathizers and supporters indicates the fate that otherwise awaits them, more pronounced with Taliban announcing amnesty! It may be ironical that Taliban may actually use the famous George Bush dialogue – Either you are with us or you are against us – in so far as the remnants of anti-Taliban forces remaining in the country!

From the time US went ahead to negotiate safe withdrawal of its troops through the Doha Talks, a number of other countries, most notably Pakistan and China, have openly courted Taliban. As for Pakistan, it is confident that TTP and its religious credentials will be the trump card in playing with Taliban. Pakistan would also attempt, if it has not already and substantially done so, to convince China that its flagship CPEC and the connectivity to Central Asian energy sources can only be guaranteed by Pakistan, not to mention the likely domino effect of an enthusiastic Taliban stepping into East Turkestan.

For China, achieving the BRI is not just a dream. President Xi has often spoken about it as the means to restore China to its ancient and domineering glory of the past. That being so, it is necessary to take a fair guess as to what are China's options in so far as Taliban-ruled Afghanistan would be.

Taliban leadership seems to have hinted fairly and clearly as to what those options are. The Talib spokesman spelt it out in unambiguous terms – Taliban will pursue a policy of non-interference in return for non-interference into Afghanistan[1]. In the light of this clear statement what are the options before China and what are the consequences?

- **CPEC**: China's investments are around USD 40 billion and the total outlay is at 60 billion, the largest in its overseas undertakings. Already at least two directed attacks have taken place on Chinese in Pakistan in which over a dozen Chinese personnel have died. TTP claimed responsibility for one and the other remains un-named[2]. Waziristan and Baluchistan are already boiling pots and the Chinese dream (and investments) of reaching out to blue sea is getting interspersed with nightmares on account of Pakistan's internal security issues[3].
- Of the 3000 km long Kashghar-Gwadar CPEC corridor, nearly half of it runs through (680 km from Chinese border to Havelian Dry Port and some 480 km in KKH II phase) Gilgit-Baltistan and Baluchistan. This corridor is TTP territory and is porous across the Durand Line. The choking of this corridor will spell doom to China's aspirations of cutting its logistics cost by 50 percent through Gwadar[4]. Whatever Pakistan may gain out of CPEC, China appears to have more to lose.
- **Mining in Afghanistan**: China announced USD 4.4 billion investment in Aynak Copper Mines projects in 2007. On ground however it has hardly expended any, much to the displeasure of Afghan government. The primary reason appears to be the internal dynamics of Afghanistan. If China had gone ahead with full investment, the Karzai-Ghani governments would have annually earned around USD 2 billion, a sum that could easily bolster their efforts against Taliban. China perhaps sat on the wall before ensuring that a powerful group that would be more amenable is actually in control[5].
- **Oil**: Three blocks in Sar-e Pul were contracted by China in a JV with Afghan companies in 2011. Like in Aynak, this project has also dragged along.
- **BRI**: Afghan government was encouraged to join BRI with a hint of over USD 1 billion in revenues. The cash strapped government however saw just an order for 1200 tons of pine nuts valued at USD 400 million[6].
- **Uyghur Issue**: China offered to conduct joint exercise in Badakshan and even raise a Brigade in the area together with Afghanistan. In return, the Afghan government was asked to round up Uyghurs slipping into Badakshan from neighboring Xinjiang. The Afghan government of course obliged. However, now with Talibs in power, this could become a reverse flow, what with a reported 20000 jihadists from all over the Muslim world fighting along the Taliban.

- **Camaraderie**: China sent its highest Diplomat to meet the top leader of Taliban, though at that time Taliban was only sweeping the rural country side and attempting to take a couple of Provincial Towns. It is quite unusual that a sovereign representative meets with a declared terrorist outfit and issues a joint statement in which he squarely notes, 'The Taliban are a pivotal military and political force in Afghanistan and are expected to play an important role in the in process of peace, reconciliation and reconstruction' and then went on to add, 'China hopes the Taliban will "deal resolutely" with the East Turkistan Islamic Movement, a group China claims is leading a push for independence in Xinjiang'. It may also be of interest to note that these statements were made when delegation led by Mullah Baradar, Taliban Religious Council Members and its Propaganda Outfit met Wang Yi, Chinese Foreign Minister in Tianjin in China on July 21, 2021.[7]

These factors point to the following suppositions that China may opt for in so far as Taliban controlled Afghanistan is concerned. These are:

1. China will recognize the Taliban Regime as the legit government of Afghanistan, sooner such a government is announced by Taliban. It may be relevant to mention that China did not recognize Taliban Regime when it seized power in 1996. The geopolitical contestations in Indo-Pacific Region were also quite different and in any case, Chinese BRI dream was yet to be spelt out.
2. Chinese recognition will render credibility to Taliban, a recognition that it badly needs. It may also be a case were such a recognition to a proclaimed terrorist organization may invite ISIS and Al Qaeda to rear their heads in other places. A lot then would depend on how China uses Taliban to keep its security interests protected.
3. China will revive its economic agenda like that of resurrecting its Aynak Project and Oil projects providing a huge economic fillip to Taliban which in any case it needs. It will also offer the BRI dream with additional concessions that Taliban would be hard put to resist. The infamous Cheque Book Diplomacy will work its part.
4. By doing so, China will hedge Pakistan out of its desire to use Afghanistan as a bargaining chip, directly or indirectly.
5. Taliban may find it convenient to underplay the Islamic card in so far as Xinjiang is concerned so as to gain an ally with veto powers in UNSC. It will help Taliban to negotiate international political pressure in its own terms. The economic gains are obvious to the eye.

Instead of exercising these options which apparently portend well for China, should it choose a boots-on-ground approach? It does not appear to be a choice due to the following factors:

- Unlike America, China has neither fostered nor fought Taliban nor any other groups in the name of 'war on terror'. It has had no externally aided attacks on its soil to serve as motivation enough, except when Britain, France, Germany as well as America joined together against Imperial China during the Opium Wars, not to mention Japanese invasion of China prior to World War II.
- As for Islamic terror is concerned, China controls Xinjiang with an iron fist. Despite the hullabaloo over Human Rights situation there, international will to intervene inside China is hardly credible.
- Should Taliban undertake to fight the cause of East Turkestan, it has to contend with Russia and the surrounding Central Asian Republics that already have a framework through SCO with China on fighting terror. Russia in any case would not be enamored with a Taliban that transgresses too close to its borders. Such an undertaking by Taliban will also isolate it, making it easy for international community to come down heavily upon it.
- The cost of boots-on-ground in Afghanistan will derail BRI. With a lucrative collaborative opportunity at hand to further its BRI dream, China to take up a contradictory approach will be detrimental to its own interests.
- In any case, Confucian wisdom dictates that an enemy's enemy should be made a friend.

China has spread its ambitious project too far wide at this juncture to risk losing its sheen by embroiling itself into the internal issues of a country that is touted as the graveyard of empires. Confucian wisdom would rather dictate that the cards should be played in a different manner. By doing so, it would also convert Afghanistan as a land bridge to energy sources in Central Asia. As for Taliban, the Chinese Cheque book will be too important a factor to ignore. Additionally, with a friendly Taliban in power, China may pay more attention to Taiwan.

As for as common Afghan citizens are concerned, they do not appear to have much choice about living with the devil. But for China, the deep sea will become easier to access by courting that devil. For once, Hobson's choice is set to work in favor of China both ways.

13. Sino-Australian Relations in the QUAD Era: Exploring the Challenges

QUAD or more precisely Quadrilateral Security Dialogue (QSD) has made a comeback to the centre stage of discussions in diplomatic, strategic and academic circles. The reason is quite obvious, given the geopolitical context in the Indo-Pacific. Interestingly, both Indo-pacific and QUAD came into wider circulation more or less at the same time, in 2006![1] Among the partners, USA, Japan, Australia and India, the later three had already coordinated on the maritime domain in the wake of Tsunami in 2004. An informal dialogue for maritime cooperation for humanitarian relief therefore already existed. Democratic ethos prevailing in them also was a factor which resulted in PM Manmohan Singh-PM Shinzo Abe issuing a Joint Statement in December 2006 indicating 'the usefulness of having dialogue among India, Japan and other like-minded countries in the Asia-Pacific region on themes of mutual interest.'[2]

The rise of China in subsequent years, led these countries to discuss modalities to expand the QUAD framework to address the emerging geopolitical challenges in Indo-Pacific, apart from mutual and multilateral cooperation. As a consequence, QUAD naval forces joined together to conduct drills apparently aimed at enforcing freedom of navigation in the region. This led to protests by China accusing the QUAD of whipping up pressure tactics in what China perceives to be its own domestic waters, the SCS[3].

Even as QUAD grabs the limelight in strategic discussions as a potential counter, an 'Asian NATO', this article attempts to understand Australia's compulsions in signing up with RCEP trade framework, raising eyebrows across the spectrum.

Brief Background

In April 2020, Australia demanded an investigation into the origins of Corona virus[4]. China-Australia relations took a down swing.

In June/July, around 70 ships carrying an estimated 10 million tons of Australian coal to China were prohibited from disembarking their cargo in Chinese ports[5]. While officially, it was said that Corona concerns were the prime reason, slapping such a convenient sanction at a time when Australia emerged at the forefront of calling for investigation into Wuhan virus does not appear to be totally unconnected.

Australian Navy joined the QUAD naval exercise MALABAR on 01-06 November 2020. Ten days later, on 15 November 2020, Australia joined the 15 country RCEP trade deal, touted to be the largest in the world, led by China[6].

China-Australia Trade Relations

President Xi Jinping visited Australia in 2014 to a hearty welcome. He addressed the Australian Parliament expressing his satisfaction at the strength of relationship that China and Australia had achieved in the preceding years[7]. His warmth was understandable considering that Australia supplies over 60% of China's iron ore imports, nearly half of its liquefied natural gas imports, and about 40% of coal imports[8]. Half of Chinese imports from Australia are of iron ore, which is critical for China's industrial and infrastructure needs.[9]

China's share of Australia's exports	%
Nickel ore	100
Timber	95
Iron ore	83
Wool	77
Lobster	76
Cotton	64
Wood chips	57
Processed food	55
Barley	54
Pharmaceuticals	47

Source: ASPI – The Strategist[10]

China accounts for more than a third of global sales for 22 of Australia's top 30 exports to the nation. Those exports with a dominant Chinese market share were worth $123 billion in 2019, which was 32% of Australia's total exports.

The impracticability of diversification is most obvious in iron ore. Australia will ship almost 800 million tonnes of iron ore to China this year. The total seaborne market in the rest of the world is only 460 million tonnes and Australia already captures around 100 million tonnes of that. If China didn't buy our iron ore, there would literally be nowhere else to send it.[11]

Apart from Australian exports, China also has substantial share in Australia's imports. As per ASPI, 'China has a dominant market share (greater than a third) account for 18% of Australia's total goods imports'.

China's share of Australia's imports	%
Lighting	76
Toys, games	74
Textiles	74
Household equipment	72
Furniture	70
Computers	70
Electronic circuits	68
Steel/aluminium structures	66
Womens clothing	66
Phones & telecom equipment	62

Source: The Strategist

In 2017-18, China had emerged as the top destination for Australian exports with USD 106.3 bn in goods, 16.9 bn in services, totaling to 123.3 bn (30.6%). In comparison, India accounted for 5.2 percent, USA 5.3 percent and UK just 2.6 percent. It is also interesting to note that Hong Kong accounted for 3.6 percent![12]

In contrast, Australia's investments in China accounted to USD 64.954 mn in 2017-18, whereas China's FDI into Australia was USD 1.491 bn, more than double of outward FDI.

Employment State in Australia

A brief look at just three major exports to China from Australia, minerals (iron ore, coal, etc.), food (beef, beverages, etc.) and pharmaceuticals reveals that nearly 24 percent of all employment (a little over 38 million)[13] in Australia depends on industries and activities related to these sectors of economy.

Advantages to Australia through RCEP

In an earlier paper on Australia joining RCEP, it was observed that perhaps its own national interest resulted in Australia joining the framework[14]. In that paper, specific reference was made to *Room for individual interests of partners and allies that* stated by Australian Prime Minister was also cited. We need to again briefly look at the perception of Australia on this trade framework:

RCEP has the potential to deliver significant opportunities for Australian businesses, with the 16 RCEP participating countries accounting for almost half of the world's population, over 30 per cent of global GDP, and over a quarter of world exports. The advantages of allying with such a framework are therefore[15]:

- Trade promotes economic growth and raises household incomes
- Trade and investment create and support Australian jobs
- Trade makes products cheaper for Australian households and businesses
- Trade gives consumers and business greater choices
- Trade and investment open global markets for Australian products
- Trade allows us to earn income on commodities that are too plentiful for Australia to consume
- Trade and investment encourage innovation, which leads to productivity benefits
- Foreign investment supports Australia's economic development
- Foreign investment has supported the growth of successful Australian industries
- Foreign investment encourages innovation

Perceptions

While QUAD is being increasingly viewed as the counter to China's growing influence in Indo-pacific, the China centric view in the discourses across the strategic and academic communities do not appear to take into consideration the ground realities and aspirations of nations involved in the region or elsewhere. Ground realities as we see, for example in Australia's export experience vis-a-vis China, appear to reveal some strong indicators:

1. China can afford to defer or even refuse imports from Australia, as has been demonstrated in the import of coal. Can Australia afford to adopt a "No Export to China" or even "Reduce exports to send a strong message" formula, given that it has over 1.2 million citizens claiming Chinese ancestry and that millions of jobs in Australia will be severely affected till it finds alternate destinations for export?
2. In a pandemic affected economic downturn around the world, can such alternatives (say No to China or play-hard-at-exports) be found with ease, especially in the stiff trade war scenario that is currently on?
3. How to address the internal political fallout of losing millions of jobs when 'the election for the House of Representatives must therefore be held by 3

September 2022; the next half-Senate election must be held between 1 July 2021 and 30 June 2022' and even elections for various territories are due' in Australia?[16]

4. Can QUAD exert enough pressure on China to respect international law and freedom of navigation in SCS, without foreseeable consequences to the members' domestic economy? The answer appears to be at best ambiguous, unless an increasing number of nations, specifically those in ASEAN expressly commit themselves to upholding an alliance that supports international rules based order, even to the peril of their domestic economies however temporarily.

International relations are a quagmire where national interests and international ambitions sometimes mix, and sometimes clash. In our understanding, pre-supposing an alliance as a deterrent against errant behavior by any one state is wrought with numerous challenges as is evident in the China-Australian relations during 2020. The developments concerning these two well developed nations and their relations in the QUAD era have important challenges that less developed or developing nations will find it difficult to address.

The most important challenge appears to be the challenge of democracy itself, for it renders the political establishment vulnerable to the compulsions of market economy in the domestic arena too.

Every discourse on QUAD or any other mechanism to address geopolitical challenges in Indo-Pacific therefore needs to take domestic and international dimensions, economic as well as political, in order to find pragmatic answers. To that extent, we may surmise that Australian membership of RCEP is pragmatic. For IR theorists, we suppose it resonates with the Realist school!

14. QUAD v. RCEP: A Geo-economic Appraisal

The QUAD Summit held on 12 March 2021 has been hailed as agenda-setting for US, Japan, India and Australia towards the geopolitical challenges prevalent in the Indo-Pacific. While the Joint Press Release did not name China directly, it said:

- Anchored by democratic values, and unconstrained by coercion
- We reaffirm our strong support for ASEAN's unity and centrality as well as the ASEAN Outlook on the Indo-Pacific

Use of these expressions as well as a specific inclusion of 'East and South China Seas', as below, leaves very little to the imagination of experts as to their import:

> We will continue to prioritize the role of international law in the maritime domain, particularly as reflected in the United Nations Convention on the Law of the Sea (UNCLOS), and facilitate collaboration, including in maritime security, to meet challenges to the rules-based maritime order in the East and South China Seas[1].

The Joint Statement further spoke on the methodology, when it said, 'We will combine our nations' medical, scientific, financing, manufacturing and delivery, and development capabilities'.

It is evident that the challenges posed by China in the SCS are at the center of QUAD's future courses of action, apart from COVID19, North Korea, climate change, cyber space, counter terrorism, quality infrastructure investments, etc., that it wishes to address.

Support to ASEAN's 'unity, centrality and outlook' are also the stated objectives of QUAD. How does ASEAN perceive and react to these intents will of course be revealed in the actions of its members in due course. It may however be worthwhile to take a look at few developments in Southeast Asia to make some deductions.

ASEAN came together as a trading bloc in 1992. In the next 25 years, it developed as a vibrant economic entity accounting for nearly 30 percent of global GDP. During these years, China emerged as the largest trading partner for ASEAN, with EU, Japan and USA coming up next in that order. With USD 134 bn and 211 bn in exports and imports, China commands a little over 15 percent of all

ASEAN trade. In comparison, Japan accounts for 10.5, US 9.4 and India 2.6 percent respectively[2].

China's investments in ASEAN at USD 108 bn (2017) is just one third of US investments in the region at 329 bn (2017)[3]. However, the nature of investments have a marked difference, with countries borrowing from China increasingly coming into a debt trap that they could ill afford to service. A telling pointer in this regard is the acquisition of the only port in Cambodia's Koh Kong Province by a Chinese firm on a 99 year lease for the cost of USD 3.8 bn[4]. China's support to Cambodia at UNSC on human rights violations case during Pol Pot Regime and Cambodia returning the favor by blocking an ASEAN statement on the Chinese affairs in SCS are again important indicators of the rules of engagement with which China is playing geopolitics in Southeast Asia.

In 1997, Asian Economic crisis created challenges for Southeast Asia which were accentuated during the global financial crisis in 2008. For ASEAN members, the Chinese BRI investments for infrastructure from 2012 onwards came as a boon, improving connectivity and promoting trade. In this scenario, Regional Comprehensive Economic Partnership (RCEP) was first floated by China in 2012. However, this partnership remained dormant in view of overwhelming American investments in the region, and the US led Trans-Pacific Partnership (TPP). America's decision to withdraw from Trans-Pacific Partnership in 2017 apparently created the vacuum into which RCEP could be housed[5]. With at least four ASEAN countries as part of TPP (Brunei, Singapore, Vietnam and Malaysia), apart from Australia and Japan, America's decision created a potential situation in which even Japan may get entangled in a trade war with USA[6].

With Trump Administrations stand on TPP, China announced RCEP with 15 members in 2017. In November 2020, the China led framework emerged as the worlds' largest trading bloc with Japan, South Korea, Australia, New Zealand, and 10 countries of the ASEAN becoming its members. It is noteworthy that Australia, at the height of QUAD led Malabar Exercise with member navies, hastened to join RCEP citing 'room for individual member's interests and priorities'. It looks like China is well set to formalize the RCEP into a reality by its intended date, 01 January 2022. It is estimated that China's exports will rise by $248 billion owing to RCEP, with Japan seeing an extra $128 billion and South Korea $63 billion[7], once it is formalized.

It is evident that the material gains RCEP is holding out to national economies of its members is more compellingly attractive than the territorial vexations that five of ASEAN members have with China. Outside ASEAN, Japan, South Korea and Australia joining the framework demonstrates the compulsions of economics vis-a-vis notions of compliance with international order.

In such an environment, the ability of QUAD to achieve its stated objectives will depend on its ability to offset the advantages of RCEP. ASEAN's capacity to keep its flock together focused on the geopolitical challenges that China is purportedly posing in the Indo-Pacific, overriding the temptations of market economics, will also be crucial to the success of QUAD.

15. RECP and Emerging Trends in the Indo-Pacific

Australian Prime Minister Scott Morrison MP was awarded the Inaugural Hugo Grotius Prize in London on 23 November 2020. The Prize is instituted by Policy Exchange UK in honor of the founding-philosopher of international law, Hugo Grotius. The award was in recognition of the Prime Minister's work in support of the international rules-based order. In his keynote address, the Australian Prime Minister welcomed the "timely publication by Policy Exchange's Indo-Pacific Commission, A Very British Tilt: Towards a new UK strategy in the Indo-Pacific Region". On this Commission's core proposal for Britain to increase the priority accorded toward the Indo-Pacific, Scott Morrison remarked: "I couldn't agree more and have conveyed the same to Boris. I endorse the report's vision for a reinvigorated community of free and independent nations with a single overriding goal. Namely, reinforce a sustainable rules-based order in the Indo-Pacific that is resilient but adaptable to the great power realities of the 21st century" (Policy Exchange UK, 2020)[1].

Covering the Prize Ceremony, AFP reported the Prime Minister as having said, with reference to China: "Morrison warned this coercive diplomacy was just "a foretaste" of what other countries -- including those in Europe -- can expect to endure in future". Further, the same report cited Morrison as having told the UK Policy Exchange that "Greater latitude will be required from the world's largest powers to accommodate the individual interests of their partners and allies. We all need a bit more room to move," (AFP News, 2020)[2].

Australia was perhaps the first country that called for international investigation into the spread of Corona virus from Wuhan. In the aftermath of protests by China to such a proposal (Guardian, 2020)[3], relations between both the countries went below normal. Having been a steadfast ally of US in the Pacific Theatre, Australia's actions and reactions were endorsed by US and UK in the trade war that ensued. In any case, led by US at the forefront, trade war on China intensified and the virulent spread of Corona aided the hardening perceptions.

While economies across the globe took a mammoth hit due to lockdown and colossal need for COVID19 containment efforts, China emerged the first nation to control and re-ignite its economic engine. Chinese registered a 4.9 percent growth in GDP (BBC, 2020)[4] in the third quarter of this FY. In the same breath as having shown pandemic-resilient growth, China-backed RECP shot into prominence on 13 November 2020. Comprised of 15 nations in the Asia-Pacific, most notably all of the ASEAN, RCEP makes up nearly a third of the world's population and accounts for 29% of global gross domestic product.

The new free trade bloc will be bigger than both the US-Mexico-Canada Agreement and the European Union. The Peterson Institute for International Economics estimates the deal could increase global national income by $186bn annually by 2030 and add 0.2% to the economy of its member states (BBC, 2020)[5]. Amongst the most notable mid-to-big economies that have joined the RECP are South Korea, Japan, New Zealand and Australia.

In the prevalent pandemic devastated global economic scenario, revival signs from China signal a ray of hope for many countries. With the lucrative tariff regimes announced by China as part of RECP, member countries would be able to avail complementary treatment helping them to boost domestic economies as well as exports perceivably in a Rules-based-Environment. In Australia's own assessment, the benefits of RECP were summarized as (Govt of Australia, n.d)[6]:

- A single set of rules and procedures for Australian goods exporters to utilise RCEP's preferential tariff outcomes across the region, and increased opportunities for Australian business to access regional value chains by allowing goods made in another RCEP party from Australian inputs to benefit from tariff preferences under RCEP when exported to a third RCEP party.
- Avenues for tackling non-tariff barriers, including in areas such as quarantine and technical standards, by promoting compliance with WTO rules and further improving cooperation and transparency. Rules on intellectual property and e-commerce will help create an enabling environment for business to trade digitally in the region and support consumer confidence in the online environment.
- New market access commitments for service suppliers and investors in China and ASEAN markets such as Malaysia, the Philippines and Thailand, and provide an additional avenue through which exporters can access those markets in which we already enjoy high quality FTA commitments, including Japan, New Zealand, Republic of Korea and Singapore.

In the backdrop of pandemic ravaged economies and the promises of RECP, it would be interesting to re-read the Australian PMs remarks:

1. I endorse the report's vision for a reinvigorated community of free and independent nations with a single overriding goal. Namely, reinforce a sustainable rules-based order in the Indo-Pacific that is resilient but adaptable to the great power realities of the 21st century.
2. Greater latitude will be required from the world's largest powers to accommodate the individual interests of their partners and allies. We all need a bit more room to move.

Having re-read these statements, when we contemplate their meanings, two important thoughts for deliberation by International Relations scholarship emerge. They are:

1. **Rules-based order in the Indo-Pacific** (for that matter elsewhere too) - The advantages stated by Australia for joining RECP obviously entail freedom to trade through SCS with littorals/ASEAN, except that this time the trade would be under the benign approval of Chinese fleet prowling in those waters. It would also mean the complementary treatment to Chinese merchandise across the RECP trade zone. The implications are clear - the very rational for FONOPS that US has mustered its resources in SCS would stand diluted. It also means that countries now not part of RECP, like India, would be indirectly compelled join RECP in order to enjoy unhindered, rather facilitated trade across SCS. Does this hollow out the debates till now held on Rules-Based Order in SCS by international community?
2. **Room for individual interests of partners and allies** - The Cold War era of compulsions for alliance to ideological blocks is long passé. However, the Uni-Polar Order that America would have perhaps dominated has come under serious challenge by the rise of China. Discourses on these aspects are essentially in the domain of geopolitics. Geo-economics, in contrast, pertains to a nation's aspiration for growth. Therefore pursuit of geo-economic interests should fit into the domain of national-interest-first. However, the means and methods of globalization prevent any one nation's interest from prevailing over the other nation's interest. Should that happen, again, the entire discourse on China's debt-trap-diplomacy would be rendered hollow. Thus, the room for individual interests of partners and allies ends in a simple question – how much of room?

These questions call for reflections on the concept of National Interest, Objectives of Regional/Multilateral Cooperation and Ideology v. Development. Successful conclusion of RECP deliberations spearheaded by China adds a new facet to the existing and expanding Chinese sphere of influence in Indo-Pacific and beyond. It calls for serious reflections on these conceptual dimensions to determine the play of geopolitics in this region in times to come.

The purpose of this article is to provoke such reflections.

16. Dragon Casts a Cashless Trap: Society, Geo-economics and Geopolitics

On 23rd November 2020, Indian Express carried an interesting piece on threats posed by Chinese Tech Giants to Western banking system (AFP, 2020)[1]. It said European banks remain wary that Chinese Tech Giants may soon be their main competitors. The article indicated as to how China pulled the rug from under the feet of Ant Group dashing its hopes of raising USD 34 billion through IPO. Alibaba's Jack Ma who holds major stakes in Ant Group has reasons to feel frustrated. In the ongoing tussle between WeChat Pay and Ant Group, the regulatory measures that Chinese government is taking on Tech Giants which facilitate e-payments outside the banking system seems to be tightening.

This apprehension by European banks by itself should not give cause to look under the surface for any relationship between Chinese Tech Giants and Chinese political ambitions. But in the author's view, there is a connectivity that belies media discourse centered only on financial sector woes.

Cashless Society – Origins and Prospects

Cashless transactions through plastic cards was imagined way back in late 19th century when Edward Bellamy in his best-selling novel *Looking Backward* (1888) 'describes a future America in which money has been banished. Instead of cash, the inhabitants of Bellamy's utopia use "credit-cards" to purchase all that they need from government depots whose interiors resemble elegant department stores' (Lauer, 2020)[2]. Bellamy's imagination of course became reality as the traditional payment system of cash or credit grew more complex with influx of immigrants and increase in population. In 1950, Diner's Club introduced the first credit card which was later followed by American Express in 1959. Stepping beyond these historical beginnings, it is Sweden, which is the first European country to introduce currency notes in 1661, that will become one hundred percent cashless by 2023 (Fourtané, 2019)[3].

Academicians, economists and analysts are having huge discourses on the pros-cons of a cashless society for quite some time now. Their discourses have pointed to the plusses like transparency and government regulation as wells as perils like loss of privacy and government control over civil liberties (Arvidsson, 2019)[4] (Bond, 2020)[5].

Cash in a Cashless Society

What happens to the cash in a cashless society? In traditional transacting societies, cash is held by financial institutions approved and regulated by the governments including banks. Government monies as well as the citizens' are held in the coffers of banks. Though increasingly intelligent monitoring systems have come into place across the globe, spate of banking scams across the world have exposed a fundamental flaw in the utilization of such funds on account of vested political, economic and personal interests by people in power. The recent debates in India over insurance coverage for bank deposits is an interesting pointer in that direction.

In contrast, China through IT enabled interventions introduced and expanded use of QR codes and e-Wallets. Monetary transactions of ordinary citizens in this system funneled the funds of citizens into the coffers of private holders like AliPay and WeChat Pay. Analysts like Aaron Klien point out that new financial technology and its application in China have created a viable alternative payments model where banks play a far less central role, and in the extreme, possibly none (Klein, 2020)[6].

Two years back, China Daily reported that mobile payments in China have reached over $41trillion (277 trillion yuan) annually. More than 92% of the mobile payments are made over the two dominant platforms: Alipay (53%) and WeChat Pay (39%). It even pointed out that with over 130 million outbound trips, travelers from China spent a whopping USD 115 billion abroad (Liu & Mingjie, 2018)[7]. In terms of conversions, the transactions which take place in US dollar are closed on the RMB exchange rate, not on the day of purchase, but on the bill day. In any other country, be it Thailand, Canada or France, the amount is converted from the local currency to USD and only then to RMB (Brown, 2017)[8]. By restricting the cash withdrawals to 1000 RMB (approximately USD 150), both Alipay and WeChat Pay have ensured that the customer funds remain within their ecosystems. With nearly 2.2 billion users between these two giants, the volume of mobile transactions in China have reportedly crossed USD 41 trillion (277 trillion yuan) annually. In other words, the funds that flow through and circulate within their ecosystems are nearly three times the GDP of China which was USD 14.4 trillion in 2019.

China reaches out to the World

Alipay's associate Ant Group has reached out with its e-payment ecosystem in a big way in Southeast Asia already. By general estimates, gross transaction value of e-wallets in Southeast Asia will increase to $114 billion in 2025 from $22 billion in 2019, according to Google, Temasek Holdings and Bain & Co (Kentaro, 2020)[9].

Ant Group's expansion in Southeast Asia

Country	Activity	Joint venture partners
Indonesia	Invested in local e-wallet Dana	Emtek *(Media and tech group)*
Myanmar	To acquire 33% stake in Digital Money Myanmar *(Wave Money)*	Yoma Group *(Conglomerate)*
Philippines	Invested in fintech firm Mynt	Ayala Corp. *(Conglomerate)*, Globe Telecom
Sinagpore	Aims to obtain a digital banking license	
Thailand	Invested in Ascend Money *(TrueMoney)*	CP Group *(Conglomerate)*

Source: Companies

Source: *Nikkei at https://asia.nikkei.com/Business/Business-Spotlight/China-s-Ant-eyes-Southeast-Asia-e-payment-dominance-with-IPO*

Chinese Tech Giants have already made deep inroads into Africa (Wang, 2019)[10] and Europe (as the Indian Express Report shows).

With even this rudimentary insight in this article, it is not difficult to surmise that these Chinese tech giants have created a funnel through which trillions of USD are circulating within the ecosystem created by them. It is important at this juncture to recognize that expert opinion and widely available inputs in public domain indicate that banks and financial institutions in China are either directly owned by the government or they are overseen by the government. In either case, the Politburo members of the CCP remain in important positions in these institutions (Elliot & Yan, 2013)[11] (McGregor, 2019)[12].

Is there a threat?

Klein observed that the Chinese payment system makes it easy to continually keep funds in digital wallets. The ubiquity of acceptance, lack of fees, and ease of commerce motivate consumers. Money brought into the digital wallet system can be moved into interest-bearing accounts, like money market funds, or invested into Chinese stocks directly through broker-dealer accounts partnered with the platform (Klein, Brookings Institution, 2019)[13]. More importantly, with Alipay becoming part of Ant Financial which has the largest mutual fund, Tianhong Yu'e Bao having 600 million investors, over $168 billion in funds, and offering short term interest of over 2%, (a better return than leaving funds in a Chinese bank), the possibility for the trillions of money brought into these ecosystems appear well within the control of Chinese government.

Such a possibility has already been set in motion by statements made by Liu He when he said "Strengthening the party's overall leadership is the core issue," alluding to a famous Mao Zedong saying. "In the party, government, military, and civil sciences, in the east, west, south, north and center, the party leads all. (Bradsher & Buckley, 2018)[14]". In the light of the report by McGregor in the Guardian (McGregor, 2019), it is evident that the controls that Chinese government would exercise would ensure that the funds within the ecosystem of e-wallets and QR codes would eventually be utilized by 'directed investments' in the shares, Mutual Funds or other state controlled lending agencies that finance projects across the world.

The **first discernable threat** therefore is, BRI dreams of China would continue to be funded by consumers across Asia, Europe, Americas and Africa using Chinese e-wallets and payment channels.

The **second threat** is much more credible. In a queer comparison, it would be interesting to look at one of the world's dangerous terrorist organizations, Aum Shinrikyo. Led by Asahara, Aum came into lime light when it carried out Sarin gas attack on Tokyo Subway on 20 March 1995. Apart from the outpouring of grief, the attack brought to light the dangers of Chemical and Biological Weapons as a tool of terrorists. The debates it created in strategic and scholarly communities drowned an important dimension of Aum's work in the field of creating financial and utility software to a number of government agencies in Japan including the Ministry of Defence, Police and banking/financial sectors. Five years after the attack, the New York Times came out with important insights into this dimension. The report said that computer companies affiliated with the Aum Shinrikyo doomsday sect developed software programs for at least 10 government agencies, including the Defense Ministry, and more than 80 major Japanese companies (Sims, 2000)[15]. There is wider unspoken apprehension that Aum Shinrikyo may still pull the financial carpet from under these companies, impacting Japan's economy critically. These debates and discussions bring out clearly that the financial ecosystem that China is assisting its Tech Giants to build across the world may as well be used to bring down the financial sector of countries that do not see eye to eye with China's ambitions. Added to this threat is the extent and reach of Chinese research in IT and AI.

What are the options?

Recently, government of India went ahead and banned 43 more Chinese Apps, specially Alipay Cashier and Alibaba Express (TOI, 2020)[16]. It had banned 59 Apps earlier (ET Bureau, 2020)[17] that included WeChat and TikTok. Predictably, China reacted vehemently, even to the extent of hinting at down swing of bilateral relations by the actions of India. Chinese foreign ministry spokesman Zhao Lijian said, "The relevant methods clearly violate market principles and World Trade Organization guidelines, and severely harm Chinese companies' legal rights and interests. India should immediately redress these discriminative methods to avoid even bigger damage to bilateral cooperation," (AT, 2020)[18].

India's actions, seen in the light of the discourse above indicate that it has actually protected its security interests by such a ban. The ability and resilience that Indian economy has shown and the stability in political dimension appear to be two important factors in taking to such recourses.

Banning Apps may appear trivial and even cause general unhappiness to segments of population that is far removed from understanding these detrimental implications. Big and small businesses that have become accustomed to easy operations, less transaction fees and even liberal loans may also feel the pinch. These are precisely the trappings of financial disaster that the widening net of Chinese business through its Tech Giants is casting across the globe.

It is also pertinent to note that Chinese interests in establishing beachheads into India's banking system are more than a reality. For example, on 18th August 2020 the People's Bank of China bought 0.006 per cent stake in private lender ICICI Bank by investing Rs 15 crore in its Rs 15,000 crore qualified institutional placement. Earlier, at the end of March 2020, the Chinese central bank held shares worth Rs 4,418 crore in HDFC, Asian Paints and Ambuja Cements (Malhan, 2020)[19]. However innocuous and procedurally right these foreign investments may appear, it is important to understand that the Dragon plays its game in a subtle and unobtrusive way which calls for greater scrutiny. In this light, the Indian government's decision to ban FDI investments through automatic route taken on 17 April 2020 (GOI, Dept of Com & Ind, 2020)[20] appears to be guided by immense foresight. However, less than six months later, that People's Bank of China acquired stakes in banks and industries indicates that greater control and action is required in this dimension. Also, Indian banking sector and industrial houses should be sensitized to the potential risk that they may generate if they are merely guided by profit orientation in the short term.

Across the world, over 70 countries appear to have already walked into the Dragon's Debt Trap. Their enthusiastic cooperation with Chinese financial and banking system, directly or indirectly, may spell disaster to their domestic economies in case leadership in those countries fails to carry out realistic evaluations. With countries like Sri Lanka negotiating for a third tranche of USD700 million loan from China, it is imperative that such awakening should happen sooner.

Section IV

Concepts, Strategies and Think Tanks

17. Large Number of Small Things: Lessons from Nagorno-Karabakh in Military Strategy

Introduction

Taiwan or the Republic of China (ROC) stands across the Taiwan Strait, preparing as it is, for the invasion from mainland China for over seventy years now. As they say, much water has flown down the strait (bridge!) with America playing eternal ally to the Island nation. Theoretically speaking, neither the South China Sea nor Taiwan would have become global concerns had China remained the China of the early 1980's. Till then, mired in its own internal issues, even China did not have the luxury of upping the ante over Taiwan but for the economic and military eminence that it has apparently gained in the international arena in subsequent times. With Xi Jinping at the helm, had China not ventured to revive the Silk Route, perhaps the world also would have relapsed into a fait accompli Uni-Polar World Order.

Nagorno-Karabakh, some 5000 kilometers away from China, again, would not have caught the imagination of the world but for involvement of Russia in mediating the affairs in Central Asia. With an estimated 1000 casualties on both sides, Armenia and Azerbaijan, the world may have remained more concerned with COVID19 that has caused millions of deaths.

Neither Taiwan nor Nagorno-Karabakh have anything in common. However, the small flash in the western corner of Central Asia appears to have a theoretical connection. More specifically, the methods and means of conflict adopted by Armenia and Azerbaijan seems to have been the testing ground for a new defense paradigm that Taiwan drafted for itself in 2017. This article probes the essential connection that belies their geographical separation and attempts to draw lessons for strategic community across the world.

Paradigm Shift in Taiwan

In 2017, Taiwan's venerable former Chief of General Staff, Admiral Lee Hsi-ming, presented the Overall Defense Concept (ODC) that represented a paradigm shift in Taiwan's strategy to prevent invasion of the island nation by PLA. The ODC postulated the means and methods of this objective through a cryptic SWOT analysis, in the words of Lee Hsi-min and Eric Lee (Hsi-min & Eric, 2020)[1]:

Taiwan must abandon notions of a traditional war of attrition with the PLA. Facing a stronger adversary, embracing an effective asymmetric defense posture and incorporating tactical asymmetric capabilities could compensate for Taiwan's disadvantage on paper and prevent the PLA from getting boots on the ground. In the face of a growing cross-strait resource imbalance and domestic budgetary constraints, Taiwan must allocate and manage its resources as efficiently and effectively as possible.

Among the three facets of the ODC, *incorporating tactical asymmetric capabilities* specifically talked about asymmetric weapon systems. His-Min and Eric ((Hsi-min & Eric, 2020) synthesized it as: Asymmetric weapon systems, on the other hand, are less visible during peacetime but essential during war. They provide non-conventional war fighting capabilities that are aimed at exploiting natural advantages and the enemy's vulnerabilities while delivering maximum tactical impact with minimal effort. Taiwan's asymmetric systems must be small, mobile, lethal and numerous for strategic dispersion. They must be cost-effective and easy to develop and maintain, yet also resilient and sustainable. They must complicate enemy operations by being difficult to target and counter. *The essence of Taiwan's asymmetric capabilities is a large number of small things.*

Drew Thompson, former Director for China, Taiwan, and Mongolia in the Office of the Secretary of Defense from 2011 to 2018, published an insightful discourse on ODC on 02 October 2018 titled HOPE ON THE HORIZON: TAIWAN'S RADICAL NEW DEFENSE CONCEPT. Thompson (Thompson, 2018)[2] went specific by stating:

"The challenge for Taiwan is ensuring that there is adequate defense funding for these large, prestige-enhancing platforms (that are the darlings of their service chiefs), as well as the small, maneuverable, and survivable asymmetric systems that are critical to Taiwan's survival"

The Nagorno-Karabakh Conflict

On 27 September, Armenia and Azerbaijan forces clashed over the control of Nagrono-Karabakh. The age old dispute between the erstwhile USSR enclaves drew the attention of the world, since a new power in Central Asia, ably assisted by Russia, was seen as emerging – Turkey. Supporting Azerbaijan openly, Turkey provided military and other assistance. The clashes ended on 10 November after Armenia apparently conceded to terms that are viewed with disenchantment by Armenians. Russia stepped in by deploying 3000 troops to keep peace while the terms of agreement between Armenia and Azerbaijan are implemented. US, though a long term benefactor of Turkey, appeared to have lost diplomatic initiative and therefore ceding 'political mileage' to Russia in Central Asian affairs.

There are two important lessons that are emerging in the conduct of Nagorno-Karabakh conflict that are of special interest to the strategic community. First, the extensive use of drones provided by Turkey to Azerbaijan. Second, use of cyber space for war. Both these figure prominently in the discourses on Taiwan's ODC discussed earlier. We will look at these two elements briefly.

Drones: Azerbaijan's highly effective use of drones and sensors indicated a "new, more affordable type of air power" (Economist, 2020)[3]. Azerbaijani forces used the Turkish drones, especially Bayraktar TB2, to carry out reconnaissance for relaying the coordinates of targets to Azerbaijani artillery. They also used Harpy or the Israeli Harop, which has the potential to loiter over TBA, search for potential targets like tanks and artillery, and strike with a precision of less than 10 meters. Commentators like Alex Gatopoulos noted that the use of drones in Nagorno-Karabakh illustrated how they enabled small countries to conduct effective air campaigns, potentially making low-level conflicts much more deadly (Gatopoulos, 2020)[4]. He also reported that Close Air Support (CAS) were conducted using specialized suicide drones such as IAI Harop, rendering tanks vulnerable and suggesting changes are required to armored warfare doctrine.

Turkish origin STM Kargu-2 was also deployed in possibly 'flocks', as reported in Turkish social media. The media account of "Divan-I Harp", reported that KARGU Kamikaze UAV was used by the Azerbaijan Army. At least 27 KARGU Kamikaze UAVs are seen in the shared images. The displayed quantities revealed the possibility that KARGU-2s could be in operational use in flocks (Mehmet, n.d)[5].

Cyber warfare and Propaganda: Both Armenia and Azerbaijan reportedly used cyber space and social media to conduct blitzing campaigns against each other and wreak havoc into each other's popular psyche. Mansur Mirovalev, reporting for Aljazeera (Mirovalev, 2020)[6], pointed to how Armenian sentiments were fired up when a post showing Armenian cello player Sevak Avanesyan playing in the snow-white and debris-covered Holy Savior Cathedral in the town of Shushi in Nagorno-Karabakh, a breakaway region in Azerbaijan dominated by ethnic Armenians since the early 1990s. The fires of centuries old enmity was fed with timbers through such portrayals.

Robin Forestier-Walker of Aljazeera (Forestier-Walker, 2020)[7] reported that digital billboards in Baku have broadcast high-resolution imagery of missiles striking Armenian tanks and other military hardware, as well as groups of soldiers caught in the open. Forester-Walker also reported Azerbaijan's President Ilham Aliyev as having told Turkish television that Turkish drones owned by Azerbaijan had "shrunk" the number of Azeri casualties. "These drones show Turkey's strength. It also empowers us," he is cited to have said. While President Aliyev was referring to Bayraktar TB2, the effect of the conflict through 'Bill Board offensive' fed the popular imagination of the public and media.

Both the countries also reportedly used own and hired cyber mercenaries from Greece, Turkey and Russia to deface government websites. Artsakh News (Artsakh, 2020)[8], for example, reported that over 80 government websites were attacked and many of them just under two hours! Misinformation, propaganda and fake news fed the public imagination for good as well as for worse.

Large number of small things

When we read the Taiwanese ODC and Nagrono-Karabakh conflict together, it is not difficult to fathom the meaning of "Large number of small things" that could obtain two primary objectives: Reduce human capital in war and reduce the enemy's will to fight. That precisely is what the Taiwanese ODC attempted to do by adopting its new paradigm. It appears that Nagrono-Karabakh validated that theory. In the light of this test case war in Central Asia, it is not surprising that Chinese President Xi Jinping appears to have given the go-ahead to PLA for testing and deploying MAM-L Unmanned Aerial Vehicles (UAV). The ANKA developed MAM-L have reportedly destroyed 100 Russian made T-72 tanks in Turkey's direct and indirect wars in Syria, Iraq, Libya, and Azerbaijan (Karabakh) (News Center, 2020)[9]. The South China Morning Post (Zheng, 2020)[10] also reported that the PLA is training with UAVs and using them for delivering ammunition, hot food and other supports in Ladakh where Sino-India talks have made little impact for disengagement on ground after the Galwan skirmish. Apart from land based drones, China has also reported deployed a dozen or more 'Sea Wing' under water drones, though allegedly for research purposes in the sea near Sri Lanka (Pandit, 2020)[11].

From the Korean War of 1950-53 to the Sino-Vietnamese War in 1979, a consistent trend that was visible to analysts was the phenomenal casualties that Chinese suffered in war. In the Korean War for example, while USA suffered 33686 deaths and 2830 non-battle deaths, China suffered 114,000 battle deaths, 34,000 non-battle deaths, 340,000 wounded, and 7,600 missing during the war. 7,110 Chinese POWs were repatriated to China. In the Vietnamese conflict, that lasted precisely thirty days, it was reported that Chinese casualties numbered over 9000 while the Vietnamese statistics was never made public.

In the Sino-Indian war of 1962, it is public knowledge that Chinese attacked Indian positions using 'wave' tactic. Many accounts of the war reveal columns after columns of Chinese attacking Indian positions in which the second wave onwards, the Chinese are said to have been without arms. When the first wave collapsed, the second wave swept forward picking up the weapons of the dead for their attack. Short of weapons and replenishments, Indian positions fell to such attacks is highlighted across available literature on the war.

The use of UAVs as evidenced in Nagrono-Karabakh could as well change the equation of human casualties incurred in conventional conflicts. Apart from suffering huge casualties, the defender nation's morale will be adversely affected if cyber space and propaganda are effectively directed from the safe environs of their originator country.

Lessons from Nagrono-Karabakh

The Taiwanese ODC and Nagrono-Karabakh conflict hold portent lessons for strategic community across the world. These lessons could be summarized as below:

1. The texture of conventional war has changed. Economical, technology-assisted platforms like UAVs or drones have come to stay. Investing in them therefore is as important as training the troops to utilize them.
2. Cyber space and propaganda are no more perceived threats. With internet and accessibility to the net reaching even far corners of the globe, punitive impact on troop and public morale could be produced. Even nations not so well developed technologically have the luxury of hiring mercenaries on this front too. Greece and Turkey, who otherwise have disputes among their territorial issues, have had no control over Greek Cyber Mercenaries being hired by either parties to the conflict.
3. Conventional game changers like heavy tanks and sophisticated artillery are highly vulnerable to cheap aerial weapons that are difficult to detect and worse, difficult to counter.
4. Weapon exporters have no ideological barriers. The example of Israeli Kamikaze UAV in the service of Turkey and Azerbaijan prove the point. Political alliances (read US-Israeli bonhomie) do not come in the way of weapon exports.
5. Nations need to re-think about the human cost of war. A country like China, with a demonstrated disregard for human cost in war, is re-drawing its game plan perhaps and ironically drawing lessons from Taiwanese thought process! Countries like USA that attach great value to human cost have a lot to worry about.

Military strategy is considered to be the domain of generals and therefore largely left out of discourse by polity. The most important lesson that emerges from Taiwan and Nagorno-Karabakh is the public discourse on strategy. When we discourse what we intend to do, it is not just the international academic community which is listening. Adversaries across the board as well as vested interests too listen in. The theories and formulations that we debate become the fodder for experimentation the results of which may impact us too. Years before, a Hollywood movie rocked the shows – Sense and Sensibility based on a novel by Jane Austen by the same title. Transplanting the title to strategic discourse should not be a strain on imagination. It is as well to recall what Sun Tzu, the grand master of strategy said:

> "Engage people with what they expect; it is what they are able to discern and confirms their projections. It settles them into predictable patterns of response, occupying their minds while you wait for the extraordinary moment — that which they cannot anticipate."

– Sun Tzu, The Art of War

18. Watch What You Speak: Think Tanks and Strategic Discourses

Sun Tzu is quoted to have said 'the opportunity of defeating the enemy is provided by the enemy himself' in his grand treatise The Art of War. The wisdom of understanding enemy's mind gains paramount when we reflect upon this saying. Understanding enemy's mind needs just one dedicated function – intelligence gathering. For ages, countries and militaries have resorted to acquiring intelligence on adversaries (as well as friends and neutrals) through various sources. The diplomatic missions for example are acknowledged as open source that countries use, apart from the news and reports published by media. It is also construed that by far the intelligence gathered through such open sources pertain to the tactical domain, though properly collated they could be of strategic value. Of course, it would depend on informed and critical analysis to distill indicators of strategic nature from the deluge of information gathered through such diverse open sources. A new dimension to intelligence gathering, more specifically of strategic nature, has become visible with the advent of Think Tanks.

In an age when the power of media and communications makes it near impossible to hide fact and fiction from public ears, let alone the luxury of time to pause and discern their difference, means of gathering intelligence through Think Tanks has become easier. The reason for ease of doing this business through the deliberations of Think Tanks is the availability of expertise that is unhindered in its analysis and expression.

Traditional intelligence schools ingrain a basic caution into the blood: Watch what you speak, the enemy is listening. Interestingly, the power of communications appears to have prodded the best kept secrets into best broadcast ideas in public domain.

This article looks at the role of Think Tanks in the dissemination of discourses on strategy into the very hands of those that the debates in the Think Tanks avowedly aim to contain!!

Taiwan adopts new defense paradigm

Taiwan was traditionally perceived to have relied more on American guarantee for its independence from Chinese occupation than on a realistic appraisal of its own capabilities to either deter or withstand such an invasion. US Naval War College in 2008 even published a detailed analysis of the necessity for Taiwan to change such a perception. The report talked about how Kuomintang and the Democratic People's Party have not framed a defense debate that could produce the open, honest appraisal that is desperately needed if domestic consensus on a viable defense is to be achieved (Murray, 2008)[1].

In 2017, having lived under the shadow of Chinese invasion and being witness to the aggressive expansion of Chinese presence in South China Sea, Taiwan's defense establishment headed by Admiral Lee Hsi-ming adopted a new and much awaited defense strategy. Modern history is witness to the threat Republic of China (ROC) at Taiwan faced from an increasingly aggressive PRC that considers itself as the rightful sovereign of ROC.

Renewed fears over defense of the island were fueled when Chinese went about conducting naval drills in Spratly's and in the close proximity of Taiwanese waters. Even though US conducted FONOPS and extended other assurances to Taiwan, the island nation was rightfully aware that its own strategic paradigm needs re-calibration. Aware that it cannot handle the immense military might of China, the Overall Defense Concept (ODC) proposed by Admiral His-ming envisaged, in broad terms, a three-prong strategy:

> The ODC's mission is to deter the PLA and, if necessary, defeat a full-scale PLA invasion. The three pillars of its concept of operations are ***force protection, decisive battle in the littoral zone*** and ***destruction of the enemy at the landing beach***. Force protection enables Taiwan's armed forces to survive and recover from the opening phase of a massive PLA strike campaign, so that units can strike back as soon as the enemy is within range. The ODC seeks to bolster the military's ability to withstand pre-invasion bombardment using tactics similar to those of force preservation. Elements of force protection include mobility, camouflage, concealment, deception, dispersion, rapid repair and blast mitigation (Hsi-min & Eric, 2020)[2].

With this development in Taiwan, the three-prong strategy was promptly picked up for immense deliberations across the Pacific. It is to be kept in mind that the discourses on ODC were driven by a genuine concern to checkmate the Chinese designs in South China Sea and the larger Indo-Pacific.

Think Tanks and ODC

Taiwan, as we know, is key to America's SCS as well as Indo-Pacific strategy. Thus, when Taiwan chalked its ODC, Think Tanks in America went on an overdrive analyzing and exploring the probability that Taiwan would thwart Chinese designs, in the process standing as the bulwark of protecting American interests in the Indo-Pacific. To sight few examples:

1. Drew Thompson who was the Director for China, Taiwan, and Mongolia in the Office of the Secretary of Defense from 2011 to 2018, published an insightful discourse on ODC on 02 October 2018 titled HOPE ON THE HORIZON: TAIWAN'S RADICAL NEW DEFENSE CONCEPT. Thompson (Thompson, 2018)[3] went specific by stating: "The new concept is animated by the most critical mission of the Taiwan military: denying China the ability to land and resupply an invasion force. Beijing can use blockades, coercion, hybrid warfare, or "gray zone" pressure, but the only thing that guarantees Beijing can achieve its political objective of Taiwan's surrender is putting Chinese boots on the ground and physically seizing control of the island. Preventing that outcome is therefore the most fundamental mission..... The challenge for Taiwan is ensuring that there is adequate defense funding for these large, prestige-enhancing platforms (that are the darlings of their service chiefs), as well as the small, maneuverable, and survivable asymmetric systems that are critical to Taiwan's survival".
2. On 09 April 2019, the Center for Strategic Analysis & International Studies (CSIS) invited the President of Taiwan to interact with experts under the title 'The Taiwan Relations Act at Forty and U.S.-Taiwan Relations: VTC Speech and Q&A with Her Excellency President Tsai Ing-wen of the Republic of China (Taiwan) (CSIS, 2019)[4]. During the course of the Q&A, Taiwan's ODC was one of the themes of discussion.
3. The Hudson Institute in August 2020 published a transcript of the talk by President Tsai Ing-wen of the Republic of China (Taiwan) (Hudson Institute, 2020)[5] in which ODC figured as an important strategy to counter a potential Chinese invasion of Taiwan.

Across the Atlantic, in UK, strategic interest on Taiwan's ODC was reflected in various discourses. To cite a couple of examples:

1. Corey Lee Bell (Bell, 2020)[6]published an Editorial in Taiwan Insight in which, apart from highlighting the play of American defense industry in shaping Taiwan's procurement interests, also spoke of ODC.

2. The Henry Jackson Society of London invited Admiral (Retd) Chen Yeong-Kang of Taiwan to specifically talk about 'Taiwan's Overall Defence Concept (ODC) and Defence Policy' (HJS, 2020)[7].

Other leading analysts and Think Tanks were not far behind in engaging in this debate at various levels and their reports and interpretations are available in public domain.

Food for Thought

War, as we know, is a game of nerves. To draw upon Sun Tzu gain, it is also a game where the objective is to dishearten the enemy and render him incapable without firing a shot oneself. It doesn't call for too much of deliberation to understand that to do so, discerning the enemy mind and intent is the first requirement.

BH Liddel Hart in his treatise The Revolution in Warfare (Hart, n.d) pointedly says, "The most virile nation might not be able to withstand another, inferior to it in all natural qualities, if the latter had some decisively superior technical appliance". Publicly available strategies outlined in ODC state that it aims to elaborately adopt to asymmetric war, by deploying *small, maneuverable, and survivable asymmetric systems* through which it aims to either deter or destroy Chinese invasion. In the discourses of the Think Tanks and expert opinions, we also find that such small, maneuverable and survivable systems have been interpreted as UAVs.

The recent conflagration in Nagorno-Karabakh demonstrated how such *small, maneuverable and sustainable technology* in the form of Turkish Bayraktar TB2, KARGU Kamikaze UAV and IAI Harop played a crucial role in obtaining victory. It would appear as though Armenian-Azeri conflict was the testing ground for some of the asymmetric capabilities that are envisaged in ODC. And the 'test' seems to have validated the theory.

The examples of extensive discussions and debates in Think Tanks and by strategic analysts provide illuminating understanding on each aspect of the new strategy that Taiwan has adopted or should adopt. The apparent aim of the strategic community is to apply its cumulative wisdom to 'theoretically' evaluate the good-bad-ugly of the elements of new strategy. More concern and excitement, if we may perceive, is added to the discourse since China is at the center of world attention for reasons that need no elaboration. While the cumulative debates may as well attract the ears of strategists in Taiwan to evaluate the potential of their new paradigm, the discourses pouring out on public platforms cannot but fail to attract the attention of Chinese too.

This is something that Think Tanks must think about!!

19. Theatre Commands: Understanding its Concepts and Implications

India's strategic community is abuzz with incisive discourses concerning the announcement by Chief of Defence Staff on the formation of theatre commands. The host of papers, opinions and discussions seem to label theatre commands as end product of the concept of joint operations that originated when Integrated Defence Staff was formed in November 2001. The line of thoughts emanating from India's first CDS, General Bipin Rawat, appear to be hinting at dissolution of existing Army, Navy and Air Force Commands in order to create three or four theatre commands under a single commander each. As anticipated, this prospect has also generated contestations and concerns over turf control.

Some of the prominent thoughts in circulation with respect to theatre commands placing joint operations as its core philosophy are from CLAWS[1], ORF[2] and in two of India's prominent newspapers, The Print[3] and Indian Express[4]. Stepping aside from these discourses in the academia and media, it is necessary to explore the concept of theatre commands first, before assessing its modalities as well as its implications.

The concept of theatre command originated obviously from the US. Till the time it was attacked on the 7th of December 1941 by Japan at Pearl Harbor, USA was merely watching the Nazi war machine sweep through Europe. However, after Japanese attack, USA stepped into the war to avenge Japan by opening the Pacific Theatre under General McArthur. In about three years' time, it also landed troops on the beaches of Normandy under General Eisenhower at the head of the Allied Forces (SHAEF). When the war ended with the atomic bombing of Hiroshima, America was already on its early stages of the Cold War with USSR, prompting it to form Supreme Headquarters Allied Powers Europe (SHAPE) or more popularly, the NATO. In due course of time, other parts of the world increasingly came within the ambit of America's interests propelling it to form theatre commands. Today, US has 11 combined combat commands covering every region or country in the world within their sphere of operations. For example, the US Africa Command 'with partners, counters transnational threats and malign actors, strengthens security forces, and responds to crises in order to advance U.S. national interests and promote regional security, stability, and prosperity'[5]. This brief historical understanding provides the following key elements that necessitate combined combat commands or theatre commands:

1. Locating and promoting substantial assets in national interest across vast and geographically separated areas across the globe.
2. Explicit intent to use armed intervention when such interests are threatened.
3. Creating partnerships with host countries where such interests and assets are located, including substantial military aid, training and joint-operational ethos.

For example, apart from addressing threats to USA emanating from the Pacific Ocean Region, protecting US' interests and alliances with Japan, Singapore, Australia, South Korea and Taiwan are embedded as the core objectives of its Pacific Command located at Hawaii. The nature of potential threats to its interests and geographical factors defining its allies or enemies necessitate that its Army, Navy and Air Force must operate under a unified command structure. In no small measure is the patently expeditionary philosophy by which US Armed Forces are trained to operate and are deployed across the globe. It is also important to note that executive decision from none other than the President of United States backed by the Senate authorize permanent deployment of American Forces all across the world.

When we look at India, we find that neither such philosophy nor any of the other factors necessitating theatre commands are present. India is surrounded by two inimical countries covering most of its land borders. Its sea borders are more threatened by conventional war from one of its neighbors. As for the other neighbors in its vicinity, except for demographic influxes, no credible threats emanate warranting permanent presence of its armed forces or even forays into their territory for specific tasks frequently. In any case, India strongly abides by the policy of negotiations than armed interventions to protect its interests in the neighborhood. Even Indian Army's surgical strikes at Balakot or across the Myanmar's borders were more due to the circumstances and national mood specifically attending on them than on account of a patented national policy.

Unlike America, India has dual control mechanism for its armed forces. The President remains its Supreme Commander. He comes into picture only when a state of war needs to be declared officially. The executive control rests with the Prime Minister through Ministry of Defence. The Parliament of India plays very little direct role in so far the deployment of armed forces is concerned, internally or otherwise. The executive control mechanism specifically keeps the armed forces away from internal as well as foreign policy making, unlike the Pentagon which works in conjunction with the Department of State or the President of USA.

Again unlike America, Indian interests abroad like ONGC, VSNL, L&T investments have no negotiated clause where either military contractors or the military are present in those areas for protection of Indian personnel or assets. They remain within the ambit of the MEA and its diplomatic framework in the host country. Even where diaspora are concerned, Americans working or residing abroad have a direct connect with their embassy which periodically reviews the security situation locally and employs forces when needed, to protect them or extract them through bilateral arrangement with the host country. The Tehran Embassy crisis in 1979-81 and America's response and the case of Daniel Pearl, an American journalist killed by Al Qaeda, that shaped America's policy towards Al Qaeda are well known.

It may be of interest to look at how India handled its crises abroad to appreciate whether boots-on-ground policy goes with national policy. To cite few examples:

- In 1972, Dictator Idi Amin specifically targeted Indians in Uganda. Nearly 75000 Indians, including 25000 who were bonafide citizens of Uganda were threatened to leave the country. The crisis had started way back in 1967-68 and even as India was winning the war in East Pakistan in December 1971, it became acute. As of 1971, Indian Armed Forces were at their prime and Indira Gandhi was not seen as a weak leader either. Yet, India kept a lukewarm silence and eventually ended up appealing to the African nations to prevail over Idi Amin. Fearing backlash from Idi Amin, neighbors like Tanzania with which India purportedly had good relations, closed their borders to Indians fleeing Uganda. The summary expulsions, harassment, detentions, disappearances and deaths combined with lack of any compensation in post-Amin era is indeed a tragic story.[6]
- Fiji, a small island nation in the Pacific, experienced four coups between 1986 and 2000. At the heart of the reasons for the coups were high decibel anti-Indian sentiments that resulted in extraordinary oppression of India diaspora. It took nearly fifteen more years for India-Fiji relations to turn around. Realizing that Fiji would remain isolated internationally, Fijian regime warmed up to India through constructive agreements in 2015 like establishing Institute for Sustainable Coastal and Ocean Research in the region, a network of marine biology research stations in various island nations and the offer to carry out hydrographic surveys by Indian Navy to help Fiji exploit its marine resources responsibly. For once and for peaceful purpose, India's naval presence became part of national strategy in the Pacific[7], although limited in its tenure.

- The Iraq (Kuwait) crisis of 1990 again saw Indian government indulging in fantastic diplomatic footwork with Saddam Husain to repatriate nearly 17000 Indians[8]. In many ways when compared with Ugandan experience, Kuwait spelt a turning point in the way India responded to crisis abroad concerning its diaspora or interests. Analysts point as to how 'the Kuwait crisis resulted in India making two critical steps that shaped its post-Cold War policy toward the region: diminishing influence of the Palestinian cause in its engagements with the Arab world and economic substance replacing political rhetoric'[9].
- The IC 814 hijack crisis of 1999 is another example when India hesitated to use its armed forces even on its own soil, handing the Taliban and Pakistan their prized terrorists. The fallout of that hesitation visited India in varied forms in the years thereafter.

These examples point to the need to evaluate India's options in multifarious dimensions before putting together its theatre commands. The aspects meriting consideration are:

1. **Need to have a stated policy that armed forces will be deployed in national interest wherever across the globe those interests are threatened.** Even though the use of force will be the last of the options, their presence in the theatre should be a matter of policy. An important case study that merits detailed appreciation is India's hesitation to accept the offer of Tajikistan to develop its international airport and house up to two squadrons of Indian Air Force there. The strategic advantage to India in Central Asia notwithstanding, a lukewarm policy let the opportunity slip away. In the current scenario in the Indo-Pacific, for example, to protect India's maritime and trade interests, will India deploy its navy or amphibious forces in conjunction with SCS littoral countries? Answers to such questions rest on the policy framework more than the capability of its armed forces.
2. **Building capabilities the armed forces need to sustain such overseas operations** over a prolonged period of time. With experiences like decades of indecisiveness over procuring or producing a couple of aircraft carriers or indigenous aerial platforms/engines, India needs to look at the concept of Atma Nirbhar more closely and pursue its proceeds in a stricter time frame. The Chinese incursion of 1962 should serve as a good example for self-sufficiency in defense production and application of innovative homegrown and sustainable technologies, not to mention the recent off-the-shelf procurements to deter Chinese in Ladakh. In the United States as well as China, it is well known that the military is deeply involved with

government and private agencies to develop and modernize its weapons and platforms though R&D collaboration.

3. **Bilateral arrangements with countries of interest** where such operations are envisaged. Bilateral agreements play an important role in shaping and preserving India's interests. It is important to identify what India can constructively offer that the host countries would be hard put to resist.
4. **Changes needed in the command and control structure**. The current command and control structure, particularly in higher defense management needs a complete revamp. The Goldwater-Nichols Act 1986[10] of the United States and the re-structuring of the Armed Forces higher command structure must be evaluated in the Indian context and with necessary modifications, adopted by an act of the Parliament.
5. **Educating the political and bureaucratic elite on the concept of military deployment**. While the military is an expression of political will that expression needs born out of concise understanding in the minds of political and bureaucratic elite as to its application. Israel's daring 90 minutes at Entebbe is a classic example for the conceptual clarity and firmness of resolve while using armed forces outside the borders in national interest. It is also an important lesson in combined command structure. It is no coincidence that America's use of military power finds its expression from its highest office the occupants of which have served directly or indirectly in uniform.
6. **Restructuring Military Training**. A firm grounding in international law of war, bilateral and multilateral process of international relations and country specific interests of India is required to be imparted to appropriate higher level of military leadership for them to work in sync with political objectives. In the same manner, civil servants and diplomatic corps need to work with the highest military formations to understand and evolve jointness of operations at all levels. They must also be in sync at field levels wherever across the globe a need for military expression emantes.
7. **Reforming and re-structuring the intelligence agencies**. In the present scheme of things, though NSA heads the complete fraternity, multiple agencies involved in the network report to as many ministries, giving rise to a tendency to play for individual turfs. Importantly, intelligence gathering abroad remains outside the domain of the military, except in an incidental manner. Smooth coordination and working together of military intelligence and civil counterparts in real time would be vital to obtain results on ground where operations are envisaged in foreign shores.

From independence onwards, India has followed its policy of non-interference instilling a paramount defensive outlook towards its military operations. The political decision makers also have played the military card only under the most compelling circumstances, that too with as many restraints as possible. India's experience of deploying IPKF in Sri Lanka is yet to be studied in detail by the strategic community to truly understand the import of theatre level operations in conjunction with policy makers, both walking side by side. Similarly, India's assistance to Maldives in times of its crisis also needs to be studied exhaustively to work out the modalities for theatre level operations.

Another country that is developing and testing its theatre command concept in India's neighborhood is China. The case of China trapping Djibouti with its Cheque book has been largely discussed within the parameters of 'String of Pearls' and 'BRI'. When we look beyond, we find that China has made investments surpassing USD 4.7 billion in Africa[11]. It even instituted a China-Africa Development Fund in 2007[12] before embarking upon a military station at Djibouti in 2017, good ten years later. Seen from the stated policy of China to protect its overseas interests arising from its ambitious BRI project, entering into Djibouti through bilateral arrangements exemplifies how the concept of theatre commands will portray power projection in national interest.

Keeping these factors in mind, it is necessary for the Indian policy establishment first to identify what are the national interests that would be served by commissioning the theatre commands to replace the internal geographical service commands that have served the nation's interest well so far. Existing command structure have also yielded substantial results in 1971 war as well as in the Kargil conflict. Given the essentially defensive philosophy that cocoons India's national security policy, explicitly excluding the military from its economic and other strategic national interests beyond its borders, critical re-appraisal of its national security policy should precede formation of theatre commands.

It is more important that India re-calibrates its policy making structures before instituting the theatre commands, if they are to serve the nation well in the emerging world order. At a time when India's growth is on the right path and the process of globalization seem to nudge it ever forward, any major shift in re-structuring its only guarantee for territorial sovereignty should be undertaken only through exhaustive and discerning evaluation. To merely treat it as a matter for the military to decide would serve little purpose towards larger national interest.

In the absence of a clear external, economic and military policy demanding explicit application of military might to protect its interests globally, disbanding the internal geographical commands will only accentuate contestations for turf control between the three forces, rendering India susceptible at a moment when geopolitical vulnerabilities in the subcontinent appear to be not in its favour.

20. Integrated Infrastructure Planning in Strategic Calculus

Rahul Bedi (Bedi, 26 February 2021)[1] wrote in the Wire that "The hoopla over the approval accorded by the Ministry of Defence (MoD) in imminently procuring 118 indigenously developed Mk-1A Arjun main battle tanks (MBTs) for the Indian Army for Rs 8,350 crore, appears misplaced, considering the operational and logistical handicaps encasing this overweight platform". The article underpinned an important dimension to strategic calculus – Integrated Infrastructure Planning. Military and other sources cited in the article point to the un-usability of tanks heavier than 50 tons in Punjab (and elsewhere) owing to the carrying capacity of the bridges, culverts and country roads in areas closer to the borders.

Infrastructure Development - Perspectives

India witnessed a mammoth push in infrastructure development from 1998 when the government launched the Bharatmala Project. Commencing from 2000-01 till 2019-20, growth in road infrastructure has visibly increased to the delight of common citizens. Brief comparative statistics in road infrastructure is given below:

Year (as on 31st March)	National Highways	State Highways	District Roads	Rural Roads	Urban Roads	Project Roads	Total (in km)
2001	57,737	1,32,100	7,36,001	19,72,016	2,52,001	2,23,665	33,73,520
2018 (Provisional)	1,26,350	1,81,531	6,14,028	44,04,404	5,31,608	3,46,505	62,04,426

Source: Ministry of Road Transport and Highways Annual Report 2019-20, Page 104 (Appendix 14)[2]

This mammoth growth has been the result of pressures of globalization, economic liberalization, political vision and executive commitment. It has also been made possible by consistent evolution of planning and executing agencies. In the preceding era, planning was largely left to central and state planning commissions which were affected by vagaries of finances, politics and executive compulsions in the controlling or competing ministries. CPWD and State PWD remained the predominant agencies that involved themselves in the execution of road works. While civilian road infrastructure was subjected to these, roads in border areas for military purposes were left to the concern of Ministry of Defence and its budgetary constraints towards allocations for the Border Roads Organization (BRO). Coordination between CPWD, State PWD and the BRO did come through on specific projects where civilian populations were involved.

The pressures of economic development in the liberalization era post-1998, as mentioned above, brought about a substantial change in the planning and executing process also. Apart from nominal changes in the name of the ministry, the Planning Commission was replaced effectively by Niti Aayog and undermentioned agencies were pressed in for road development across the country:

- National Highways Authority of India (Autonomous under Ministry of Road Transport and Highways), formed in 1988
- Indian Road Construction Corporation (Public Sector Corporation), formed in 1976
- National Highways and Infrastructure Development Corporation Ltd[3]. – NHIDC (Public Sector Corporation), formed in 2014

In the framework of institutional developments, formation of NHIDC is significant and consistent with the Look and Act East Policy. It is especially focused on North Eastern states and border areas, thus giving specific impetus to India's strategic concerns in the North East[4].

While at the national level, the institutions for planning and execution underwent changes, on ground level viz., the State, district and Panchayat levels also new institutions came up due to the strengthening of the third pillar of governance, the Panchayati Raj, through the 73rd Amendment to the Constitution. Briefly, they encompassed Village-Block-District Panchayat Standing Committees, District Planning Committees, and State Planning Committees[5]. Through these agencies, developmental projects including that of roads[6] (which is in the Concurrent List of Indian Constitution) are projected to State and Central Finance Commissions for allocation of funds.

Strategic Calculus and Infrastructure

In their present format, the above frameworks do not have any provision for consultation with field or formation level military organizations. Thus, the planning process for road infrastructure is essentially based on extant and anticipated civilian use hinging on popular demands, political compulsions or expanding demands of economic infrastructure needs. The observation made in the cited news item in the Wire needs to be understood in this context. This understanding is also equally applicable to states/UTs that are on LOC, LOAC and IB.

In the context of Sino-Indian stand-off in eastern Ladakh, government of India announced INR 784 cr Border Area Development Program (BADP), essentially aiming to enhance connectivity[7]. Similarly, in the budget presentation on 01 February 2021, a total outlay of INR 4.78 lakh caror was made for defense out of which a total of Rs 1,35,060 crore has been set aside for capital expenditure that includes purchasing new weapons, aircraft, warships and other military hardware[8].

The government also announced purchase of MiG 29s, SU 30s, Tejas LCA, MBT Arjun Mk IA and a variety of other military hardware. Implicit in effective deployment of these weapon and support systems is the movement of logistics and troops by road, rail and air to wherever they need be, especially the border areas up to the lines of control. By common understanding, it is also important to appreciate that amongst the three modes, roads play a vital role since bulk of the logistics, especially closer to border areas, moves by road.

In the current and foreseeable future where India will be a dominant regional player and major global player (if not already), connectivity for economic as well as strategic objectives will become crucial for it to pursue its national interests. This observation is not a fall-out of the recent lessons from Sino-Indian stand-off. It essentially rises from India's own objectives for economic and regional-multilateral cooperation frameworks. For example, in the 14 priority areas of BIMSTEC, India is the lead country in four areas, viz Counter-Terrorism and Transnational Crime, **Transport & Communication**, Tourism, and Environment and Disaster Management.

It is not a matter of supposition or presumption that the ability to defend own frontiers and enforce own will on recalcitrant adversaries in our national interest is a necessary precondition for stability, growth, and progress. To do so, the nation's armed forces become the tool. However, for this tool to discharge its intended tasks, sound infrastructure remains a prerequisite. India suffered ignominious defeat in 1961, despite having the most battle proven armed forces in Asia-Pacific (aside Japan). When the sentiments are set aside, lack of critical infrastructure in border areas stands as one of the fundamental lessons from the 1962 episode. This was highlighted by Bhartendu Kumar Singh (Singh, 2013)[9] in his analysis of the Henderson Brooks Report on the 1962 war in the following words:

> **Logistics and Infrastructure**. The ground reality is that India has made only marginal progress since sixties. The efforts of dedicated organization like the Border Roads Organization (BRO) notwithstanding, India still doesn't have fair-weather roads to ensure round the year movement of troops and supplies. While

there have been a further push to road building plans in the Northeast, the Central tracts still remain neglected. The Terai area adjacent to Nepal still remains poorly served. If China were to attack India alternatively through (in collusion with) Nepal, it would be a cakewalk for them to reach the Gangetic plains.

In the present times, when India has demonstrated its will to safeguard its interests (whether in terms of Balakot strikes or the who-blinks-first Dokhlam or even the Ladakh stand-off or otherwise), the time is ripe for India to reformat the energetic infrastructure initiatives that have come to define it as a country on the move – in top gear.

Recommendations

In the context of the opinion expressed above, it is necessary that the planning process considers integrating the military establishment into the calculus of infrastructure development for strategic gains. The following are specifically suggested:

1. At the national level, MoD and MoRTH must have a consultative mechanism with representatives at senior level from the Services HQs. All road network and enhancement plans across the country must be studied by Services HQ reps and recommendations made by them for strategic use of portions of those plans are to be dovetailed into the overall ministerial plans, apart from civilian transport needs. This especially applies to NHIDC and its plans for projects in North East.
2. At the field level (so to say in military terms), State and District Planning Authorities must have representatives from Corps, Division or Brigade level officers. The need for extension, upgradation or integration of local development plans for military use should form a fundamental part of the planning process. The Lucknow-Agra Expressway with dual use capability by Indian Air Force aircraft (TOI, October 24, 2017)[10] is a classic example of how this is possible. However, such practices of developing multi-purpose infrastructure needs to become the norm.
3. Institutionalized framework for such coordination needs to be put in place specifically in States that have LAC/LOAC/IB in so far as Railways and airports are also concerned.
4. The Integrated Defense Staff under CDS is obviously the best suitable nodal military institution since CDS already has appropriate civilian officers of required seniority blended into it. Appropriate level civilian officials of the MoRTH, MoCA, MoS and Ministry of Railways could be either seconded to CDS or military officers of required seniority seconded

to these ministries. This would facilitate addressing of strategic concerns related to infrastructure in a comprehensive manner.

The mechanisms suggested above have an additional advantage since perspective planning through the integrated mechanism will minimize specialized needs spurred by momentary circumstances, resulting in better utilization of budgetary resources.

War and armed confrontation will, and should, always remain the last tool that the polity should employ to protect and further its national interests. However, from Chanakya, Clauswitz and Sun Tzu to eminent strategic thinkers, being prepared is the first dictum stated above all other precepts. In an era when India is poised to emerge as a lead nation in Asia-Pacific, integrating civilian infrastructure planning with military necessities will sit well with such derived wisdom.

Notes

China's Internal Political Dynamics and its Impact on India

1 Antonakis, John; Bendahan, Samuel; Jacquart, Philippe & Lalive, Rafael (2010). On Making Causal Claims: A Review and Recommendations, The Leadership Quarterly, Yearly Review Issue 2010, Pp. 1-94.

2 Lake, David, A. (2010). The State and International Relations in The Oxford Handbook of International Relations, Christian Reus-Smit and Duncan Snidal (Eds), Pp. 41-61.

3 Gourevoitch, Peter (2002). Domestic Politics and International Relations in The Handbook of International Relations, Sage: London, Pp.309-328.

4 Srinivasan, Dr R (2021). China's Unilateral Withdrawal in 1962: Did China Have an Internal Compulsion? C3S Issue Brief IV, March 12, 2021. Retrieved from: https://www.c3sindia.org/defence-security/c3s-issue-brief-iv-chinas-unilateral-withdrawal-in-1962-did-china-have-an-internal-compulsion-by-dr-r-srinivasan/

5 Madan, Tanvi (Sep 13, 2017). How the U.S. viewed the 1967 Sikkim skirmishes between India and China, The Print: https://www.brookings.edu/opinions/how-the-u-s-viewed-the-1967-sikkim-skirmishes-between-india-and-china/

6 Though strategically important with portent lessons, 1967 remains vague in Indian memory. Sagat Singh was to be instrumental in brilliant victories again in 1971, as a General in the Eastern Theatre in the Indo-Pak Conflict of 1971.

7 Kleinman, Arthur & Kleinman, Joan (1994). How Bodies Remember: Social Memory and Bodily Experience of Criticism, Resistance, and Delegitimation following China's Cultural Revolution New Literary History, Vol. 25, No. 3, 25th Anniversary Issue (Part 1) (Summer, 1994), pp. 707-723

8 The tumult of the Cultural Revolution after 1966 is often blamed on a few leaders in Beijing, or on long-term egalitarian ideals, or on communist or Chinese political cultures. Lynn White shows, however, that the chaos resulted mainly from reactions by masses of individuals and small groups to three specific policies of administrative manipulation: labeling groups, designating bosses, and legitimating violence in political campaigns. These habits of local organization were common after 1949 and gave the state success in short-term revolutionary aims, despite scarce resources and staff--but they also drove millions to attack each other later.

First, measures accumulated before 1966 to give people bad or good names (such as "rightist" or "worker"); these set a family's access to employment, education, residence, and rations--so they gave interests to potential conflict groups. Second, policies for bossism went far beyond Confucian patronage patterns, making work units tightly dependent on Party monitors--so rational individuals either pandered to local bosses or (when they could) deposed them. Third, the institutionalized violence of political campaigns both mobilized activists and scared others into compliance. These organizational measures were often effective in the short run before 1966 but accumulated social costs that China paid later. The book ends with comparisons to past cases of mass urban ostracism in other countries, and it suggests how such tragedies may be forecast or prevented in the future.

See: White III, Lynn T. (1989). Policies of Chaos: The Organizational Causes of Violence in China's Cultural Revolution, Princeton University Press.

9 Bhattacharya, Abhijit (June 27, 2017). "China's Bhutan push to fulfill Mao's old dream", Deccan Chronicle, Op-Ed, For the full article see: https://www.deccanchronicle.com/opinion/op-ed/270617/chinas-bhutan-push-to-fulfill-maos-old-dream.html

10 Singh, Teshu (2013). India, China and the Nathu La India, China and the Nathu La: Understanding Beijing's Larger Strategy towards the Region Understanding Beijing's Larger Strategy towards the Region, IPCS Issue Brief 204, January 2013.

11 Dasgupta, Probal (2019). Watershed 1967: India's Forgotten Victory Over China, Jaggeurnat: New Delhi.

12 Singh, V.K. (2005). Leadership in the Indian Army: Biographies of Twelve Soldiers, Sage: New Delhi, Pp.198-199

13 Gazette of India, No.51, dated December 19, 1964. See: http://egazette.nic.in/WriteReadData/1964/O-1799-1964-0051-82054.pdf

14 https://history.state.gov/milestones/1953-1960/seato#:~:text=In%20September%20of%201954%2C%20the,Asia%20Treaty%20Organization%2C%20or%20SEATO.

15 Wilson Centre (n.d). "Minutes of Chairman Mao Zedong's Third Meeting with Nehru," October 26, 1954, History and Public Policy Program Digital Archive, PRC FMA 204-00007-17, 135-142. Obtained by Chen Jian and translated by Chen Zhihong. http://digitalarchive.wilsoncenter.org/document/117828

16 Clare, Hollingworth (1985). Mao and the Men Against Him, Jonathan Cape: London, pp. 297–298

17 Wang, James C.F. (1980). Contemporary Chinese Politics: An Introduction, Prentice-Hall: New Jersey, p. 36

18. Hornby, Lucy (November 15, 2018). Xi versus Deng, the family feud over China's reforms, The Financial Times (online), Retrieved from: https://www.ft.com/content/839ccb0c-e439-11e8-8e70-5e22a430c1ad

19 Liu, Allan, P.L. (1982). Social Change on mainland China and Taiwan, 1949-80, Contemporary Asian Studies Inc., University of Maryland.

20 McGregor, R. (2019, July 25). How the state runs business in China. The Guardian, The Long Read. Retrieved May 21, 2020, from https://www.theguardian.com/world/2019/jul/25/china-business-xi-jinping-communist-party-state-private-enterprise-huawei

21 Ching, Frank (March 19, 2018). "With Xi Jinping's lifetime presidency, China could become more powerful than ever", Scroll, https://scroll.in/article/872209/with-xi-jingpings-lifetime-presidency-china-could-become-more-powerful-than-ever

22 BBC News (March 11, 2018). China's Xi allowed to remain 'president for life' as term limits removed, BBC News (online). Retrieved from: https://www.bbc.com/news/world-asia-china-43361276

23 Fisher, Harriet E. (2015). The Chinese Inquisition: Xi Jinping's War on Corruption. Honors Theses. 375.

https://egrove.olemiss.edu/hon_thesis/375

24 Tiezzi, Shannon (October 15, 2020).Xi Pays Tribute to Reform and Opening – and Deng Xiaoping, The Diplomat (online). Retrieved from: https://thediplomat.com/2020/10/xi-pays-tribute-to-reform-and-opening-and-deng-xiaoping/

"Xi's CCP has been crystal clear that loyalty to the Party is the ultimate criteria for success. Xi demands more efforts to "unify members of the private sector around the Party".

25 Gueorguiev, Dimitar D. (2018). Dictator's Shadow: Chinese Elite Politics Under Xi Jinping, China Perspectives

[Online], 2018/1-2 | 2018. Retrieved from: http://journals.openedition.org/chinaperspectives/7569

26 Wani, Ayjaz (November 25, 2020). Pakistan: Why has China halted CPEC projects, Raisina Debates: ORF Online. Retrieved from: https://www.orfonline.org/expert-speak/pakistan-why-has-china-halted-cpec-projects/

27 Idrees, Rao Qasim, Shapiee, Rohimi & Ahamat, Haniff (September, 2018). Energy Cost Saving and Economic Prospective of China Pakistan Economic Corridor, International Journal of Energy Economics and Policy, 2018, 8(6), Pp. 217-226.

28 Hailiang Gu. (2018). The Chinese Wisdom of Contemporary Political Economics. *World Review of Political Economy,* 9(1), 5-20. doi:10.13169/worlrevipoliecon.9.1.0005

29 Haider, Suhasini & Srinivasan, Meera (June 27, 2020). With India yet to respond on debt freeze request, Sri Lanka turns to China, The Hindu (Online). Retrieved

from: https://www.thehindu.com/news/international/four-months-on-sri-lanka-still-waits-for-indian-decision-on-debt-moratorium/article31934947.ece

China's Unilateral Withdrawal in 1962: Did China Have an Internal Compulsion?

1 Nehru, Jawaharlal (1982). Glimpses of World History, Jawaharlal Nehru Memorial Fund & Oxford University Press: New Delhi, P.267.

2 Ibid, p.663.

3 Singh, Maninder (Dec 10, 2017). '62 war: When a DC lost confidence of the President, The Trbune India (online). Retrieved from: https://www.tribuneindia.com/news/archive/features/-62-war-when-a-dc-lost-confidence-of-the-president-510868

4 For more graphic descriptions, read Brigadier Dalvi's Himalayan Blunder. In our opinion, critics of this work like Lt Gen LP Sen, (GOC in C at that time and overall commander of troops in NEFA sector) or Maj Gen BM Kaul (The Untold Story by B. M. Kaul) may have been guided by their urge to salvage their pride by punching holes into the picture that evolves from Dalvi's narrative. We also understand that poetic imagination is liable to the charm of vivid fictional fantasies. But then, Dalvi was no poet and in any case he was not attempting to create another Iliad or Odyssey. He was commander of 7th Infantry Brigade, fought the Chinese in Kameng Division, was taken prisoner in October 1962 and repatriated to India in May 1963. See: https://www.thestatesman.com/opinion/a-soldier-forgotten-1502907006.html for a brief portrait of one of India's distinguished but forgotten soldiers.

5 See also: Noorani, A., & Dalvi, J. (1970). India's Forward Policy. The China Quarterly, (43), 136-141. Retrieved March 8, 2021, from http://www.jstor.org/stable/652088

6 https://www.history.com/topics/china/china-timeline

7 https://www.sjsu.edu/faculty/watkins/greatleap.htm

8 Sangay, Lobsang (2003). Tibet: Exile's Journey, Journal of Democracy Volume 14, Number 3, P 121.

9. Wagner, Christian and Stanzel, Angela (2020). Redrawing the Maps in Kashmir: New Geopolitical Realities in the Conflict between China, India, and Pakistan, SWP Comment No.52, November 2020, Stifftung Wissenschaft and Politik, German Institute for International and Security Affairs. Retrieved from: https://www.swp-berlin.org/10.18449/2020C52/

10 PTI (Mar 08, 2021). China & India should not "undercut" each other; must create 'enabling conditions' to resolve border issue: Chinese FM, The Economic Times (online). Retrieved from:https://economictimes.indiatimes.com/news/

defence/china-india-should-not-undercut-each-other-must-create-enabling-conditions-to-resolve-border-issue-chinese-fm/articleshow/81378411.cms?utm_source=contentofinterest&utm_medium=text&utm_campaign=cppst

11 Sinha, S.K. (May 20, 2015). The unreasonable fear of a coup, The Deccan Chronicle (online). Retrieved from: https://www.deccanchronicle.com/150520/commentary-op-ed/article/unreasonable-fear-coup

12 Raghavan, KN (2017), Dividing Lines, Platinum Press: Wadala, Maharashtra. Chapter 7.

13 Verma, Shiv Kunal (2016). 1962: The War That Wasn't, Aleph: New Delhi. See: https://www.theweek.in/theweek/leisure/the-war-that-wasnt-by-shiv-kunal-verma-gives-a-total-picture-of-the-1962-war.html?fb_comment_id=767695863335890_770588849713258

14 Garver, John W, (2006). China's Decision for War with India in 1962, in New Directions in the Study of China's Foreign Policy, Alastain Iain Johnston & Robert S. Ross (Eds.), Stanford University Press: Stanford, Chapter 4, P.124.

15 https://www.britannica.com/place/China/Readjustment-and-reaction-1961-65

16 Ibid.

17 Ibid.

18 Kakkar, R. (1977). The Role of the PLA during the Cultural Revolution. China Report, 13(5), 29–36. https://doi.org/10.1177/000944557701300503

19 Andrew, Martin K. (2009). Tuo Mao: the Operational History of the People's Liberation Army, Thesis submitted to Bond University, P.206. Retrieved from: https://pure.bond.edu.au/ws/portalfiles/portal/18370976/Tuo_Mao.pdf

20 Srinivasan, R (2019). Borders and the Concept of Sovereignty: A South Asian Perspective, in Adluri Subhramanya Raju (Ed), Borders in South Asia, Studera Press: New Delhi, P.67.

21 US Dept of Justice (January 28, 2020). Harvard University Professor and Two Chinese Nationals Charged in Three Separate China Related Cases. Retrieved from: https://www.justice.gov/opa/pr/harvard-university-professor-and-two-chinese-nationals-charged-three-separate-china-related.

22 Mehra, Parshotam (1992). An "agreed" Frontier: Ladakh and India's Northernmost Borders, 1846-1947, Oxford University Press: New Delhi

Flipside View of Sino-Indian Troop Disengagement: Victory or Lesson?

1 Singh, Rahul (January 10, 2021). China pulls back 10,000 troops from Ladakh theatre, Hindustan Times, India News (online). Retrieved from: https://www.hindustantimes.com/india-news/china-pulls-back-10-000-troops-from-ladakh-theatre-101610382216148.html

2 Gupta, Shishir (February 12, 2021). China surprises India with its speed, moves out 200+ tanks from Pangong Tso, Hindustan Times (online). Retrieved from: https://www.hindustantimes.com/india-news/china-surprises-india-with-pace-of-withdrawal-pulls-out-200-tanks-in-2-days-101613088444899.html

3 Trager, Frank. (1964). Burma and China. Journal of Southeast Asian History, 5(1), 29-61. Retrieved March 8, 2021, from http://www.jstor.org/stable/20067475

4 Ibid. P.38.

5 Fan, Hongwei (2012), China–Burma Geopolitical Relations in the Cold War, in: Journal of Current Southeast Asian Affairs, 31, 1, 7-27.

6 Wilson Centre (n.d). "Minutes of Chairman Mao Zedong's Third Meeting with Nehru," October 26, 1954, History and Public Policy Program Digital Archive, PRC FMA 204-00007-17, 135-142. Obtained by Chen Jian and translated by Chen Zhihong. http://digitalarchive.wilsoncenter.org/document/117828

7 Van Ness, Peter (1970), Revolution and Chinese Foreign Policy, Los Angeles and London: University of California Press.

8 Fan, Hongwei (2012), China–Burma Geopolitical Relations in the Cold War, in: Journal of Current Southeast Asian Affairs, 31, 1, 7-27.

9 https://www.bbc.com/news/world-asia-pacific-12992883

10 BBC News (July 27, 2019). Aung San Suu Kyi's Myanmar dam dilemma with China. Retrieved from: https://www.bbc.com/news/world-asia-48857781

11 https://www.nytimes.com/2017/11/30/world/asia/china-myanmar-aid-sanctions.html

12 Yun, Sun (February 19, 2021). China's Stakes in the Myanmar Coup, Interview published by Institut Montaigne. Retrieved from: https://www.institutmontaigne.org/en/blog/chinas-stakes-myanmar-coup

13 Regan, Helen, (February 8, 2021). Why the generals really took back power in Myanmar. https://edition.cnn.com/2021/02/06/asia/myanmar-coup-what-led-to-it-intl-hnk/index.html

14 Edwards, Laura (Feb 10, 2021). Myanmar coup, explained, Retrieved from: https://penntoday.upenn.edu/news/myanmar-coup-explained

15 Cheetham, Joshua (March 09, 2021). Myanmar coup: The shadowy business empire funding the Tatmadaw, BBC News (online). Retrieved from: https://www.bbc.com/news/world-asia-56133766

16 Mitchell, Travis (2012). Chinese Foreign Direct Investment in Myanmar: Remarkable Trends and Multilayered Motivations, Lund University. Retrieved from: https://lup.lub.lu.se/luur/download?func=downloadFile&recordOId=2756649&fileOId=2756655

17 Lwin, Nan (26 July 2019). China Leads Investment in Yangon, The Irrawaddy (online). Retrieved from: https://www.irrawaddy.com/business/china-leads-investment-yangon.html#:~:text=Currently%2C%20China%20is%20Myanmar's%20second,country%2C%20according%20to%20the%20MIC.

18 PTI (Mar 08, 2021). China & India should not "undercut" each other; must create 'enabling conditions' to resolve border issue: Chinese FM, The Economic Times (online). Retrieved from: https://economictimes.indiatimes.com/news/defence/china-india-should-not-undercut-each-other-must-create-enabling-conditions-to-resolve-border-issue-chinese-fm/articleshow/81378411.cms?utm_source=contentofinterest&utm_medium=text&utm_campaign=cppst

19 These statements are surprisingly similar to the Chinese official statements issued preceding and after the 1962 war.

20 PTI (Mar 08, 2021). China & India should not "undercut" each other; must create 'enabling conditions' to resolve border issue: Chinese FM, The Economic Times (online). Retrieved from: https://economictimes.indiatimes.com/news/defence/china-india-should-not-undercut-each-other-must-create-enabling-conditions-to-resolve-border-issue-chinese-fm/articleshow/81378411.cms?utm_source=contentofinterest&utm_medium=text&utm_campaign=cppst

21 Dutta, Prabhash K (February 26, 2021). What led to India-Pakistan ceasefire at LoC and will it hold for long?, India Today (online). Retrieved from: https://www.indiatoday.in/news-analysis/story/what-led-to-india-pakistan-ceasefire-at-loc-and-will-it-hold-for-long-1773379-2021-02-26

22 The Freepress Journal (March 1, 2021). China role in Myanmar coup under scanner https://www.freepressjournal.in/world/china-role-in-myanmar-coup-under-scanner

Resolving Indo-Pak and Sino-Indian Border Disputes: Considerations and Prospects

1 Easterly, Grace and Threlkeld, Elizabeth (August 12, 2021). Afghanistan-Pakistan Ties and Future Stability in Afghanistan. See: https://www.usip.org/publications/2021/08/afghanistan-pakistan-ties-and-future-stability-afghanistan

2 Mirza, Nasrulla M (2006). Indus Water Disputes and India-Pak Relations, PhD Dissertation, University of Heidelberg. https://archiv.ub.uni-heidelberg.de/volltextserver/20915/1/Mirza%20PhD%20Dissertation%20for%20heiDOK.pdf

3 Noorani, AG (1994). Easing the Indo-Pakistani Dialogue on Kashmir: Confidence Building Measures for the Siachen Glacier, Sir Creek and the Wular Barrage Disputes, Stimson Centre Occassional Papers, No. 16, April 1994. https://www.stimson.org/1994/confidence-building-measures-siachen-glacier-sir-creek-and-wular-barrage/

4 Trivedi, Abhishek (July 8, 2019). Why the 1963 Sino-Pakistan Boundary Agreement Is Unlawful in Light of the Recent ICJ Advisory Opinion on the Chagos Archipelago, 2019. https://www.jurist.org/commentary/2019/07/abhishek-trivedi-sino-pakistan-boundary/

5 Riedel, Bruce (Dec 14, 2015). Lessons from 1963 for India-Pakistan relations, Op-Ed Brookings. https://www.brookings.edu/opinions/lessons-from-1963-for-india-pakistan-relations/

6 The Tribune (July 5, 1969). India, Pakistan Settle Kutch Border Dispute. https://www.tribuneindia.com/news/archive/this-day-that-year/india-pakistan-settle-kutch-border-dispute-797198 Also see: Uhtawale, M. G. (1971). *Cooperation within conflict: international relations in South Asia* (Doctoral dissertation, University of California, Berkeley).

7 The Indian Express (June 26, 2021). Pakistan to remain on FATF grey list. https://indianexpress.com/article/pakistan/fatf-pakistan-grey-list-terror-financing-7375835/

8 Gravitas Desk (Nov 26, 2020). Organisation of Islamic Cooperation snubs Pakistan on Kashmir again. https://www.wionews.com/south-asia/organisation-of-islamic-cooperation-snubs-pakistan-on-kashmir-again-345655

9 Roy, Shubhajit (February 24, 2019). After 50 years, India invited to OIC meet, Sushma Swaraj to attend. https://indianexpress.com/article/india/after-50-years-india-invited-to-oic-meet-sushma-swaraj-to-attend-5598336/

10 Zhang, D., Sial, M. S., Ahmad, N., Filipe, A. J., Thu, P. A., Zia-Ud-Din, M., & Caleiro, A. B. (2020). Water Scarcity and Sustainability in an Emerging Economy: A Management Perspective for Future. Sustainability, 13(1), 144. MDPI AG. Retrieved from http://dx.doi.org/10.3390/su13010144

11 Calderas, Isabel (n.d). Pakistan: Jihadism and drug trafficking, the threats from within https://www.unav.edu/web/global-affairs/detalle/-/blogs/pakistan-jihadism-and-drug-trafficking-the-threats-from-within# Also see: https://www.unodc.org/documents/regional/central- asia/Illicit%20Drug%20Trends%20Report_Pakistan_rev1.pdf

12 Middle East Institute (2009). Islamization of Pakistan https://www.mei.edu/sites/default/files/publications/2009.07.Islamization%20of%20Pakistan.pdf

13 Riedel, Bruce (Dec 14, 2015). Lessons from 1963 for India-Pakistan relations, Op-Ed Brookings. https://www.brookings.edu/opinions/lessons-from-1963-for-india-pakistan-relations/

14 Fravel, Taylor M (Fall 2005). Regime Insecurity and International Cooperation, International Security, 30, no. 2 (fall 2005): 52.

15 Maxwell, Neville (2007). How the Sino-Russian boundary conflict was finally settled, Critical Asian Studies, 39:2, 229-253, DOI: 10.1080/14672710701340079

16 Gerson, Michael S (November 2010). The Sino-Soviet Border Conflict: Deterrence, Escalation, and the Threat of Nuclear War in 1969, Center for Naval Analyses: Arlington (Va). https://www.cna.org/cna_files/pdf/d0022974.a2.pdf

17 Hung, N. M. (1979). The Sino-Vietnamese Conflict: Power Play among Communist Neighbors. Asian Survey, 19(11), 1037–1052. https://doi.org/10.2307/2643953

18 Brimelow, Benjamin (March 02, 2021). What China's last major war tells us about how it will fight the next one. https://www.businessinsider.in/international/news/what-chinas-last-major-war-tells-us-about-how-it-will-fight-the-next-one/articleshow/81296094.cms

19 Yee, H. S. (1980). The Sino-Vietnamese Border War: China's Motives, Calculations and Strategies. China Report, 16(1), 15–32. https://doi.org/10.1177/000944558001600103

20 Allen, Kenneth W; Krumel, Glen & Pollack, Jonathan D (1995). China's Air Force Enters 21st Century, Santa Monica (CA): Rand. See https://www.rand.org/content/dam/rand/pubs/monograph_reports/2005/MR580.pdf

21 Ghatate, N. M. (1968). The Sino Burmese Border Settlement, India Quarterly, 24(1), 17–49. http://www.jstor.org/stable/45069250

22 ibid

23 The Tribune (Jul 09, 2020). Pact with China no guarantee of peace. https://www.tribuneindia.com/news/comment/pact-with-china-no-guarantee-of-peace-110383

24 The New York Times (2004), The 9/11 Report published by St Martin's Press: New York, Pp XCIV to C

25 Srinivasan, R (Jan 11, 2022). Bridges, Villages and Sovereign Claims: Playing the Chinese Way, Chennai Centre for China Studies: Chennai. https://www.c3sindia.org/defence-security/bridges-villages-and-sovereign-claims-playing-the-chinese-way-by-gp-capt-dr-r-srinivasan/

Implications of Recent Border Dispute between India and China through the lens of a Military Personnel

1 https://www.britannica.com/place/Kashmir-region-Indian-subcontinent

2 British interest in China began in the mid-17th century. The first trading concession was secured by East India Company in Taiwan in 1672. While trade grew in volumes over the next 150 years, opium produced in India by the Company was illegally used flood Chinese markets, eventually resulting in the Opium war of 1840. The war resulted in Hong Kong being given to Britain for 150 years and five Chinese ports, Canton, Amoy, Foochow, Ningpo and Shanghai to be opened to foreign traders (Fay, 1998). The eventual result of second Opium war of 1856-60 was the burning of the Summer Palace in Beijing by the combined armies of Britain and France. In the aftermath of this slight to Chinese pride, Boxer Rebellion broke out in 1899 that saw the end of Qing dynasty. China also faced wars with Japan between 1894-5. Nearly five centuries earlier, the Ming dynasty had attempted to define the northern borders of China by constructing the Great Wall. Now the humiliating defeat at the hands of European powers drove home the necessity to modernize and strengthen its economic and military might (Lei, 2017).

3 4 Assam Riffles jawans were killed when their patrol was ambushed by Chinese soldiers at Tulung La in Arunchal Pradesh on October 20, 1975. Officially, India claimed on 20 October 1975, Chinese forces had crossed over into Indian Territory in south of Tulung La, and ambushed Assam Rifles jawans. The Chinese troops also fired at them, resulting in death of 4 Indian soldiers.

4 Sumdorong Chu incident in 1987 is biggest face-off after 1962 war in north of Tawang in Arunachal Pradesh between. It is one such stand-off between the Indian Army and Chinese People Liberation Army (PLA) where India-China came close to a war. Army chief General KSundarji airlifted a large number of troops to Sino-Indian border under 'Operation Falcon' to Zimitang to counter China's aggressive moves. These forces occupied the Hathung La, across the Namka Chu from Thag La.

In May 1987, the then Indian Minister of External Affairs, N.D. Tiwari went to Beijing en route to Pyongyang, North Korea. In order to de-escalate the tension, Tiwari gave a clear message that New Delhi had no intention of aggravating the situation. As a result, the first formal flag meeting to discuss 'the freezing of the situation' since 1962, took place on the 5th of August, 1987 at Bum La in the aftermath of the Wangdung affair. Both countries also decided to resume bilateral talks to solve border disputes.

5 A 21-day face-off saw two armies pitching tents and indulging in banner drills after PLA troops intruded 19 km into India territory in Depsang Bulge area of the DBO sector in Ladakh.

On 15 April 2013, a platoon of 50 Chinese troops established an encampment of four tents 30 km southeast of Daulat Beg Oldi at about 16,300 feet in elevation in the RakiNala valley. The Indian military followed a policy of restraint, attempting to keep the issue "localized" and "tactical", in order to give the Indian government the opportunity to resolve the issue through diplomacy. The military and diplomatic tensions was resolved after hectic round of negotiations following which the Chinese troops withdrew.

In 2014, Chinese army admitted 2013 incursion at Depsang Valley for 1st time and said such incidents occurred due to different perception about the Line of Actual Control.

6 The 2017 China India border standoff or Doklam standoff refers to the military border standoff between the Indian Armed Forces and the People's Liberation Army of China over Chinese construction of a road in Doklam near a trijunction border area, known as Donglang, or Donglang Caochang in Chinese. Indian soldiers blocked Chinese troops from extending an existing road southward in Doklam. It was a 73-day confrontation on Bhutanese territory of Doklam near the Sikkim-Bhutan-Tibet trijunction.

7 On June 15, twenty members of the Indian armed forces, including a colonel were killed in a clash with Chinese forces along the disputed border in Ladakh, making them the first fatalities on what is known as the Line of Actual Control in 45 years. The troops were apparently killed in close-quarter combat in the Galwan Valley as more than a month-long hostilities along the border went into a full-blown conflict. The Indian Army said both sides suffered casualties.

8. Boxer Protocol on September 7, 1901 "Austria-Hungary, Belgium, France, Germany, Great Britain, Italy, Japan, Netherlands, Russia, Spain, United States, and China—Final Protocol for the Settlement of the Disturbances of 1900."

9 Chinese filmmakers crank out anti-Japanese war films faster than Michael Bay can produce *Transformers* sequels, constantly reminding the public of the suffering the Chinese people experienced under two successive Japanese invasions.

10 One prominent topic brought up again and again about the "century of humiliation," is China's numerous naval failures in the era. Chinese professors and strategists

repeatedly point to the failures of the Qing Navy as justification for a 21st century naval buildup.

11 https://www.thehindu.com/news/international/china-repeats-claim-on-bhutans-east/article32153665.ece

Bridges, Villages and Sovereign Claims: Playing the Chinese Way

1 Som, V. (Dec 06, 2020). *NDTV*. Retrieved December 06, 2020, from Exclusive: China Sets Up 3 Villages Near Arunachal, Relocates Villagers: https://www.ndtv.com/india-news/exclusive-china-sets-up-3-villages-near-arunachal-pradesh-relocates-villagers-2334869

2 TNIE (Dec 31, 2021). A strategy of assertion: Why China is inventing names for places in Arunachal Pradesh, The New Indian Express, Explained Desk, New Delhi. https://indianexpress.com/article/explained/a-strategy-of-assertion-why-china-is-inventing-names-for-places-in-arunachal-pradesh-7699576/

3 UNGA. (n.d). UNGA. Retrieved December 01, 2020, from Resolution 181 (II). Future government of Palestine 29 Nov 1947: https://unispal.un.org/DPA/DPR/unispal.nsf/0/7F0AF2BD897689B785256C330061D253

4 Lazcano, Santiago (April 2005). Ethnohistoric Notes on the ancient Tibetan kingdom of sPO BO and its influence on the Eastern Himalayas, Revue d'Etudes Tibétaines, Vol 7, April 2005, Pp 51. https://citeseerx.ist.psu.edu/viewdoc/download?doi=10.1.1.508.2403&rep=rep1&type=pdf Retrieved 06 January 2022.

5 Bray, John (1991). Ladakhi History and Indian Nationhood, South Asia Research, Volume 11, No. 2, November 1991, Pp 117.

6 Ibid, Pp

7 Srinivasan, R (2021*). BRI, Neo-Tribute System and International Financial Assistance: Perspectives for South Asia*, South Asia and China, A Subramanyam Raju (Ed), Routledge India: New Delhi, 2021.

Fencing the Dragon Out: Cyber Security Challenges for India

1 Sharma, Deepak (2011). China's Cyber Warfare Capability and India's Concerns, *Journal of Defence Studies*, Vol 5. No 2. April 2011, IDSA: New Delhi, P 73

2 Ball, D. (2011). China's Cyber Warfare Capabilities. *Security Challenges*, 7(2), 81-103. Retrieved March 1, 2021, from https://www.jstor.org/stable/26461991

3 Kannan, Saikiran and Bhalla, Abhishek (August 06, 2020). Inside China's cyber war room: How PLA is plotting global attacks, India Today (online). Retrieved from: https://www.indiatoday.in/world/story/inside-china-s-cyber-war-room-how-pla-is-plotting-global-attacks-1708292-2020-08-06

4 ibid

5 Madhavan, N (November 07, 2019). Is India cyber security ready?, The Hindu Businessline (online). Retrieved from: https://www.thehindubusinessline.com/opinion/columns/is-india-cyber-security-ready/article29911679.ece

6 ET Bureau (October 13, 2020). Rare power outage throws Mumbai out of gear for hours, Economic Times. Retrieved from: https://economictimes.indiatimes.com/news/politics-and-nation/rare-power-outage-throws-mumbai-out-of-gear-for-hours/articleshow/78630968.cms?utm_source=contentofinterest&utm_medium=text&utm_campaign=cppst

7 Prasad, Rachita (October 12, 2020). Tata Power says tripping of state transmission line led to Mumbai power outage, Economic Times. Retrieved from: https://economictimes.indiatimes.com/industry/energy/power/tata-power-says-tripping-of-state-transmission-line-led-to-mumbai-power-outage/articleshow/78622922.cms?utm_source=contentofinterest&utm_medium=text&utm_campaign=cppst

8 Sanger, David E. & Schmall, Emily (February 28, 2021). China Appears to Warn India: Push Too Hard and the Lights Could Go Out, The New York Times. Retrieved from: https://www.nytimes.com/2021/02/28/us/politics/china-india-hacking-electricity.html

9 Laskar, Rezaul H and Venkatraman, Tanushree (Mar 01, 2021). Chinese hacker groups target at least dozen Indian organisations, Hindustan Times (online). Retrieved from: https://www.hindustantimes.com/india-news/chinese-hacker-groups-target-at-least-dozen-indian-organisations-101614572360610.html

10 China's National Defense in the New Era. Retrieved from: http://eng.mod.gov.cn/publications/2019-07/24/content_4846452.htm

11 Jinghua, Lyu (April 01, 2019). What Are China's Cyber Capabilities and Intentions?, Carnegie Endowment papers. Retrieved from: https://carnegieendowment.org/2019/04/01/what-are-china-s-cyber-capabilities-and-intentions-pub-78734

12 Libicki, Martin C (2009). Cyberdeterrence and Cyber War, Rand Project Air Force, Rand Corporation: Santa Monica.

13 Srinivasan, Gp Capt (Dr) R (Feb 11, 2021). Lessons from Nagrono-Karabakh and Taiwan ODC, Defence Research and Studies (online). Retrieved from: https://dras.in/lessons-from-nagrono-karabakh-and-taiwan-odc/

Pawns in a Board Game: China, India and Prisoners of War

1 Spl Corr. (Oct 19, 2020). *Army apprehends Chinese soldier in Demchok sector—The Hindu*. https://www.thehindu.com/news/national/army-apprehends-chinese-soldier-in-demchok-sector/article32892047.ece

2 Krishnan, A., & Peri, D. (Oct 21, 2020). India hands over Chinese soldier who crossed LAC. *The Hindu*. https://www.thehindu.com/news/national/india-hands-over-chinese-soldier-who-crossed-lac/article32906023.ece

3 ICRC. (n.d.). *Treaties, States parties, and Commentaries—China*. Retrieved October 21, 2020, from https://ihl-databases.icrc.org/applic/ihl/ihl.nsf/vwTreatiesByCountrySelected.xsp?xp_countrySelected=CN

4 Arpi, C. (2019, December 6). *Exclusive! How China released Indian troops after the 1962 War—Rediff.com India News*. https://www.rediff.com/news/special/how-china-released-indian-troops-after-the-1962-war/20191206.htm

5 Ibid.

6 *Clausewitz: War as Politics by other Means—Online Library of Liberty*. (n.d.). Retrieved October 21, 2020, from https://oll.libertyfund.org/pages/clausewitz-war-as-politics-by-other-means

Postcolonial Approach to Understanding China's Quest for Maritime Power

1 Turner, Jonathan H; Beeghly, Leonard & Powers, Charles H (2002). The Emergence of Sociological Theory (5th Ed), Belmont CA: Wadsworth Thomson Learning, Pp 54-89

2 https://www.britannica.com/science/survival-of-the-fittest

3 Twitchett, Denis and Fairbank, John K. (Eds.) (2008). The Cambridge History of China, Volume 10, Late Ch'ing 1800-1911, Part I. Cambridge University Press: Cambridge NY, Pp

4 Ching, Frank (2018). With Xi Jinping's lifetime presidency, China could become more powerful than ever, Scroll, 19 March 2018, https://scroll.in/article/872209/with-xi-jingpings-lifetime-presidency-china-could-become-more-powerful-than-ever, accessed 16 October 2018.

5 Jones Jr., Charles C. (1878). The Life and Services of Commodore Josiah Tattnall, Morning News SteamPrinting House, Savannah, Georgia, Pp 99-100.

6 For a detailed report covering how the burning and looting of the Yuan Ming Yuan has come to occupy a central theme being used by the Chinese Communist Party

to impress upon its population the importance of strong government, see British Broadcasting Corporation's report: Chris Bowlby (February 02, 2015). The palace of shame that makes China angry, BBC News, Beijing (online) at https://www.bbc.com/news/magazine-30810596

7 From Yung Wing Biography. Retrieved from: https://www.liquisearch.com/yung_wing/biography#:~:text=In%201863%2C%20Yung%20Wing%20was%20dispatched%20to%20the,western%20powers.%20The%20arsenal%20later%20became%20Jiangnan%20Shipyard.

8 Yung Wing persuaded the Qing Dynasty government to send young Chinese to the United States to study Western science and engineering. With the government's eventual approval, he organized what came to be known as the Chinese Educational Mission, which included 120 young Chinese students, to study in the New England region of the United States beginning in 1872. The Educational Mission was disbanded in 1881, but many of the students later returned to China and made significant contributions to China's civil services, engineering, and the sciences.

9 Wang, H. (2009). Discovering Steam Power in China, 1840s–1860s. Technology and Culture, 51, 31 - 54.

10 Day, Jenny Huangfu (2015). From Fire-Wheel Boats to Cities on the Sea: Changing Perceptions of the Steamships in the Late Qing, 1830s-1900s, Australasian Journal of Victorian Studies 20.1. Retrieved from: https://openjournals.library.sydney.edu.au/index.php/AJVS/article/download/9407/9306

11 Lai, Benjamin (2019). Chinese Battleship vs Japanese Cruiser: Yalu River 1894, Bloomsbury Publishing

12 Jiayao, Li (Ed.) (2019). China's National Defense in the New Era, Ministry of National Defence. Source: Xinhuanet

13 The reason to say so comes from the age old cardinal belief in deception that Chinese appear to firmly rely on and practice.

14 Office of Naval Intelligence (ONI), United States of America (2009). The People's Liberation Army Navy: A Modern Navy with Chinese Characteristics. Retrieved from: https://fas.org/irp/agency/oni/pla-navy.pdf

15 Ibid. P.9.

16 Fanell, James E. (2019) "Asia Rising: China's Global Naval Strategy and Expanding Force Structure," Naval War College Review: Vol. 72: No. 1, Article 4. Available at: https://digital-commons.usnwc.edu/nwc-review/vol72/iss1/4

17 Yu, Miles Maochun (2018). Did China Have A Chance To Win The Opium War?, Hoover (online). Retrieved from: https://www.hoover.org/research/did-china-have-chance-win-opium-war

18 Twitchett, Denis and Fairbank, John K. (Eds.) (2008). The Cambridge History of China, Volume 10, Late Ch'ing 1800-1911, Part I. Cambridge University Press: Cambridge NY, P 191.

19 Twitchett, Denis and Fairbank, John K. (Eds.) (2008). The Cambridge History of China, Volume 10, Late Ch'ing 1800-1911, Part I. Cambridge University Press: Cambridge NY, P 195.

20 Srinivasan, Dr R (December 01, 2020). RCEP and Emerging Trends in the Indo-Pacific, Chennai Centre for China Studies (online). Retrieved from: https://www.c3sindia.org/business-economics/rcep-and-emerging-trends-in-the-indo-pacific-by-dr-r-srinivasan/

21 Fanell, James E. (2019) "Asia Rising: China's Global Naval Strategy and Expanding Force Structure," Naval War College Review: Vol. 72: No. 1 , Article 4. Available at: https://digital-commons.usnwc.edu/nwc-review/vol72/iss1/4

22 Srinivasan, Gp Capt (Dr) R (December 28, 2020). Chinese Aircraft Carrier – From Macau, with Love, Defence Research and Studies (online). Retrieved from: https://dras.in/chinese-aircraft-carrier-from-macau-with-love/

23 Vavasseur, X. (Jan 24, 2019). Naval News. Retrieved December 04, 2020, from Liaoning Aircraft Carrier, Returns To Sea After Refit: https://www.navalnews.com/naval-news/2019/01/liaoning-aircraft-carrier-returns-to-sea-after-refit/

24 BBC. (July 29, 2019). BBC. Retrieved November 15, 2020, from China profile – Timeline: https://www.bbc.com/news/world-asia-pacific-13017882

25 Dahl, R. A. (2007). The concept of power. *Behavioral Science*, *2*(3), 201–215. https://doi.org/10.1002/bs.3830020303

26 Sevastopulo, Demetri and Hille, Kathrin (Feb 10, 2021). US admiral says Chinese military activity is rising in S China Sea, Financial Times (online). Retrieved from: https://www.ft.com/content/93294101-be11-41ef-8b54-c4bd83d559e5

27 Li, Jiayao (Ed.) (2019). China's National Defense in the New Era, Ministry of National Defence. Source: Xinhuanet

28 Chan, P. (2014). China's Approaches to International Law since the Opium War. Leiden Journal of International Law, 27(4), 859-892. doi:10.1017/S0922156514000399

29 McLeod, John (2012). Beginning: Postcolonialism, Viva Books: New Delhi, P 33.

30 Twitchett, Denis and Fairbank, John K. (Eds.) (2008). The Cambridge History of China, Volume 10, Late Ch'ing 1800-1911, Part I. Cambridge University Press: Cambridge NY, P 185.

From Macau, with Love: The Story of Chinese Aircraft Carrier

1 Mizokami, K. (Jan 24, 2019). *National Interest.* Retrieved December 04, 2020, from The 1996 Taiwan Crisis Shows Why China Wants Aircraft Carriers so Badly: https://nationalinterest.org/blog/buzz/1996-taiwan-crisis-shows-why-china-wants-aircraft-carriers-so-badly-98152

2 Global Security. (July 05, 2011). *Global Security.* Retrieved December 04, 2020, from Taiwan Strait: 21 July 1995 to 23 March 1996: https://www.globalsecurity.org/military/ops/taiwan_strait.htm

3 ARKIB. (Nov 11, 1998). *Utusan Online.* Retrieved December 04, 2020, from Macau Company Denies Buying Carrier For China: https://web.archive.org/web/20170224132150/http://ww1.utusan.com.my/utusan/info.asp?y=1998&dt=1111&pub=Utusan_Express&sec=World_Trend&pg=wt_09.htm

5 Vavasseur, X. (Jan 24, 2019). *Naval News.* Retrieved December 04, 2020, from Liaoning Aircraft Carrier Returns To Sea After Refit: https://www.navalnews.com/naval-news/2019/01/liaoning-aircraft-carrier-returns-to-sea-after-refit/

4 China Power Team. (Aug 26, 2020). From What Do We Know (so far) about China's Second Aircraft Carrier?: https://chinapower.csis.org/china-aircraft-carrier-type-001a/

6 BBC. (July 29, 2019). *BBC.* Retrieved November 15, 2020, from China profile - Timeline: https://www.bbc.com/news/world-asia-pacific-13017882

7 Sanskrit Roots. (n.d). *Sanskrit Roots.* Retrieved October 18, 2020, from National Integration Through Thirukkural And Sanskrit: https://sanskritroots.com/thirukkural-couplets/601-700/651-660/655-introspection/

Regime Change in Pakistan and Chinese BRI Dream

1 Express News Service (March 31, 2022). Imran's Fate Sealed as Key Ally Bolts. TNIE Coimbatore, p 1.

2 MFA PRC (March 24, 2022). Wang Yi Meets with Chief of Army Staff Qamar Javed Bajwa of Pakistan. https://www.fmprc.gov.cn/eng/zxxx_662805/202203/t20220324_10654933.html

3 PTI (March 22, 2022). Chinese Foreign Minister Wang Yi in Pakistan for OIC conference amid Opposition efforts to overthrow Imran.

https://www.newindianexpress.com/world/2022/mar/22/chinese-foreign-minister-wang-yi-in-pakistan-for-oic-conference-amid-opposition-efforts-to-overthrow-2432893.html

4 Greenfield, Charlotte (March 24, 2022). China's foreign minister visits Afghanistan, Reuters. https://www.reuters.com/world/asia-pacific/chinas-foreign-minister-visits-afghanistan-2022-03-24/

5 ANI (Dec 04, 2021). Pakistan struggles to pay Chinese debts amid ballooning external payments. https://www.aninews.in/news/world/asia/pakistan-struggles-to-pay-chinese-debts-amid-ballooning-external-payments20211204202039/

6 Siddiqa A.(2007). 'Military Inc. - Inside Pakistan's Military Economy', Pluto Press, London. See also: ANI (Nov 12, 2020). Pakistan's economy controlled by a ruthless conglomerate – The Army. http://timesofindia.indiatimes.com/articleshow/79183808.cms?utm_source=contentofinterest&utm_medium=text&utm_campaign=cppst

7 Mohammad Taqi (March 14, 2022). In Dumping Imran Khan, Pakistan Army Seeks Face-Saving, Not Course-Correction. https://thewire.in/south-asia/in-dumping-imran-khan-pakistan-army-seeks-face-saving-not-course-correction

Between the Devil and the Deep Sea: China's Options in Afghanistan

1 Mohammad Naeem, the spokesman for the Taliban's political office said the Taliban would adopt a policy of non-interference in others' affairs in return for non-interference in Afghanistan. Reuters (August 16, 2021). Taliban declare 'war is over' as president and diplomats flee Kabul, India Today (online). Retrieved from: https://www.indiatoday.in/world/story/taliban-declares-war-is-over-as-president-diplomats-flee-kabul-1841232-2021-08-16

2 Xin, Liu and Han, Zhang (July 16, 2021). China, Pakistan confirm terrorist attack; who is the most likely perpetrator? Global Times (online). Retrieved from: https://www.globaltimes.cn/page/202107/1228870.shtml

3 Rifaat, Hamzah and Maini, Tridivesh Singh (2016). The China-Pakistan Economic Corridor, A Visiting Fellows Working Paper (Winter 2016), The Stimson Center: Washington DC. Retrieved from: https://www.stimson.org/wp-content/files/file-attachments/The%20China-Pakistan%20Economic%20Corridor%20-%20Final.pdf

4 Alam, Khalid Mehmood; Li, Xuemei & Beg, Saranjam (2019). "Impact of Transport Cost and Travel Time on Trade under China-Pakistan Economic Corridor (CPEC)", Journal of Advanced Transportation, vol. 2019, Article ID 7178507, 16 pages, 2019. https://doi.org/10.1155/2019/7178507

5 Huasheng, Zhao (March 2012). China and Afghanistan: China's Interests, Stances and Perspectives, CSIS (online). Retrieved from: https://www.csis.org/files/publication/120322_Zhao_ChinaAfghan_web.pdf

6 Kartha, Tara (July 21, 2021). China in Afghanistan: Balancing Taliban, Uighurs, & Ghost Investments, The Quint. Retrieved from: https://www.thequint.com/voices/opinion/china-in-afghanistan-balancing-taliban-uighurs-ghost-investments#read-more

7 AP (July 29, 2021). China's top envoy, Taliban meet, Arkansas Democrat Gazette. Retrieved from: https://www.arkansasonline.com/news/2021/jul/29/chinas-top-envoy-taliban-meet/

Sino-Australian Relations in the QUAD Era: Exploring the Challenges

1 Kuo, Mercy A. (January 25, 2018). The Origin of 'Indo-Pacific' as Geopolitical Construct: Insights from Gurpreet Khurana. The Diplomat (online). See for more interesting insights: https://thediplomat.com/2018/01/the-origin-of-indo-pacific-as-geopolitical-construct/

2 Madan, Tanvi (November 16, 2017). The Rise, Fall, and Rebirth of the 'QUAD', War on the Rocks (online). Retrieved from: https://warontherocks.com/2017/11/rise-fall-rebirth-quad/

3 Rasheed, Zaheena (November 25, 2020). What is the Quad and can it counter China's rise?, Al Jazeera (online). Retrieved from: https://www.aljazeera.com/news/2020/11/25/what-is-the-quad-can-us-india-japan-and-australia-deter-china

4 Kelly, Lida (April 19, 2020). Australia demands coronavirus enquiry, adding to pressure on China. Reuters (online). Retrieved from: https://www.reuters.com/article/us-health-coronavirus-australia-idUSKBN221058

5 Zhuang, Yan (Dec. 26, 2020). Sailors Stranded for Months as China Refuses to Let Ships Unload Australian Coal. The New York Times (online). Retrieved from: https://www.nytimes.com/2020/12/26/business/coal-ships-china-australia.html

6 Doran, Matthew (November 15, 2020). Australia signs Regional Comprehensive Economic Partnership, the world's largest trade deal, abc news. Retrieved from: https://www.abc.net.au/news/2020-11-15/australia-joins-signing-of-worlds-largest-trade-deal/12885666

7 Xi Jinping, "Address to the Parliament of Australia," (speech, Australian, November 17, 2014), https://parlinfo.aph.gov.au/parlInfo/search/display/display.w3p;query=Id%3A%22chamber%2Fhansardr%2F35c9c2cf-9347-4a82-be89-20df5f76529b%2F0005%22;src1=sm1.

8 "China Fact Sheet," Australian Department of Foreign Affairs and Trade.

9 Kassam, Natasha; McGregor, Richard & Rajah, Roland (June 30, 2020). "Changing Australia's conversation about Chinese economic coercion," Lowy Institute, June 30, 2020, https://interactives.lowyinstitute.org/features/covid-recovery/issues/china/; Darren Lim and Victor Ferguson, "China's 'boycott diplomacy' over calls for coronavirus inquiry could harm Australian exporters," ABC, April 29, 2020, https://www.abc.net.au/news/2020-04-29/china-boycott-diplomacy--coronavirus-comes-more-government/12194482.

10 Uren, David (November 10, 2020). Australia's asymmetrical trade with China offers little room to move, ASPI – The Strategist (online). Retrieved from: https://www.aspistrategist.org.au/australias-asymmetrical-trade-with-china-offers-little-room-to-move/

11 Ibid.

12 Department of Foreign Affairs and Trade, Australia (2019). Trade and Investment at a Glance 2019. Retrieved from: https://www.dfat.gov.au/about-us/publications/trade-investment/trade-at-a-glance/trade-investment-at-a-glance-2019/Pages/default

13 Vandenbroek, Penny (April 10, 2019). Snapshot of employment by industry, 2019. Parliament of Australia (online). Retrieved from: https://www.aph.gov.au/About_Parliament/Parliamentary_Departments/Parliamentary_Library/FlagPost/2019/April/Employment-by-industry-2019

14 Srinivasan, Dr R (December 01, 2020). RCEP and Emerging Trends in the Indo-Pacific, Chennai Centre for China Studies (online). See: https://www.c3sindia.org/business-economics/rcep-and-emerging-trends-in-the-indo-pacific-by-dr-r-srinivasan/

15 Department of Foreign Affairs and Trade, Australia (2019). Trade and Investment at a Glance 2019. Retrieved from: https://www.dfat.gov.au/about-us/publications/trade-investment/trade-at-a-glance/trade-investment-at-a-glance-2019/Pages/default

16 Lundie, Rob; Schatz, Laura, & Muller, Damon (January 13, 2020). 'So when is the next election?': Australian elections timetable as at January 2020, Parliament of Australia (online). Retrieved from: https://www.aph.gov.au/About_Parliament/Parliamentary_Departments/Parliamentary_Library/pubs/rp/rp1920/NextElection

QUAD v. RCEP: A Geo-economic Appraisal

1 White House Press Release (March 12, 2021). Quad Leaders' Joint Statement: "The Spirit of the Quad". See for full text: https://www.whitehouse.gov/briefing-room/statements-releases/2021/03/12/quad-leaders-joint-statement-the-spirit-of-the-

quad/#:~:text=1.,Japan%2C%20and%20the%20United%20States.&text=On%20this%20historic%20occasion%20of,defining%20challenges%20of%20our%20time.

2 https://asean.org/wp-content/uploads/2016/11/Table20_as-of-6-dec-2016.pdf

3 https://www.usasean.org/why-asean/investment

4 https://www.ft.com/content/23968248-43a0-11e6-b22f-79eb4891c97d

5 https://www.reuters.com/article/asia-trade-rcep-china/china-says-members-of-rcep-pact-aim-for-deal-to-take-effect-from-2022-idUSL1N2LN08W

6 https://money.cnn.com/2018/03/08/news/economy/tpp-trump-tariffs/index.html

7 https://asia.nikkei.com/Spotlight/Asia-Insight/RCEP-China-to-gain-as-trade-pact-ripples-across-post-COVID-world

RECP and Emerging Trends in the Indo-Pacific

1 Policy Exchange UK. (Nov 23, 2020). *Policy Exchange UK*. Retrieved November 24, 2020, from Inaugural Grotius Prize presented to Hon Scott Morrison MP: https://policyexchange.org.uk/pxevents/inaugural-grotius-prize-scott-morrison/

2 AFP News. (2020, November 23). *Barrons*. Retrieved November 24, 2020, from Australia Hits Back At 'Needless' Worsening Of China Ties: https://www.barrons.com/news/australia-hits-back-at-needless-worsening-of-china-ties-01606184705?refsec=afp-news

3 Guardian. (Apr 29, 2020). *The Guardian*. Retrieved November 24, 2020, from China bristles at Australia's call for investigation into coronavirus origin: https://www.theguardian.com/world/2020/apr/29/australia-defends-plan-to-investigate-china-over-covid-19-outbreak-as-row-deepens

4 BBC. (Nov 16, 2020). *BBC News*. Retrieved November 24, 2020, from China's economy continues to bounce back from virus slump: https://www.bbc.com/news/business-54594877

5 BBC. (2020, November 16). *BBC News*. Retrieved November 24, 2020, from RCEP: Asia-Pacific countries form world's largest trading bloc: https://www.bbc.com/news/world-asia-54949260

6 Govt of Australia. (n.d). *Australian Government-Department of Foreign Affairs and Trade*. Retrieved November 24, 2020, from RCEP outcomes documents: https://www.dfat.gov.au/trade/agreements/not-yet-in-force/rcep/rcep-outcomes-documents

Dragon Casts a Cashless Trap: Society, Geo-economics and Geopolitics

1 AFP. (Nov 23, 2020). Chinese Tech Giants Pose a Threat to Western Banks. *The New Indian Express*, p. 9.

2 Lauer, J. (2020). Plastic surveillance: Payment cards and the history of transactional data, 1888 to present. *Big Data & Society*, 1-14. doi:10.1177/2053951720907632

3 Fourtané, S. (Feb 20, 2019). *interestingengineering.com*. Retrieved Decemeber 01, 2020, from Sweden: How to Live in the World's First Cashless Society: https://interestingengineering.com/sweden-how-to-live-in-the-worlds-first-cashless-society

4 Arvidsson, N. (2019). *Building a Cashless Society: The Swedish Route to Cashless Society*. Stockholm: Springer. doi:https://doi.org/10.1007/978-3-030-10689-8

5 Bond, C. (Mar 08, 2020).*Huffington Post*. Retrieved December 01, 2020, from Why The Idea Of A 'Cashless Society' Is So Dangerous: https://www.huffpost.com/entry/cashless-society-dangers-racist_l_5f234e95c5b68fbfc880de22

6 Klein, A. (Apr 2020). *Global China*. Retrieved December 01, 2020, from China's Digital Payment Revolution: https://www.brookings.edu/wp-content/uploads/2020/04/FP_20200427_china_digital_payments_klein.pdf

7 Liu, C., & Mingjie, W. (Oct 19, 2018). New ways to pay make life easier on the road. *China Daily*. Retrieved from http://global.chinadaily.com.cn/a/201810/19/WS5bc93a59a310eff303283525.html

8 Brown, A. (Nov 05, 2017). *Finance Feeds*. Retrieved December 01, 2020, from AliPay Vs WeChat Pay vs UnionPay – Important research: https://financefeeds.com/alipay-vs-wechat-pay-vs-unionpay-important-research/

9 Kentaro, I. (Sep 04, 2020). *Nikkei*. Retrieved December 01, 2020, from China's Ant eyes Southeast Asia e-payment dominance with IPO: https://asia.nikkei.com/Business/Business-Spotlight/China-s-Ant-eyes-Southeast-Asia-e-payment-dominance-with-IPO

10 Wang, B. (July 30, 2019). *Equal Ocean*. Retrieved December 02, 2020, from Alipay Expands Payment Business in Africa, A Strategic Area for Chinese Tech Players: https://equalocean.com/news/2019073011475

11 Elliot, D. J., & Yan, K. (2013). *The Chinese Financial System*. Washington DC: Brookings. Retrieved November 20, 2020, from https://www.brookings.edu/wp-content/uploads/2016/06/chinese-financial-system-elliott-yan.pdf

12 McGregor, R. (July 25, 2019). How the state runs business in China. *The Guardian*. Retrieved November 15, 2020, from https://www.theguardian.com/world/2019/

jul/25/china-business-xi-jinping-communist-party-state-private-enterprise-huawei

13 Klein, A. (June 2019). *Brookings Institution*. Retrieved November 16, 2020, from Is China's new payment system the future?: https://www.brookings.edu/wp-content/uploads/2019/06/ES_20190620_Klein_ChinaPayments.pdf

14 Bradsher, K., & Buckley, C. (Mar 12, 2018). China's Communist Party Centralizes Power Over Finance and Pollution Control. *The New York Times*. Retrieved from https://www.nytimes.com/2018/03/12/business/china-consolidates-power-financial-industry.html

15 Sims, C. (Mar 02, 2000). Japan Software Suppliers Linked to Sect. *The New York Times*. Retrieved December 02, 2020, from https://www.nytimes.com/2000/03/02/world/japan-software-suppliers-linked-to-sect.html

16 TOI. (Nov 24, 2020). Government bans 43 more mobile apps 'prejudicial' to India's Sovereignty, Integrity. *The Times of India*. Retrieved November 24, 2020, from https://timesofindia.indiatimes.com/business/india-business/government-blocks-access-to-43-mobile-apps/articleshow/79389252.cms

17 ET Bureau. (July 29, 2020). India bans 59 Chinese apps including TikTok, WeChat, Helo. *The Economic Times*. Retrieved from https://economictimes.indiatimes.com/tech/software/india-bans-59-chinese-apps-including-tiktok-helo-wechat/articleshow/76694814.cms

18 AT. (Nov 26, 2020). China protests Indian apps ban. *Asian Times*. Retrieved November 27, 2020, from https://asiatimes.com/2020/11/alibaba-apps-banned-in-latest-india-security-move/

19 Malhan, A. (Aug 20, 2020). A look at Chinese central bank's growing India footprint. *Economic Times*. Retrieved November 28, 2020, from https://economictimes.indiatimes.com/industry/banking/finance/a-look-at-chinese-central-banks-growing-india-footprint/articleshow/77631615.cms?from=mdr

20 GOI, Dept of Com & Ind. (2020). *Review of Foreign Direct Investment (FDI) policy for curbing opportunistic takeovers/acquisitions of Indian companies due to the current COVID-19 pandemic*. New Delhi: DPIIT. Retrieved November 20, 2020, from https://dipp.gov.in/sites/default/files/pn3_2020.pdf

Large Number of Small Things: Lessons from Nagorno-Karabakh in Military Strategy

1 Hsi-min, L., & Eric, L. (Nov 03, 2020). *The Diplomat*. Retrieved November 09, 2020, from Taiwan's Overall Defense Concept, Explained: https://thediplomat.com/2020/11/taiwans-overall-defense-concept-explained/

2 Thompson, D. (Oct 02, 2018). *War on the Rocks*. Retrieved November 08, 2020, from Hope on the Horizon: Taiwan's Radical New Defence Concept: https://warontherocks.com/2018/10/hope-on-the-horizon-taiwans-radical-new-defense-concept/

3 Economist. (Oct 20, 2020). *The Economist*. Retrieved November 10, 2020, from The Azerbaijan-Armenia conflict hints at the future of war: https://www.economist.com/europe/2020/10/10/the-azerbaijan-armenia-conflict-hints-at-the-future-of-war

4 Gatopoulos, A. (Oct 11, 2020). *Aljazeera*. Retrieved November 09, 2020, from The Nagorno-Karabakh conflict is ushering in a new age of warfare: https://www.aljazeera.com/features/2020/10/11/nagorno-karabakh-conflict-ushering-in-new-age-of-warfare

5 Mehmet, F. (n.d). *defenceturk.net*. Retrieved November 10, 2020, from STM's indigenous kamikaze UAV KARGU seen in Azerbaijan: https://www.defenceturk.net/stmnin-yerli-kamikaze-ihasi-kargu-azerbaycanda-goruldu

6 Mirovalev, M. (Oct 15, 2020). *Aljazeera*. Retrieved November 10, 2020, from Armenia, Azerbaijan battle an online war over Nagorno-Karabakh: https://www.aljazeera.com/features/2020/10/15/karabakh-info-war

7 Forestier-Walker, R. (Oct 13, 2020). *Aljazeera*. Retrieved November 10, 2020, from Nagorno-Karabakh: New weapons for an old conflict spell danger: https://www.aljazeera.com/features/2020/10/13/nagorno-karabakh-new-weapons-for-an-old-conflict-spell-danger

8 Artsakh. (Sep 12, 2020). *Artsakh News*. Retrieved November 10, 2020, from Greek hackers from Anonymous Greece hacked 159 state websites of Azerbaijan: https://artsakh.news/en/news/190391

9 News Center. (Oct 22, 2020). *Turkish Defese News*. Retrieved November 10, 2020, from The number of tanks hit by the MAM-L exceeded 100: https://www.turkishdefencenews.com/the-number-of-tanks-hit-by-the-mam-l-exceeded-100/

10 Zheng, W. (Sep 11, 2020). *SCMP*. Retrieved November 10, 2020, from China tests drones, new rocket launcher near disputed India border area: https://www.scmp.com/news/china/military/article/3101193/china-tests-drones-new-rocket-launcher-near-disputed-india

11 Pandit, R. (Mar 24, 2020). *Times of India*. Retrieved November 10, 2020, from India on alert as China deploys dozen underwater drones in IOR: https://timesofindia.indiatimes.com/india/india-on-alert-as-china-deploys-dozen-underwater-drones-in-ior/articleshow/74783818.cms

Watch What You Speak: Think Tanks and Strategic Discourses

1 Murray, W. S. (2008). Revisiting Taiwan's Defense Strategy. *Naval War College Review*, 1-28. Retrieved November 22, 2020, from https://digital-commons.usnwc.edu/cgi/viewcontent.cgi?article=1814&context=nwc-review

2 Hsi-min, L., & Eric, L. (Nov 03, 2020). *The Diplomat*. Retrieved November 09, 2020, from Taiwan's Overall Defense Concept, Explained: https://thediplomat.com/2020/11/taiwans-overall-defense-concept-explained/

3 Thompson, D. (Oct 02, 2018). *War on the Rocks*. Retrieved November 08, 2020, from Hope on the Horizon: Taiwan's Radical New Defence Concept: https://warontherocks.com/2018/10/hope-on-the-horizon-taiwans-radical-new-defense-concept/

4 CSIS. (Apr 09, 2019). *CSIS*. Retrieved November 08, 2020, from The Taiwan Relations Act at Forty and U.S.-Taiwan Relations: https://www.csis.org/analysis/taiwan-relations-act-forty-and-us-taiwan-relations

5 Hudson Institute. (Aug 12, 2020). *Hudson Institute*. Retrieved November 09, 2020, from Transcript: President Tsai Ing-wen Discusses the Diplomatic, Security, and Economic Challenges Facing Taiwan: https://www.hudson.org/research/16300-transcript-president-tsai-ing-wen-discusses-the-diplomatic-security-and-economic-challenges-facing-taiwan

6 Bell, C. L. (Apr 23, 2020). Taiwan Insight. Retrieved November 10, 2020, from Taiwan's Defense Quandary – American Ally or Protectorate?: https://taiwaninsight.org/2020/04/23/taiwans-defence-quandary-american-ally-or-protectorate/

7 HJS. (Sep 12, 2020). *Henry Jackson Society*. Retrieved November 09, 2020, from invitation-only roundtable discussion: https://henryjacksonsociety.org/event/invitation-only-roundtable-taiwans-overall-defence-concept-odc-and-defence-policy/

8 Hart, L. B. (n.d). *Good Reads*. Retrieved from The Revolution in Warfare Quotes: https://www.goodreads.com/work/quotes/3081537-the-remaking-of-modern-armies-the-revolution-in-warfare

Theatre Commands: Understanding its Concepts and Implications

1 https://www.claws.in/theatre-commands-a-conceptual-approach/

2 https://www.orfonline.org/expert-speak/theater-commands-prospects-and-challenges/

3 https://theprint.in/defence/what-are-military-theatre-commands-and-why-does-india-want-to-switch-to-them/690487/#:~:text=These%20theatres%20referred%20to%20the,largely%20led%20by%20the%20Army.

4 https://indianexpress.com/article/explained/proposed-integrated-theatre-commands-what-we-know-so-far-7374555/

5 https://www.africom.mil/

6 Patel, H. (1972). General Amin and the Indian Exodus from Uganda. Issue: A Journal of Opinion, 2(4), 12-22. doi:10.2307/1166488

7 Weber, E. (2017). Looking north or looking anywhere? Indo-Fijian international relations after the coups of May 2000 and December 2006. Bandung J of Global South 4, 2 (2017), P 04. https://doi.org/10.1186/s40728-017-0039-4

8 Fabian, K., & Indian Foreign Affairs Journal. (2012). Biggest Ever Air Evacuation in History. Indian Foreign Affairs Journal, 7(1), 93-107. Retrieved August 17, 2021, from http://www.jstor.org/stable/45341807

9 Quamar, M. M., & Kumaraswamy, P. R. (2019). The Kuwait Crisis of 1990–1991: The Turning Point in India's Middle East Policy. Contemporary Review of the Middle East, 6(1), 75–87. https://doi.org/10.1177/2347798918812287

10 Locher, James R. (2017). Transformative Leadership on Capitol Hill: The Goldwater-Nichols Defense Reorganization Act, in Bradley Lynn Coleman, Kyle Longley , eds. Reagan and the World: Leadership and National Security, ch 4, Pp. 81-110.

11 Park, Yoon Jung (April 17, 2021). Chinese investment in Africa involves more than megaprojects. Private enterprises also are making their mark, Washington Post (online). Retrieved from: https://www.washingtonpost.com/politics/2021/04/17/chinese-investment-africa-involves-more-than-megaprojects-private-enterprises-also-are-making-their-mark/

12 Chen, James (May 09, 2021). China-Africa Development Fund (CADFund), Investopedia (online). Retrieved from: https://www.investopedia.com/terms/c/china-africa-development-fund.asp

Integrated Infrastructure Planning in Strategic Calculus

1 Bedi, Rahul (Feb 26, 2021). Why the Arjun MK-1A Main Battle Tank May Prove to Be a Costly Mistake for the Army, The Wire (Online). Retrieved from:https://thewire.in/government/defence-arjun-mk-1a-main-battle-tanks-indian-army

2 https://morth.nic.in/sites/default/files/Ministry%20Annual%20Report_2019-20.pdf

3 The National Highways & Infrastructure Development Corporation Limited (NHIDCL) is a Public Sector Undertaking under the Ministry of Road

Transport and Highways, Govt. of India. It was incorporated on 18 July 2014 with the objective to develop National Highways and other infrastructure at a fast pace in the North East and Strategic areas of the country sharing International Borders.

4 See:https://morth.nic.in/sites/default/files/Ministry%20Annual%20 Report_2019-20.pdf for specific road projects by NHIDC in the North East.

5 Manual for Integrated District Planning, Planning Commission of India, See: http://www.mpplanningcommission.gov.in/distplan/Infopack_of_DPP_MP/ Resource_Documents/Integrated%20District%20Planning%20Manual%20 English.pdf

6 Article 243G, 11th Schedule to the Constitution, Item 13 puts Roads, culverts, bridges, ferries, waterways and other means of communication, within the purview of the Panchayat Union. See: https://legislative.gov.in/constitution-seventy-third-amendment-act-1992

7 Singh, Vijaita (June 03, 2020). India to boost infrastructure in areas along China border, The Hindu (online). Retrieved from: https://www.thehindu.com/news/national/india-to-boost-infrastructure-in-areas-along-china-border/article31741145.ece

8 PTI (February 01, 2021). Defence Budget 2021: Rs 4.78 lakh crore allocated for defence, 19 percent increase in capital outlay, Economic Times. Retrieved from: https://economictimes.indiatimes.com/news/defence/defence-budget-2021-rs-4-78-lakh-crore-allocated-for-defence-19-percent-increase-in-capital-outlay/articleshow/80632540.cms?utm_source=contentofinterest&utm_medium=text&utm_campaign=cppst

9 Singh, Dr. Bhartendu Kumar (2013). Henderson Brooks Report and India's China Challenge, Journal of the United Service Institution of India, Vol. CXLII, No. 591, January-March 2013. See: https://usiofindia.org/publication/usi-journal/henderson-brooks-report-and-indias-china-challenge/

10 TOI (October 24, 2017). IAF jets land on Lucknow-Agra Expressway: 10 points, Retrieved from: https://timesofindia.indiatimes.com/india/iaf-jets-to-land-on-agra-lucknow-expressway-today-10-points/articleshow/61195274.cms

Index

C

D

J

K

L

M

Q

R

S

V

W

X

Y

Z